Explaining Criminal Justice

Explaining Criminal Justice
Community Theory and Criminal Justice Reform

David E. Duffee
*State University of New York
at Albany*

 Oelgeschlager, Gunn & Hain, Publishers, Inc.
Cambridge, Massachusetts

Copyright © 1980 by Oelgeschlager, Gunn & Hain, Publishers, Inc. All rights reserved. No part of this publication may be reproduced, stored in a retrieval system, or transmitted in any form or by any means, electronic mechanical photocopy, recording or otherwise, without the prior written consent of the publisher.

International Standard Book Number: 0-89946-058-5

Library of Congress Catalog Card Number: 80-17465

Printed in the United States of America

Library of Congress Cataloging in Publication Data

Duffee, David.
   Explaining criminal justice.

   Includex index.
   1. Criminal justice, Administration of—United States. 2. Criminal justice, Administration of.
I. Title.
HV8138.D83   364′.973   80-17465
ISBN 0-89946-058-5

To B. D.

Contents

Preface ix

Introduction xi

Chapter 1 Criminal Justice: A Concept in Search of a Theory 1
  Social Complexity and Legal Specialization 6
  Stateless Societies and Reactions to Deviance 9
  The Rise of the State 12
  Distributive and Retributive Justice 16

Chapter 2 Retribution and Deterrence as Goals of Criminal Justice 23
  Justifications for Punishment 24
  Packer's Rationale for Deterrence 26
  Packer's Two Models of the Criminal Process 31
  Packer's Limits 33
  Retribution: Van den Haag's Chocolate-Coated Bullet 37

Chapter 3 Social Welfare and Criminal Justice in Search of a Theory 47
  The Evolution of the Welfare Approach 48
  Ramsey Clark's *Crime in America* 51
  Menninger's Punishment for the Punishers 56

viii / Contents

Chapter 4	**Assumptions and Implications about Society in Moralist and Welfare Approaches**	**63**
	The Social Moralist Conception of the Present	65
	The Social Moralist Conception of the Future	69
	The Social Welfare Conception of the Present	70
	The Social Welfare Conception of the Future	74
Chapter 5	**Systems Analysis and Criminal Justice**	**77**
	The Problem of Getting from "Here" to "There"	77
	The Concept of Control	80
	Welfare, Morals, and Social Stability	92
	The Development of Systems Analysis and Our Conception of Criminal Justice	93
	The Consequences for Criminal Justice	95
Chapter 6	**Searching for the Context of Criminal Justice**	**99**
	Criminal Justice as a Unitary System	102
	Criminal Justice as an Integrated System	108
	Reactions to Pressure for Integration	111
	The Assumed Integration of Society	113
Chapter 7	**Problems with Definition of Social Order, or Models of Community Conflict**	**117**
	Goal Polarity Within Communities	119
	Rancorous Conflict in Community Decisionmaking	125
	The Community as a Forum for Games	128
	The Community as the Context of Criminal Justice	136
Chapter 8	**Toward a Descriptive Theory of Criminal Justice—The Community as a Model of a Differentiated Social System**	**139**
	Community Defined	141
	Industrialization, Urbanization, and Bureaucratization	144
	Warren's Model of Community	148
	The Vertical and Horizontal Axes and Criminal Justice	154
	Summary	158
Chapter 9	**Criminal Justice Functions in Various Settings—Production, Socialization, and Social Control**	**159**
	The Production Function	159
	Production Functions of Criminal Justice	162
	The Socialization Function	166
	Moralist and Welfare Misconceptions	168
	Criminal Justice Socialization	169
	Impact of Criminal Justice on Other Socialization Auspices	171
	The Social Control Function	172
	Criminal Justice Agencies and Social Control	177

Chapter 10 Criminal Justice Functions in Various Settings-
Social Participation and Mutual Support 181
Social Participation Function 181
Criminal Justice and Social Participation 183
The Mutual Support Function 187
Mutual Support by Criminal Justice 189
Chapter 11 Criminal Justice Reform in the Context
of Social Change 199
A Comparison of Frameworks 204
Relationship Between Frameworks 206
Some Key Research Areas 211
Potential Shifts in Social Policy and Action 214

Notes 221

Bibliography 243

Index 255

About the Author 263

Preface

This is an introduction to criminal justice, not for the novice, but for persons somewhat familiar with the criminal process, with the agencies of criminal justice, and with the typical statements made about criminal justice goals and criminal justice problems. The book probably demands a good bit from the reader; it certainly did from the writer. I call it an introduction because it is, I believe, a first attempt to provide a systematic and comprehensive theory of criminal justice. And while I think it offers significant advances over previous attempts to analyze criminal justice as a facet of American society, it offers no conclusions. It is an introduction to a comprehensive theory.

I have reviewed a variety of conservative, liberal, and radical approaches to American criminal justice and have found all these approaches deficient in major respects. I have found that the analysts and proponents of criminal justice reform too often allow their own desires for the system to get in the way of their descriptions of it. I prefer a more complete and accurate description of criminal justice before I can subscribe to any systematic revision of criminal justice policy and practice. Right now, while it may be that criminal justice is a substantial and politically significant engine, I am not sure what track it is on. This work is an attempt to outline some tracks for analysis and some tracks for social action.

As with all such endeavors, I owe some thanks and recognition to those who helped me work through this "introduction." For their specific, insightful, and at times aggravating, comments I wish to thank Professors Patrick McAnany, Lawrence Sherman, Leslie T. Wilkins, Thomas Phelps, and Paul Brantingham. I did not agree with everything they said, but I think the work has been the better for their suggestions.

In addition, I will always feel indebted for the quality of the "postgraduate" education I received during my first academic post in the Division of Community Development at the Pennsylvania State University. I'm not sure I could have completed this work there, but my association with Professors R. Richard Ritti and Peter B. Meyer, among many others, made possible my exploration of the societal context of criminal justice. This work was completed, either appropriately or ironically, at my alma mater—the School of Criminal Justice of the University of Albany. The intellectual stimulation and excitement of my colleagues here certainly played a significant part in reshaping and finalizing the manuscript I brought with me. For the heroic typing and retyping, thanks to Mitzi Jeffrey and Jo Anne DeSilva, who perhaps were not in a position to appreciate the results of comments by Sherman, et al., as much as I was.

Finally, I thank Roland Warren, whose brief but positive review of my use of his work revived my spirits when I was having doubts, and my wife Barbara, to whom I have dedicated this work because she helped turn me around and look forward when I was looking down.

Introduction

In 1969 at the Graduate School of Criminal Justice, the University at Albany, the seven initial doctoral students in the program were completing our first year of study. Our Korean colleague turned to several of his fellows and proceeded to summarize a year of education with consummate Oriental terseness. He said, "Crime affects criminal justice; criminal justice does not affect crime." At the time, I think most of us passed off Joo Shin's remark as evidence that he was punchy from comprehensive examinations. Since then, however, I have returned to that observation over and over again as a rather accurate and comprehensive statement about criminal justice. It is only a slightly less accurate generalization to say that this work is an explication of that statement of relationship between crime and criminal justice.

Another orienting proposition, cast off in the same year as Shin's proposal, was Donald J. Newman's comment that there is no comprehensive theory of criminal justice administration. I accepted that statement when I first heard it, although I did not quite understand why it had to be so. Coming as I had from a background in English literature, I was accustomed to the symmetry, comprehensiveness, and closure associated with the works of John Milton and William Blake. I thought that if those giants could come to grips with eternity, why should a mundane little system such as criminal justice provide behavioral scientists with so much trouble?

Newman's statement provided me with both a challenge and a goal. This work is a measured acceptance of the challenge, although it is only a first step toward the goal of a comprehensive theory.

Finally, Leslie Wilkins provided a grounding for the method used here. In a number of different seminar contexts, he said that when a problem is unsolvable with current information, one possible strategy is to make the problem more complex! Complexity can be particularly helpful, it turns out, when one is dealing with highly uncertain, probabilistic, and relativistic phenomena. For example, there may be no absolute answers to the degree of punishment to be imposed for an act. But one might arrive at an acceptable answer by comparing degrees of punishment to each other and to the perceived seriousness of the crimes involved. In this case, I have concluded both that criminal justice does not affect crime and that there is no comprehensive theory of criminal justice administration for relatively similar and related reasons. Our ability to affect crime with criminal justice operations has been minimal because we use assumptions about crime and criminal justice that are too simplistic and too monolithic to be accurate either about the nature of criminal behavior or about the nature of criminal justice behavior. Our ability to formulate a comprehensive theory of criminal justice has been deficient because we have generally discounted or ignored significant kinds and sources of information about variations within and across real, operating criminal justice systems.

This book has three basic objectives: (1) to review and critique the traditionally predominant modes of analyzing criminal justice goals, functions, and processes; (2) to compare traditional descriptions of criminal justice to data about actual operating agencies; and (3) to provide a new theoretical framework for describing criminal justice operations in specific settings and for predicting how specific criminal justice systems will respond to attempts to make them more coherent, consistent, and efficient.

The traditional approaches to criminal justice are reviewed in Chapters 1 through 5. While a number of approaches to criminal justice analysis and reform certainly exist, I believe the two predominant threads or schools of thought can be characterized as the Moralist and Welfare approaches to criminal justice. These two groups are quite critical of each other, and therefore their contrasting assumptions and descriptions of criminal justice are presented in Chapters 2 and 3. Chapter 1 introduces these schools as separate attempts to rationalize and justify criminal justice activity as a type of "social control" activity, and sets the stage for the contrasting emphases of Moralist and Welfare versions of social control by tracing the use of that term in American social philosophy and sociology.

Chapter 4 combines the Welfare and Moralist traditions by examining the underlying assumptions that each makes about the nature of American society, the nature of principal influences on criminal justice, and the nature of man. The thrust of Chapter 4 is that although different analysts have placed varying weights on goals such as deterrence, retribution, rehabilitation, and social reconstruction, behind much of this superficial debate and conflict lies essential agreement on the relationship between man and society and on the role of criminal justice as a mediating collection of processes that should reduce deviance, if the processes were properly implemented.

Chapter 5 then contrasts the Welfare and Moralist beliefs in criminal-justice-as-a-social-control to a number of theoretical and empirical positions concerning the characteristics of social control in a complex society. After reviewing the evidence, I conclude that the traditional means of criminal justice analysis are deficient in a number of respects. Perhaps most important, the Moralist and Welfare analyses attempt to use a normative framework for describing criminal justice operations and the relationship between criminal justice and the American social system. By "normative" I mean that much analysis and reform effort proceeds from the notion that the criminal justice system *should* accomplish a particular set of goals that are seen as particularly desirable to the analyst or reformer. The emphasis on what *should* happen therefore confounds efforts at describing what in fact *does* happen.

Behind the normative approach operate three overriding assumptions about criminal justice and American society. These assumptions are (1) that there is a uniform conception of criminal justice operation applicable to any and every actual social setting; (2) that there is in fact a coherent criminal justice system in any particular social setting; and (3) that there is in fact a coherent, consensual version of American society and consequentially a single version of social order that most, if not all, persons in the United States would accept, had they the opportunity.

The descriptive accuracy of these assumptions are serially addressed in Chapters 6 and 7. Chapter 6 focuses primarily on the first two. Data are brought to bear on the issues of criminal justice uniformity and coherence. My conclusions are that there are several separate types of criminal justice operating in the United States and that in many of these real "systems" some non–criminal justice goals and constraints are more influential on criminal justice agencies than are other criminal justice agencies. Chapter 7 focuses primarily on the all-important assumption that there is a consensus conception of social order in the United States. Data presented in this chapter suggest that the American social system is too variegated and fragmented for uniform criteria of social harmony and social order to apply. Moreover, I argue that continuing attempts to unify and standardize both a normative order and a set of criminal justice operations may reduce still further the perceived legitimacy of criminal justice in the United States.

In Chapters 8, 9, and 10, a "new" framework for criminal justice analysis is presented. "New" is qualified because the framework is not necessarily new, although the application of that framework to criminal justice analysis may be novel. In these chapters I suggest how criminal justice analysis might proceed if the analyst began with some stipulations about the structure of American society rather than stipulations about the goals of criminal justice. I examine the ways and the extent to which criminal justice agencies, alone or in combination, may contribute to a number of social functions. Nothing very esoteric is meant by "social function" in this context. Basically I am referring to classes of needs for group survival that have been documented in any number of political, anthropological and sociological observations about life in complex but communal settings.

Chapter 11 then reassesses the review, the analysis, and the new theoretical framework. The basic conclusion is that criminal justice may continue to be irrelevant to social order if analysis and policymaking continues to be made from "inside" the alleged criminal justice system rather than outside this system in the context of social structure and human needs. A new framework can make analysis more fruitful and reform more substantial—but only if our anchor point is in the tradition of social order and social control rather than in the tradition of criminal justice agencies and programs.

Explaining Criminal Justice

Chapter 1

Criminal Justice: A Concept in Search of a Theory

"Criminal justice" is a term used to denote the distribution of penal sanctions and the administration of agencies involved in law enforcement, prosecution, and punishment. Whereas the term may have been around for some time, rarely has it had the political and social significance that it enjoys today. Very recently, about half of the fifty states convened statewide conventions to adopt standards and goals for criminal justice operations. Since 1967, the number of colleges and universities offering degrees in criminal justice has grown from a handful to several thousand. Publishers who several years ago may have included a few criminal justice texts in their sociology series now boast dozens of volumes on police, courts, corrections, and juvenile justice. Fifteen years ago federal agencies sponsoring research in criminal justice did so as a secondary interest. Now the National Institute of Law Enforcement and Criminal Justice and the National Institute of Correction specialize in system-oriented research and training. In the last several years, the emphasis on criminal justice education has seeped down to high school and junior high school levels, where "modules" on criminal justice have become regular fare in history and social science courses.

The point is that criminal justice as a career objective, a political issue, and a topic of study is now so widespread that we can easily lose perspective in groping with the meaning and significance of the term. Criminal justice as a *national* political issue came into vogue with the Goldwater presidential campaign of 1964. The notion of a criminal justice *system* did not gain significant academic and professional acceptance until 1965, when President Johnson convened the President's Commission on Law Enforcement and the Administration of Justice. It is interesting, and should be cautionary, that the other national commission dealing with criminal justice, the Wickersham Commission, neither used the term "criminal justice system," nor expended a great deal of energy interrelating police, court, and penal agency activities. That commission, in 1933, tended to analyze the operations of each agency separately.

The theme of this book is related to the above observations in the following sense. "Criminal justice" and "criminal justice system" are not scientific terms, coined by social scientists to refer to a set of processes or social functions that practitioners and lay people could not see for themselves. Both terms—but particularly the notion of "criminal justice system"—have political and popular origins. These notions are utilized to describe matters of importance to policymakers, administrators, offenders, victims, newspaper reporters, and the like. Scientists have arrived in this field late, and apparently have disembarked without a great deal to offer.

Social scientists, somewhat unlike nuclear physicists, biochemists, or astronomers, are always dealing with phenomena "close to home"—with material, questions, and problems that may appear too mundane to the Shakespearean scholar and too complex and/or value-laden to physical scientists and mathematicians. Nevertheless, the social sciences have established a widely recognized domain, and their impact in a variety of areas is increasing rapidly.

But social *scientists* as *scientists* have achieved their present status because of their ability to analyze everyday occurrences in ways that most people find unusual and uncommon. They do so by employing everyday concepts such as "status" and "group" in new ways, or by employing new terms such as "norm" or "manifest" and "latent" function to refer to aspects of behavior that have not been categorized before. It is only through the imaginative elaboration of constructs and the theoretical arrangement of these constructs that social science progresses beyond common sense observation to the useful ordering of phenomena for their explanation, prediction, and control.

It is the construction and testing of theory that associates social and other sciences, no matter how disparate atoms, enzymes, and racial prejudice may be as objects of scientific study. However, the examination of criminal justice and the criminal justice system has not progressed to the stage where scientific explanation, prediction, and control are possible. There are many reasons for this problem, only a few of which will be addressed in this volume. The reasons I wish to focus on are those that have tended to detract from the ability of scientists to behave scientifically about the entity that is called criminal justice.

One objective of social science is to describe criminal justice agencies and processes accurately, to understand how and why they operate as they do. But social scientists have not been very adequate in their descriptions thus far because scientists, among others, have been too preoccupied with how they *want* the system to work. In fact, applying the word "system" to criminal justice agencies and processes may be itself a good example of wishful thinking. Many students of criminal justice have used the term "system" to refer to those agencies occasionally working in consort around the legal notion of the criminal process. But to designate police, judicial, and penal agencies as a system of criminal justice can be misleading. This approach arbitrarily isolates and designates as a system a set of activities in organizations that perform many other activities as well, and have many other, perhaps more significant, systemic relationships.

While *some* people may want "police-courts-corrections" to be a system, and may strongly desire more systemic interaction among these agencies, many other people may prefer, with justification, that these agencies never become cohesively related. By concentrating on the preferences of the first group, many social scientists behave *as if* "police-courts-corrections" were right now a unified, integrated system. And they pose for themselves questions such as how to make "it" more effective and more efficient. This concentration tends to downplay some facts of life that I find rather significant. Police, judicial, and penal agencies—even those operating in the same locality under the same law—often have such contradictory objectives, and such independent sets of constraints, that it becomes very hard to imagine that the *primary* determinates of criminal justice agency action are the actions and needs of other criminal justice agencies. These machines are built by different hands, quite possibly for different purposes. Moreover, "criminal justice systems" across localities differ significantly. The police problem in Dallas may not be the police problem in New York City and certainly not the problem in rural towns, and likewise for other justice agencies. If in fact public organizations serve their constitutent social systems, it seems quite possible that the services rendered or functions performed may be significantly different in different areas.

The basic aims of this work are: (1) to provide a critical, analytical review of what social scientists and legal scholars expect that the criminal justice system can and cannot do and what the same system should and should not do; (2) to examine the scientific and ideological underpinnings of these expectations and recommendations for reform of criminal justice; and (3) to suggest a new starting point for the analysis of criminal justice activity and the formulation of policy concerning the social control of behavior in American society. Unlike some other recent works that have promised to rethink the crime problem, or reorganize the administration of criminal justice, I do not offer new justifications for present policy or justifications for changing policy related to criminal justice administration. My assumption is that much of the scientific investigation of criminal justice and many of the policies that have allegedly utilized social science findings have been conducted or formulated prematurely. Whether the analysis of criminal justice has been done by radicals, liberals, or conservatives, most analysts from Van den Haag, to Packer, to Quinney[1] have assumed that (1) there is a centralized, unified criminal justice system (in varying states of disrepair) and (2) that this system influences significantly the frequency with which crime is committed, the proportion of offenders who are apprehended, and the degree to which punishment for crimes would feed back on the political, economic and social conditions that give rise to crime and the means with which society responds to it.

Radicals frequently deplore the new trends in criminal justice planning and administration, assuming that "strengthening the system" will include more frequent and intrusive control of individuals and, in effect, will punish human beings for the "sins" of the system. Conservatives have generally deplored the slowness with which reform or "strengthening" measures have been conceived and implemented, feeling that the societal inability to act upon the increasing evidence of social disruption will eventually result in the decay of our social institutions and way of life. Liberals stand, as usual, somewhere in between, unwilling to accept the "causes" of social disruption and deviance as totally seated in the lap of an elitist or capitalist system nor as totally seated in the minds of evil individuals who need to be controlled. Liberal reforms therefore generally aim to ameliorate dissident or deprived groups to the American way of life while at the same time "rehabilitating" the system so that, to some extent, power and resources are more widely shared.

In any case, all groups apparently believe that the interagency network that investigates crime, apprehends offenders, prosecutes, convicts, and punishes, as well as the legislative system that proscribes certain conduct and provides the criminal process agencies with the authority and resources to act, has a significant (positive or negative) impact upon human beings who commit crimes, experience punishment, or contemplate the crime and punishment of others. Of course, from the "no man is an island" perspective, such impact exists, but we have as yet little evidence that the criminal justice network can do much to deliver what its proponents desire or its critics deplore.

I shall not assume that these connections between a system of agencies and individuals do not exist, any more than I will assume they do. Rather, I feel that it is time to try to place such assumptions in perspective by examining their origins as well as to reflect upon the feasibility of criminal justice reform as a significant venture in social planning and social change. By and large, this work is *not* concerned with whether an individual caught up in the criminal process is influenced by decisions made about him and the paths of action he adopts in order to survive. Instead, the focus will be on the question of whether the criminal justice network provides, or can provide, a means of dealing with criminal behavior.

This examination obviously cannot begin with a clean slate. It, too, will be shaped by certain predispositions, the most basic of which is that previous attempts to analyze criminal justice have taken too simplified an approach. Conservative and liberal approaches generally assume some rather direct connection between laws, the threat of punishment, and agencies that implement criminal law, and an ideal individual who can choose between committing and not committing crime. Radicals, on the other hand, often assume that there is a direct connection between societal level systems of economics and politics and the behavior of individual officials interacting with persons defined as criminal. In either case, I think that the literature underestimates the importance of two levels of social grouping, both of which "intervene" or mediate between individuals and states. These two other levels are complex public organizations and communities. Liberals and conservatives tend to suggest that systematizing the criminal justice system (if not nationalizing it) will make the system more effective and efficient. Radicals generally suggest that the nationalization of criminal justice is already well underway and that the resultant increase in efficiency and effectiveness will contribute to the eventual decay of the capitalist system that "needs" to control the deviant persons who are "produced" by the system.

While the conservative and liberal positions may differ considerably over what efficiency and effectiveness in criminal justice may consist of, both positions ignore the possibility that the criminal justice networks of different jurisdictions may be critically different in terms of social functions performed, and therefore that standardizing the criminal process across jurisdictions may conflict with the efficiency and effects of other political and social systems within any jurisdiction. Radical positions on criminal justice tend to ignore the other side of the same coin, that the many and expensive attempts to nationalize and standardize criminal justice activities have not proven very successful, even within the definitions set up by the national policymakers.[2] The agencies and agency officials in the criminal justice networks simply do not respond to national guidance as one would expect them to, if these public organizations were in fact no more than cogs in a capitalist machine.[3] The public organizations of criminal justice often conflict with each other, and often resist attempts at "systematization" because their own goals conflict with the goals of the "strengthened" or the "nationalized" system.[4]

Not only are criminal justice agencies public organizations frequently operating against each other, perhaps for individual rather than systemic purposes, and often at great cost and perhaps small gain for the state, but in addition, criminal justice organizations operate within environmental contexts, "playing fields," perhaps, that can be called communities. Communities, like public organizations, may have *some* relationship to the state—and to national level political and economic systems—but communities, like public organizations, display a tantalizing, infinite variation in climate, structure, process, and in the problems they suffer. Again, it would be simplistic, and I imagine dangerous, to assume that the type of criminal justice operation that seems beneficial in one community will be beneficial in another. Many criminal justice analysts and policymakers pay lip service to this last statement, but in operation betray its implications. If communities are in fact remarkably different, and criminal justice agencies form integral parts of those communities, it is essential to understand the variety of relationships that criminal justice agencies may have with other components of community. Much criminal justice analysis bypasses the study of these relationships to make judgments about how the "criminal justice system" can be more effective in serving "the community." I have difficulty accepting these generalizations and their hidden assumptions. What real criminal justice agencies do in real communities is relatively unknown.

Many recent studies of criminal justice assume that criminal justice agencies, and the interagency network, perform a "social control" function for the American social system.[5] This work seeks to analyze that assumption. I will start in this chapter with a review of the development of the study of social control, tracing its origins in social psychology, to its adoption and redefinition in current social policy.

SOCIAL COMPLEXITY AND LEGAL SPECIALIZATION

In the early twentieth century, a number of social scientists and social philosophers began in earnest the study of social control. They asked questions concerning why social systems were cohesive units, and why most people in a system behaved in similar fashion and had roughly similar values. The earliest examinations of social control read more like justifications for the existing type of social system than either critical essays on the problematic nature of control or empirical investigations of variations in social order. Among the most interesting differences between these early works and current examinations of social control are the relatively small concern of the early theorists with planned social control by public organizations in general, and the small amount of interest they displayed in criminal justice specifically. The early theorists did not see crime as a major problem, nor the control of crime as a primary form of "social control." Most took the approach that social control was an informal process and that public agencies responsible for criminal punishment were generally ineffective and unimportant to the maintenance of social stability.[6] Most of the early attempts to conceptualize social control recognize law and punishment but focus instead on social processes that have come to be recognized in later sociology as processes of socialization. Crime and official processing of criminal offenders was often handled in the social control literature as a subspecialty, reflecting perhaps the much smaller influence at the time of government and public organizations in the control of social problems.[7]

In some other respects, the earlier views of punishment as a form of social control were similar to some views popular today. For example, the early theorists assume that punishment is necessary. That the punishments as implemented were "good" was justified, the theorists felt, by their existence. The purpose of punishment, said McConnell in 1918, was "to secure such an organization of society that in it all persons may have full opportunity to live their largest lives."[8]

How we are to define "full opportunity" or "largest lives" is unknown, but McConnell and others were certain that social control *existed* almost by definition: if a particular social system survived it was "under control"; if the system was disrupted or disorganized, it was evidence that social control had broken down.

Such arguments are, of course, tautological. They define a given set of institutionalized patterns of living as "orderly" and make the assumption that identified social organizations responsible for the control of deviance have contributed to this type and level of order. Indeed, the assumption that the existing social control systems were both necessary and properly functioning was carried to extremes: "Crime—not too much of it—is needed; it keeps the controls in good working order. Control is not effective unless it is tested."[9] With this strange comment, Homans twisted around the older Durkheimian idea that deviance was inevitable[10] into a moral justification for both certain levels of crime *and* the means used to control it: without a certain amount of disorder, the social mechanisms of order would atrophy and decay. The implication, apparently, is that even in a deviance-free society, controls would be necessary. Why, is not explained.

Such "studies" of social control gradually became unpopular. Many social scientists argued that the notion of social control was so vague and general that it was synonymous with sociology itself.[11] Gradually interest in social control was replaced with more modest concerns: explanation of certain types of crime, studies of certain types of social responses, etc. This fragmentation of the study of social control into smaller specialties has become very marked since the 1960s: there are now separate systems, separate system specialists, and separate languages to discuss adult crime, juvenile delinquency, mental illness, social welfare and other social problems. The earlier social control experts tended to lump together all these different types of deviances, along with discussions of immigration, small group conflict, religious differentiation, political conflict, family organization, and other social phenomena to which the discussion of cohesion and control was applicable.[12]

Perhaps the most interesting distinction between the modern studies of "social controls" and the earlier study of "social control" is that while the earlier studies assumed that control was effective, the newer studies usually assume that the controls are ineffective. For example, many modern studies of criminal justice begin by stating that the "system" of criminal justice is failing. Very few studies seriously ask *why* the system acts the way it does. The earlier studies began with the value position that society was "good" as it was. Many present studies begin with the value position that society is "bad" as it is. In either case, the analysts presumably have some notion both of how society *should* be structured (relative to their own desires) and some idea of how society did (or can) arrive at that structure. While some Marxist criticisms of the present criminal justice system are very explicit about *some* of these assumptions, most critics are not Marxists and *most* are not clear about *why* the present social structure is *better* (or worse) than some alternative structure.

In the works cited above on social control, from Ross's in 1901 through LaPiere's in 1954, it is baldly assumed that society *is* under control. These analysts took it as their task merely to examine the social and psychological processes that contributed to the level of stability they perceived. The writing since 1965 generally assumes the society is not "under control" and that the various formal control mechanisms, such as criminal justice and social welfare, fail to bring that control about. One could argue that the United States has undergone considerable change between the 1901–54 period and the one since 1965, and that these changes explain the different attitudes about control in the two periods. However, many examples of social disruption, such as massive immigration, a Great Depression, and two world wars, would suggest all was not well with the earlier world. And yet the assumption persisted that social control was effective.

As the historical analyses of Platt and Rothman make clear, much turmoil of urbanization and industrialization took place during or prior to the time of the early social control studies.[13] Moreover, the earlier theorists also assumed that the formal public mechanisms of control, such as criminal justice, were then ineffective and relatively unimportant to the degree of social integration they observed. The major difference between the earlier examinations of social control and the more current analyses of control organizations lies not so much in the facts that they observe, but in their interpretations of those facts. Those studies that concentrate on the processes that serve to integrate the social system have usually begun with the notion that that integration was real. Analysts who have focused instead on formal organizations or interorganizational networks that are supposed to contribute in some degree to that social control or social integration have usually begun with some belief that the organizations in question are *not* effective, and, moreover, that the larger social system is not well integrated and is relatively disorderly.

Whether a particular social control study has assumed that society is good or bad, or has assumed society is under or out of control, many studies of social control have been deficient in the following respect. Studies that have begun with the assumption that the social system is "in control" have not been able to relate particular mechanisms of control (i.e., the police) to that general system characteristic. Studies that have examined particular control systems, such as the police or public welfare, have not demonstrated *how* any particular control organization failure has contributed to the alleged disorder in the social system. Wamsley and Zald suggest that the inability to relate organizational operations to societal outcomes is *not* characteristic *alone* of criminal justice or other "social control" studies. They see this inability to relate one set of variables to another as a fundamental fault of almost all research concerned with public organizations.[14]

An effective theoretical framework for the analysis of criminal justice structure and processes will not evolve until analysts are willing (or able) to separate personal and public perceptions of value from hypothetical statements of relationship. If we are not able to understand why criminal justice activity operates as it does, and to relate these activities empirically to operations in related social systems, we will have no chance to assess the *value* of the system, no matter whose values we choose to advance.

STATELESS SOCIETIES AND REACTIONS TO DEVIANCE

Most of the rigorous empirical work in criminal justice has been guided by relatively constricted, limited theory (such as police patrol practice X yields faster police response time than patrol practice Z, or institution of civilian review boards increases public satisfaction with police services). While such hypotheses are both interesting and valuable, they do not address the kinds of questions that seem to be of greatest concern either to the public or to policymakers. These larger questions concern the relationship between the criminal justice system and incidence of crime in general, or variation in perception of the severity of crime, public perception of the general quality of life, etc. In other words, they concern relationships *of* the criminal justice system *to* society, rather than relationships *between* two or more aspects or behaviors *in* the criminal justice system. Theory that would guide research about causality *of* rather than *in* the system is lacking. Therefore, we are unable to make informed assessments about the value of criminal justice for the life experience of American citizens.

In order to build a testable theory of the social functions of criminal justice, we need to be in a position to observe changes over time in both social definitions of deviance and disorder and changes in the manner of handling or responding to disorder. Two important points are relatively certain: (1) a criminal justice apparatus *is not the only means* of handling interpersonal or intergroup conflicts in any society and (2) the predominant means utilized vary considerably over time in one society or across societies at any one time. Stated more generally, all societies seem to have certain standard responses by which to enforce adherence to standard social arrangements, but the "things" we today recognize as the "criminal justice system" are not always the same, nor even always present. Moreover, while the operations of American criminal justice are now seen by many people as quite important to the quality of life in American communities, the imputation of this importance to formal organizations in social integration is relatively new.

As late as 1950, George Homans could state, "The student of social control will go hopelessly wrong if he thinks of it as always lying in the hands of policemen, district attorneys, judges and their like. Historically, this kind of control, which we shall call external control appears late."[15] But there was little if any evidence then to support Homans's position—or the contrary one. And that inability to assess the social value (if any) of criminal justice is still with us, presidential commissions and political hoopla to the contrary notwithstanding. If we are concerned with the contribution (or output) of criminal justice for a larger social system, then our *first* concern should be with an adequate definition of this consequence or contribution. In other words, there is little agreement on what social order supposedly is. Therefore it is understandably difficult to assess the contribution of social controls, including criminal justice, to social order.

Hollingshead has argued that "the essence of social control is to be sought in the organization of a people," not in particular mechanisms adopted to handle crises or particular disturbances.[16] This statement is perhaps so basic as to appear useless—*of course* an orderly, agreeable, peaceful group of people will employ one type of police while an argumentative, conflicting, violent group may employ another type. But at another level, this observation is quite challenging to persons concerned with criminal justice. It suggests that criminal justice organizations may not be so much a *means* of establishing social control as they are *products* of the type of social control or "organization of a people" that exist.[17]

One study that tends to confirm this point of view attempted to relate measures of social and legal complexity in fifty-one societies. Schwartz and Miller measured the complexity of the legal system in terms of the existence of: (1) formal means of dispute mediation; (2) police; and (3) specialized counsel.[18] These measures of legal complexity were related to independent measures of social complexity, which included: (1) degree of urbanism; (2) existence of a written language; (3) utilization of money as a means of exchange; and (4) concepts of property and damages. They found that specialized counsel was the last aspect of the legal system to develop, and formalized mediation the first. Societies that lacked even means for mediating disputes also lacked a concept of damages (as well as money and personal property).[19] Of the twenty societies that had police, all but two also had formalized mediation as well as a concept of damages. Only in seven of the fifty-one societies was there specialized counsel. All of these seven had both mediation and police, as well as high degrees of literacy and urbanism. Schwartz and Miller suggest that only in complex, advanced societies with a high division of labor are there penal sanctions and elaborate mechanisms for implementing them. Simpler societies (without specialization of labor) apparently rely more heavily on restitutive sanctions (e.g., exacting damages or mediating disputes) to correct the social disturbance, but do not have formalized official positions or roles for carrying out this activity. Moreover, these societies neither rely on punitive controls nor recognize the roles of victim and offender.[20]

The observations of Chambliss and Seidman lead to quite similar conclusions, although these authors stress the emergence of the state (rather than social complexity) in explaining the emergence of punitive sanctions and a criminal justice apparatus.[21] They focus principally on African tribal societies, and emergent conflicts between tribal norms and norms imposed under British colonial rule. The primary distinction they found between stateless societies and states was the existence in the latter of "winner-take-all" reactions in dispute settlement, whereas the former emphasized mechanisms of compromise in which all participants in a dispute negotiated a settlement satisfactory to all. A key difference, according to Chambliss and Seidman, was the "need" or "desire" in stateless situations for all participants to continue their relationship upon conclusion of the dispute. In state societies, in contrast, the emphasis has been on winning the dispute; there is generally little need or desire for the disputants to continue their relationship. Perhaps equally important would appear to be the emphasis in stateless societies for immediate and practical corrections of disturbing situations. The aim was to restore order in a manner so that all participants in the society could continue to participate. States, in contrast, tend to emphasize symbolic reactions as well as or in place of practical, face-to-face solutions. While it does not directly help the victim to have an offender isolated or punished, punitive rather than restitutive corrections are frequently relied upon.

Leslie Wilkins also remarks on the differences between reactions to deviance in simple and complex systems. Using the simple British village as his model of a simple society, and an urban center as his model of a complex one, Wilkins suggests that deviance is handled informally in the former system and formally in the latter system. According to Wilkins, deviants are included in the simple system while they are excluded in the complex one. Simple societies can tolerate deviance because all the members of the system have a great deal of information about the deviant. While the behavior of the deviant might be recognized as "strange" for other people in the system, the deviant, as a person, is a recognized member of the social group. Complex societies have less information about the deviant as a person, and simply respond in standardized ways to the deviant person in the role of deviant.[22]

The distinctions between social control in simple and complex societies, then, are quite marked. It is not merely that complexity has given rise to more elaborate and sophisticated reactions to social disturbances. More importantly, the division of labor in states means that social disruption will be handled in a particular way: persons involved in causing or reacting to the disruption are assigned specialized roles associated with the disturbing events. Deviants are assigned particular roles, as are particular officials responsible for acknowledging the status of the deviant and directing the processing of the deviant. Simple societies may recognize deviance, that is, events that are out of the ordinary or that do not conform to standard expectations. But by and large, the persons affected by the event are not fragmented into competitive, conflicting roles in which one side must win and the other side lose.

THE RISE OF THE STATE

The rise of the state is extremely important to the examination of social control and criminal justice, because it is only with the state that a criminal justice system per se comes into existence. Concomitant with the emergence of the state (or really, arising as important aspects of the state itself) are the law (and, therefore, *crime*) and the monopoly on coercion.

While it is clear that stateless societies do respond effectively to deviance, they do so without the utilization of written procedures to follow and without the location of raw power resting in only one member or one part of the group. "Government . . . possesses a control characteristic which differentiates it from other . . . units performing a control function: the power of ultimate coercion."[23] Criminal justice, then, as a means of responding to social disturbance requires several elements of the social system lacking in simple societies. It requires that a people will recognize the state, and act in its behalf or acknowledge that others are doing so. It requires that all people in a certain locality recognize this abstract entity as superordinate. And, it requires that the state can implement its dictates, or notions of order, independent of what any particular individual or group would do for itself: it requires the structure and operation of complex, public organizations.

The operation of some semblance of a criminal justice system has always been associated with states. Strong states have generally had strong criminal justice organizations; they are apparently among the first public organizations to emerge. Chapman traces the term "police" from the Greek city-state and the Roman imperium.[24] The Latin term, *politia*, means the survival and welfare of the inhabitants of the city. Police power (or the legalized coercion monopolized by the state) was at the very heart of state authority in Rome. This power was seen as the authority of the state to govern, or to maintain the welfare of the inhabitants. Police *force* was the use of armed coercion to enforce the welfare policy of the state.[25]

The sociological studies of social control between 1900 and 1950 focused on informal, normative processes and tended to ignore or underestimate the role of the police and, therefore, the role of legitimate coercive power in social control.[26] The reasons for this oversight in sociology are unclear. It is possible that the operation of public organizations and the formation of public policy were left to political science and public administration. It is also true that the area of "macrosociology," examining the state, the law, and interorganizational networks, was slow to develop; and, therefore, the conceptual tools necessary to appreciate the functions of the police and other criminal justice organizations were lacking until after World War II. It is not surprising, then, that while there are now many texts and studies that describe what the criminal justice apparatus of the state "does" (in the sense of what the actors in the system believe, value, and do), there is still little, if any, consensus about what the system "is good for" (in the sense of what it produces, or how it functions for the social structure).

In many ways, it is apparently the police, and the integral connection of "police power" with the concept of the state, that is central to criminal justice, as opposed to other means of handling social disturbances and disputes. A variety of stateless societies have mediator or judgelike roles.

But, dispute settlement becomes something quite different when officials of the state are empowered to go out among the citizenry and pull into court the disputants or the offenders and more importantly, to prevent or break up disputes *before* individuals would voluntarily seek out mediation or intervention. Moreover, the police, operating under state law as a guide to what should and should not happen, are *enforcing* a predetermined policy established by an abstract, nonhuman entity.

> The function of the police power of the state is to maintain a threshold of force to deter and/or contain the ever-present margin of antisocial acts by individuals and groups. . . . . Even when isolated outbreaks contain germs of larger social issues . . . they may be contained at acceptable costs by the appropriate and measured application of police power.[27]

It is important to underscore in the preceding passage that "antisocial acts" are behaviors defined as antisocial by a particular organization called the state. The state is not an organism, let alone a human being. We cannot properly speak of the state "needing" or "wanting" a particular state of affairs or a particular organization of social situations. The state, however, as part of its existence, enforces written rules, or applies en masse to a variety of situations and people a set of standards. These standards, because they can be coercively enforced, are superordinate to the desires, needs, wants, or goals of any individual or group. Equally important to remember, however, is that the state actions of enforcement, through police power, are not necessarily good or helpful or desired by any group or individual, let alone by society in its entirety. Furthermore, it would be foolhardy to assume that the organizations that are empowered to act on state authority always do so "for the good of the state," let alone the good of society. Implementation within complex organizations is like a golf game. No matter how well it is done, it is still a series of mistakes.

Mistakes, however, can change appearance as their viewer changes viewpoint. Criminal justice organizations can fail to implement plans from the state's point of view. The policeman can fail to arrest a suspected felon because of personal fear, mechanical failure of his pursuing patrol car, personal belief that the felon would not be convicted in an overly liberal court, lack of knowledge that the event he witnessed was a crime, or any number of other reasons. Or, an officer can mistakenly make an arrest—of an innocent person, or in an event that does not turn out to be a crime, or out of personal motives, etc. Or, an officer can make a mistake in not following the procedures for application of coercion that the state requires in the implementation of its rules.

Many of these possibilities that can arise during the performance of the police rules may be mistakes from the point of view of the rules that are to guide official behavior. On the other hand, many of them, such as arresting on personal motives when no crime has occurred, or allowing an offender to go free because the officer is cynical about the court system, are still intended acts. They may be evidence that that particular officer does not agree with the official role he is to perform. Some of these "mistakes" may not be personal ones, but signs that the role the officer is playing has been altered from the role prescribed in law by the organization for which the police officer works. If a policeman knowingly arrests by using a procedure that will not permit a conviction, he may be conforming to informal norms in *his* police department that certain persons should be harassed because their behavior, while objectionable to the police, is quite difficult to prosecute. In this case, there may be conflict between the police department's goals and the rules for police behavior established by the state.[28]

Lastly, even mechanical failure of a pursuing patrol car may be the manifestation of "mistakes" in the implementation of police power, rather than evidence of a random error or accident. Perhaps the police budget requires that police cars are in service overly long or that a sufficient number of mechanics cannot be hired.

These are only very simple examples intended to highlight the complexity and uncertainty involved in relating any particular official's behavior in specific situations to the relatively remote processes by which the state empowers complex bureaucracies to implement state policy. In some cases the intervening variables may be purely personal or situational. No matter how critical the judgment of such events, few critics would attribute such personal or situational factors to some characteristics inherent in the organization of the state. No large, complex, and abstract ordering of roles and rules can account for all the uncertainties of future events or all the proclivities of the individuals who will play a part in or be confronted by the system.

One key question in the analysis of criminal justice would appear to be just where the analyst draws the line between those events and behavior that are attributable to characteristics of the state and those that are attributable to other forms of institutionalized behavior. In other words, a strong theory of criminal justice must be able to delineate between those actions and outcomes that manifest the state's monopoly on legal coercion and those that manifest the characteristics of groups, organizations, and communities independent of their relationship to the state. To what extent, for example, is a police department norm to harass prostitutes or drug addicts (rather than prosecute solicitation or drug possession or use) an example of state rather than organizational behavior?[29] To what extent can a corrections department's behavior in instituting a series of halfway houses be considered part of the state plan to punish criminal offenders rather than an organizational move to accommodate public dissatisfaction with state prisons?[30] Neither the informal norm of harassment nor the departmental policy to establish reintegration facilities are manifestations of personal proclivities or situational factors. These are *organized* behaviors. They are behaviors that occur during the implementation of state authority. But, should they be taken to mean that any negative or positive organized criminal justice behavior is something that occurs *only* because criminal justice agencies are agencies of the state?

While this analysis holds out no firm answers to such questions, these questions provide a basic frame of reference. They ask for a systematic inquiry into the functions of criminal justice that can deal with *both* states and legal systems *and* with factors of social organization, bureaucracy, and community structure and conflict. They ask for an examination of institutionalized behaviors (or socially patterned behavior) that occur within a mix of the state-originated police power and the socially earlier tendency of people to deal with social disturbance and disagreement through norms of compromise and negotiation.

DISTRIBUTIVE JUSTICE AND RETRIBUTIVE JUSTICE

Interwoven in many treatises on criminal justice are the two themes of distributive justice and retributive justice. Both terms are relatively vague, and the relationship of the criminal justice system to the meting out of either sort of justice seems ambiguous. Some scholars, such as Van den Haag, attempt to distinguish between the distribution of social goods and rewards on the one hand and the distribution of penalties for the breaking of laws on the other.[31] Other scholars, such as George Homans, apparently see the two as relatively synonymous, the distinction being more in the eye of the beholder than in the events that take place: "We can describe control in the language of reward and punishment, or we can describe it in the language of the distribution of goods, provided that in this case we consider both tangible goods, such as money, and intangible goods, such as the enjoyment of high social rank."[32]

Many legal scholars make a clear distinction between "distributive" or "social justice" on the one hand and "retributive" or "criminal justice" on the other. For example, John Rawls barely mentions criminal justice in his major treatise on the fair distribution of social resources.[33] Rawls is concerned with the elaboration of principles by which social goods would be fairly distributed, if men were ignorant of their position in life when such principles were devised. He then goes on to elaborate the social institutions, or the patterns of behavior controlled by law that would instill a sense of justice and distribute social rewards based on his principles.

This is not a mere academic exercise for Rawls, since he assumes that the current social institutions and distributive patterns could be effectively utilized and altered, if justice, in the pure case, could be defined. For Rawls, criminal justice is irrelevant to the discussion, since all men would comply with rules of distribution if they were seen to be just. He does, however, suggest that even in a just or fair society a system of criminal sanctions might be necessary in order to lend stability to the system (or to maintain the system), even though events recognized as crimes might theoretically be absent.[34]

Criminal justice, states Rawls, in terms of its actual operations, is only relevant "under conditions of partial compliance" with principles of social justice.[35] But, it is precisely with these conditions of partial compliance (or, as some might argue, noncompliance) that I am interested here. To what extent are criminal justice and the distribution of social advantages related, under conditions in which distributive justice is admittedly incomplete or imperfect? Will criminal justice in this instance still perform the function of providing stability to the system, as Van den Haag suggests? Or is criminal justice, under these conditions, to be viewed as another means of distributing social advantages, as Homans implies?

Distributive justice is a broader term than retributive justice. The latter will be used here only to denote the administration of penal sanctions as the official reaction to the commission of criminal offenses.[36] Distributive justice, in contrast, refers to the broader range of political and economic processes by which goods, services, and symbolic rewards are distributed to classes and groups of people. An organization or an individual can gain a good deal of wealth, power, and prestige utilizing relatively immoral and unscrupulous means without breaking a penal law or being subject to a penal action. On the other hand, some relatively well respected, honest, kind and considerate people can and do commit crimes and may be punished, regardless of their status within a broader scheme of distributive justice.

While the distribution of social rewards and the distribution of penal sanctions are clearly different, most recent criminal justice literature assumes that the use of the criminal law is clearly related to the existing type of distributive justice. Karl Menninger and Ramsey Clark, whose work we shall discuss in Chapter 3, vehemently argue that the present system of penal sanctions does not achieve justice, nor contribute to social order, because penal sanctions are applied to control groups who have been deprived within the distributive system.[37] Herbert Packer and Ernest Van den Haag, whose works are discussed in Chapter 2, argue that the penal system is inappropriate to the task of altering distributive justice, and can only be expected to deal with control of criminally offensive behavior. Nevertheless, both Packer and Van den Haag suggest that when a distributive justice system is unfair, then the criminal justice system may be less effective.[38]

These two views of the nature and purpose of the criminal sanction do not *necessarily* conflict. Menninger and Clark are not suggesting that the criminal justice system should be used as a means of altering the distribution of social resources. Packer and Van den Haag admit that there may well be injustices in the allocation of social resources. However, these two views conflict considerably in terms of their diagnosis of the relationship between distributive and penal justice and, therefore, in their proposed strategies for dealing with the inequities and ineffectiveness of either system of sanctions. Menninger and Clark would apparently argue that inequities in the distribution of social resources can continue to exist *because* the penal system is available as a means to control dissatisfaction with the present distributive system. Packer and Van den Haag apparently argue that there are certain irrationalities in penal justice that must be dealt with immediately, and that a strengthened retributive justice system must be maintained whether or not correctives in the larger political-economic institutions are ever undertaken.

More detailed examinations of these very different attitudes toward criminal justice will have to wait. The point here is that sufficient disagreement exists among learned and well-intentioned scholars concerning the function of criminal justice in both retributive and distributive systems of social control, that exactly what this collection of agencies does, has the potential to do, and whether and in what order change should come are matters very open to question. Both Clark and Packer are lawyers, Menninger and Van den Haag are psychiatrists, and none of them are radicals, anarchists, or Marxists. Yet, their intellectual opposition to each other would suggest that none of them knows exactly what is going on here and that each has grasped very different parts of an unseen elephant. Their selective attention to different facts and different problems in criminal justice might lead one to suspect that their individual conclusions and recommendations for change could have been made without examination of the elephant at all.

In 1901, Ross made an observation about distributive and penal justice that has apparently escaped the attention of more current debaters: "While conceivably we might procure obedience to the laws by reward as well as by punishment, we do in fact use punishment alone.... However preferable a scale of prizes to a scale of dooms, the latter will be used so long as it is so cheap to give pain and so expensive to confer pleasure."[39] Several years ago, the author attended a graduate seminar on the administration of criminal justice in which the same point was made in a very different way. The professor had asked his students whether they would grant or deny parole to fictitious offenders, based on summary case histories. One of these offenders had committed grand larceny by stealing a $500 set of drums. When asked whether he should be paroled after his one year minimum, some students agreed and others disagreed. But, all the students except one took the decision task as given. One seminar participant dissented from the entire process and suggested that the parole board, if interested in preventing such crimes in the future, should provide this offender with a set of drums and a job in a rock band. The laughter that followed this suggestion was both immediate and uncomfortable. The notion that there were conceivable alternatives to the administration of the penal sanction as traditionally done, a notion that is usually submerged, had become too suddenly evident.

What connection with criminal justice does this student's suggestion or Ross's more literary turns of phrase have, one might ask? Several, might be the answer. Would an individual concerned with social control be more effective legislating changes in federal economic regulations or in drafting parole regulations? Should he aim at being a parole officer who can provide sympathetic supervision to a drum thief, or should he become a booking agent specializing in placing ex-offenders? Can a social system that has a monopoly on coercion also expend sufficient energy in the political process, which determines who will receive what proportion of material and cultural wealth? Chambliss and Seidman contend that stateless societies have relied on informal distributive justice rather than retributive justice because the limits of their subsistence economies made every individual necessary to the group. States, by their nature, not only subordinate whole groups and classes to the maintenance of a hierarchy of power and control, but also differentially distribute access to force and power (or the means by which to object as well as to obtain compliance).

Perhaps the coercive alternatives available through criminal justice may reduce both the organized effort available to deal with differential and perhaps unfair allocations of distributive justice. However, it would be a mistake to think that the relationship between the two systems is unidirectional. For example, Reith argues that the British police made social reform in England possible in two ways. First, through impartial enforcement of unfair laws, they made visible the injustices in legislation, resulting in both riot and revision of the law. Second, they enforced with equal impartiality the social reform legislation, coercing a fairer distribution of social resources than some Englishmen apparently would have agreed to voluntarily.[40]

In the United States, Ross observed a reverse relationship between criminal justice and socially unpopular laws. He suggested that because American police had (in 1901) a very similar set of values to those of the majority of the people they policed, they frequently acted as a buffer between unpopular or unjust state rules and public sentiment. The police practice of nonenforcement of unpopular laws increased the legitimacy of the legal system by reducing the impact on citizens of laws they did not favor.[41]

While we have thus far concentrated on police power in examining the connection between retributive and distributive sanctioning systems, indications that the criminal justice network contributes to both are also available in court and correctional organizations. Prosecutors and public defenders are evidently quick to ascertain an offender's status in terms of distributive justice symbols when they are deciding how to handle a case.[42] Judges and parole boards apparently consider the impact that a penal sanction (or the continuation of it) will have on an offender and his family's access to social resources.[43] Correctional organizations expend a good deal of energy in the distribution of educational, medical, and other services, and the staff efforts during the reintegration process may include attempts to alter normal employment opportunity patterns, to the benefit of the offender.[44]

Of course, the impact of the criminal justice system upon a society's political economy is probably minimal. Walter Nord would argue that no matter how committed operators in the criminal justice system are to reallocation of social resources, they work within a macrosystem that sustains the very situations that officials attempt to change. Consequently, criminal justice reform that "takes the edge off" the stark realities of coercive social control, through minor alterations in distributive patterns, merely prolongs the status quo.[45]

The criminal justice system itself, however, cannot be blamed for the perpetuation of distributive injustice. The criminal justice system is a network of agencies that seek to achieve their own goals, not the "will of the people" or "the goals of the state." It is true that criminal justice policy, like other public policy, is determined in large part by factors and forces outside the bureaucracies themselves. And, there are strong indications that retributive justice rather than redistributing social rewards is the favored means of social control. "More police, more stringent policing, less leniency by the courts—this is how a substantial segment of the population would undertake to reduce crime—except when they are confronted with the necessity of deciding the fate of a particular individual."[46] It is apparently more popular to resort to punishments than to alter the distribution of social resources in an attempt to prevent deviance. The election of punishment, however, is apparently less strong when an individual is given facts concerning a particular offender who is liable to punishment. The preference for penal rather than distributive sanctions is stronger when judgments can be made on an abstract, general level.

It would seem to be another characteristic of the state and retributive justice that they tend to depersonalize the sanctioning decision. The criminal sanction offers the symbolic satisfactions of retribution as an alternative to correcting social disturbances on a practical, face-to-face level.

The criminal justice system, however, is more than the implementation of penal sanctions. It is a network of complex organizations that must operate between the tendencies legalized by the state toward symbolic, retributive reactions to deviant individuals, and the tendencies of social groups to negotiate and compromise solutions to deviant events. The extent to which these organizations will focus on coercive control or upon nonlegal, informal controls should be expected to vary considerably. In the next two chapters we will examine two major positions vis-à-vis the role of criminal justice in the production of social stability.

Chapter 2

Retribution and Deterrence as Goals of Criminal Justice

In this and the following chapter, I will briefly survey two positions on the purposes of the criminal justice system by examining in detail the work of four authors, Herbert Packer, Ernest Van den Haag, Karl Menninger, and Ramsey Clark. The reasons for this selection are somewhat arbitrary, but ideally the four works compared provide useful indications of the current conflict and confusion in understanding the criminal justice system and illustrate four different ways in which criminal justice reform has been approached, based upon four different value positions concerning punishment. The high sales and wide citation of these four particular authors suggest that these works are well regarded and have a considerable following and indicate that these works may be articulate statements of commonly held points of view. Finally, these four authors' works were chosen because none of the four can be rejected as radical, and yet they take radical departures from each other. Comparison of these works is evidence of the distance in value and policy prescription that exists in the field where criminal justice decisions are most frequently made.

I should emphasize that these particular authors have not been selected because they are paragons of virtue, analytical wizards, or exemplary scholars. I am reasonably sure that more scholarly and perhaps better constructed arguments concerning criminal justice may be found elsewhere.

But the works selected for discussion here represent or characterize widely held opinions about the purposes, value, and problems of criminal justice. The position taken by Packer and Van den Haag I shall call the "Moralist" position because both authors seem convinced that in one way or another the criminal justice system can uphold the morals, or the cultural fabric, of society. The position taken by Menninger and Clark I shall call the "Welfare" position because they believe that public organizations such as criminal justice ones are primarily concerned with improving the public welfare. They have little regard for criminal justice as retribution or as a deterrent force; in fact they have strong doubts that criminal justice operations can have much impact on crime.

The major purposes of reviewing these two positions are as follows. I am interested in investigating the possibility of determining the value—perhaps the social utility—of criminal justice. These representative "Moralists" and "Welfarists" have little doubt about the value of the system, so their arguments are worth reviewing. Second, a key concern will be to distill from their arguments their underlying assumptions about the American social system so that I can examine how they relate criminal justice to that system. Third, I wish to review how the downplaying of the complexity of social structure and process by all four authors limits the accuracy of their descriptions and the feasibility of their recommendations. As I stated in Chapter 1, I think that most studies of the criminal justice system downplay or ignore the substantial influences of complex organizations and communities. What happens when these elements of the social system are discounted can be observed in both the Moralist and Welfare approaches to criminal justice.

JUSTIFICATIONS FOR PUNISHMENT

The Moralist position on criminal justice recognizes that criminal justice agencies may have many purposes and may serve a variety of functions. In fact, proponents of this position usually argue that one of the major difficulties with the current criminal justice system is that it has too many purposes, some of which conflict. Moralist reviews of criminal justice usually include attempts to define and compare these various purposes and then to identify from that number a smaller range of purposes that have social value and that may be effectively achieved through criminal justice operations. The basic argument of this position can be stated briefly: punishment, as a purpose of criminal justice, is unavoidable and therefore only those purposes consonant with punishment can rationally remain as purposes of criminal justice. In addition, the Moralist writers, by and large, assume that criminal justice is basically the same social operation, wherever it is found, and moreover that society and the criminal justice system would be better off if the departures from this basic set of operations were stripped away.

Van den Haag and Packer clearly favor (justify) punishment, although on somewhat different grounds. Packer seeks to raise general deterrence as the predominant justification for punishment, while Van den Hag is currently famous (or infamous) for attempting to "rehabilitate" the status of retribution as a legitimate penal goal.

While deterrence and retribution are usually summarily distinguished in elementary texts,[1] there is evidence in both the social control literature and social philosophy that these terms are ambiguous, taken separately, and may be more difficult to distinguish when they are put side by side.

In 1912, McConnell, a social Darwinist, "justified" punishment on the basis that it was a fact of life: "Punishment is but an aspect of the struggle for existence. Society's right to punish is based upon the necessity of punishment from the viewpoint of social utility, a necessity imposed by the struggle for existence."[2] McConnell goes on to say punishment is founded on the "social will," which he defines as the will of those in power. (This, too, is acceptable in the social Darwinist view, since those in power have, by gaining it, demonstrated evolutionary superiority).[3] From this perspective, deterrence and retribution seem substantially the same. Invocation of "social will" seems reminiscent of the satisfaction of "retributive urges," but social utility presumably implies some future benefits, similar to those of deterrence.

In 1901, E. A. Ross "dismissed" retribution as barbaric and nonscientific, and suggested that without the power to deter, punishment would not be used.[4] One of Ross's followers, L. L. Bernard, accepted the equation of retribution with vengeance (or an "anger reaction"),[5] but defined punishment itself in words that made it virtually synonymous with retribution: "Punishment is commonly regarded as a deliberate act undertaken for the purpose of reestablishing a normal or equitable relationship between two or more persons when such a relationship has been disturbed or violated . . . persons who undertake to administer it have a legal right or obligation to do so."[6] If this definition can stand, it would suggest that all punishment is by definition retributive and, therefore, that deterrence either precedes retribution (a threat used to prevent the need to punish or be retributive), or that deterrence follows retribution as a consequence of other people's having observed its occurrence.

Radzinowicz connects the two in a different way. He argues that insistence is made on the effectiveness of deterrence, frequently against the facts, so that people will not lose their commitment to the norms to which they conform: "There is a reluctance . . . to admit the implication of any other view—to accept, or appear to accept, that the threat of punishment is ineffective, at least for some offenses. This is related in turn to a fear, attached to the repeal of any criminal provisions, of increasing the sense of collective insecurity."[7] Admitting that deterrence alone does not require the notion of legal responsibility, Radzinowicz goes on to suggest that retribution (which does require *mens rea*) is itself a deterrent in that it reinforces the belief that people are responsible for their actions and can therefore resist the temptation to violate the law.[8] The publication in 1968 of *The Limits of the Criminal Sanction*[9] was regarded by many as an end to this confusion.

PACKER'S RATIONALE FOR DETERRENCE

Packer states that his work is written in layman's terms for the general reader: "The rhetorical question that this book poses is: how can we tell what the criminal sanction is good for?"[10] He divides the answer into three parts: (1) a rationale, positing basic assumptions and defining terms, including the generally recognized purposes of punishment; (2) a middle section—the most noted part of the book—dealing with the process by which the criminal sanction is applied; and (3) his recommendations for appropriate limits to the criminal sanction, based on his argument in Part I about the appropriate purposes of punishment and Part II about the means by which this process is implemented.

Packer's intention, then, was somewhat broader than is ordinarily the case in jurisprudential writing about the criminal law. Part II is one approach to the analysis of certain aspects of the criminal justice system (most notably its value orientations). Part III is not a justification for the penal law as it stands, but prescriptions for change in the scope of the criminal law. He does not address the administration and organization of the criminal justice system and does not cover corrections or the implementation of punishment. In other words, the basic question—what is the criminal sanction good for?—really asks who should be liable to criminal penalties for what behaviors, and how the determination of this liability should be established.

Packer defines Punishment (with a capital P), or the criminal sanction, as a processing of people that has these characteristics:

> (1) The presence of an offense; (2) the infliction of pain on account of the commission of the offense, (3) a dominant purpose that is neither to compensate someone injured by the offense nor to better the offender's condition, but to prevent further offenses or to inflict what is thought to be deserved pain on the offender.[11]

Note that this definition presumably requires (1) the existence of the state (or an entity that establishes offenses); (2) a negative reaction (the infliction of pain); and (3) manifest purposes of deterrence (prevention of further offenses) or retribution (infliction of *deserved* pain). The disavowal of compensation to the victim probably strengthens the implication of state involvement, although Packer is not explicit about who or what administers punishment.

Packer's review of the common purposes of punishment tends to clarify his definition. He reviews in turn retribution, deterrence, incapacitation, and rehabilitation, ends up rejecting all of the common definitions as inaccurately describing what actually happens, and then concludes that deterrence and retribution, properly defined, are very much the same thing and together justify the use of what is still, in his view, a lamentable and ambiguous practice.[12] Exactly why he qualifies a "necessary" or inevitable phenomenon as "lamentable" is unclear. Of course, punishment is necessary only within the context of the state, a point that Packer does not emphasize. It is not clear whether he is lamenting the existence of the state, or the apparently frequent conflict between the behavior of individuals and the rules of the state.

Some of Packer's conclusions about punishment are quite rational and commendable, if unremarkable. Concluding that the process is both necessary but ambiguous, his major recommendation is that it be used sparingly and with utmost caution in the deliberation of who is culpable (or punishable) in order to prevent "this human agency from becoming tyrannical and in the end destructive."[13]

He begins by rejecting the traditional definitions of retribution. These are: (1) retribution as *revenge*, meaning that the offender is paid back or that society fulfills the promise (threat) made in the criminal law; and (2) retribution as *expiation*, meaning that the offender pays back in return for something he has taken.[14] Packer argues that distinguishing which of these processes takes place is a silly exercise and that the proper meaning of retribution is "the criminal is to be punished simply because he has committed a crime."[15] This definition, of course, *does* make retribution and punishment synonymous. The value of doing so, suggests Packer, lies not in what it justifies, but in what it prevents: retribution defined in this way means that punishment can only be applied for demonstrated legal wrongs, not merely in response to objectionable behavior, and certainly not because someone may be dangerous or objectionable in the future.

Deterrence, Packer admits, is a problem. It is frequently broken into two types: *general deterrence*, or the application of punishment to one person so that others will not offend, and *special deterrence*, or the application of punishment to an individual so that the individual will not reoffend.[16] Packer takes the helpful step of reserving the term *deterrence* for the impact of punishment on the nonoffender and using the term *intimidation*, to refer to the application of penalties to the offender.[17]

Packer criticizes those who attack deterrence for being ineffective. "Unless we know what the crime rate would be if we did not punish criminals, the conclusion (or ineffectiveness) is unfounded," he correctly observes.[18] But, obviously, the same argument holds against those who state deterrence *is* effective, yet Packer clearly believes that penalties operate as deterrents. The material used to "demonstrate" this effect is weak.

> When the threat of punishment is removed or reduced, either through legislatve repeal . . . or through the inaction of enforcement authorities, conduct that has previously been repressed . . . tends to increase. We are so familiar with the phenomenon that there may be no more convincing demonstration than this of the effectiveness and complexity of deterrence.[19]

Packer is observing a correlation between high frequency of a certain behavior and repeal or nonenforcement of laws prohibiting that behavior. That *lifting* or relaxing the prohibition *caused* the high frequency would require, in addition to correlation, the demonstration that the change in enforcement *preceded* the change in behavior *and* that some other variable did not cause both the behavior and enforcement change. Packer can do neither of these and, indeed, the reverse interpretation seems equally or more likely true. For instance, prohibition of alcohol did not reduce the consumption of alcohol, and repeal of prohibition did not increase it. Similarly, reduction of the severity of sanctions for, and the nonenforcement of, marijuana laws followed the higher frequency of marijuana use, particularly by middle-class white people. Crimes of abortion, homosexuality, and vices provide similar examples. Generally, the change in law tends to lag behind the change in behavior rather than the reverse.[20] Moreover, evidence exists that the law not only lags behind changes in cultural valuation of behavior, but that the enforcement patterns lag considerably behind the cultural expectations of what is appropriate or deserved punishment.[21]

Packer rejects the notion that intimidation actually occurs by citing the high rates of recidivism.[22] But this rate, whether people characterize it as high or low, says nothing about the effect of special deterrence unless we know what reoffense rates would be had there been no punishment. This data is generally lacking, unless we would take as evidence that first offenders placed on probation generally do not recidivate. If probation in these instances is minimal or nominal supervision, this phenomenon may indicate that intimidation would not have been necessary in these cases. But, of course, it was not used in these cases.

Packer cites as evidence of the ineffectiveness of intimidation "that those subjected to the qualitatively less severe sanctions of probation or of early release from prison on parole have a lower rate of recidivism than do persons subjected to more severe punishment."[23] On the contrary, the majority of studies that control for type of offender demonstrate that variation in severity makes little difference.[24]

Packer also objects to intimidation because it cannot be uniformly applied; its efficacy will vary for different offenders. This observation seems correct. Rigorous criminological research demonstrated long ago that an equal amount of punishment may, in interaction with different offender characteristics, have negative, positive, or no effect.[25] But, if Packer is to insist on the differential results of intimidation, how can he presume that deterrence can be uniformly applied? His insistence on the variability of individual offender response to penalties combined with his denial of the same variability for the impact of general deterrence would indicate either or both of two false beliefs: (1) that offenders are socially isolated individuals whose varying response to punishment is unrelated to their social group membership, or (2) that all citizens are single units of action directly subject to the threat of state proscriptions, but unaffected by their community status and roles.

Packer does make some distinctions concerning various individuals' susceptibility to deterrence. He suggests that deterrence has its greatest effect on those people who are most completely socialized and, therefore, most accepting of the rules they are to follow.[26] There is probably some truth in this view. It suggests that punishment has been with us for so long that it has become part of the general cultural symbols employed in the primary socialization process. However, it is doubtful that the majority of law-abiding persons utilize punishment or the threat of it as a primary ingredient in socialization. A variety of child-rearing studies have demonstrated that middle-class parents depend much more on guilt formation for the demonstration of personal approval than they do on symbols of, or actual, punishment.[27]

Another point to remember when considering Packer's claims for deterrence is that most offenders are not caught and that most behaviors that are legally defined as crimes do not come to the attention of the police. Do the greater proportions of racial minorities—uneducated, poor, city dwellers—in reported arrests than in the general population mean that "those people" commit more crimes than the "law-abiding," or merely that the behavior of the "law-abiding" is less open to the scrutiny of the criminal justice officials?

As Stinchcombe points out: "There is a fundamental difference between conducting the affairs of a small social system in such a manner that no crimes committed shall come to the attention of the police, and conducting them so that a physically present policeman will approve."[28] But, more importantly, the benefit of being wealthy enough to commit crimes in private extends much further than to differential probability of being observed. Stinchcombe argues that because of the laws of evidence, crimes committed in private are more difficult to demonstrate in court because they are likely to have happened prior to police intervention (when it does come) and are likely to require the testimony of relatives, friends (and victims) of the private offender—something that is extremely difficult to obtain. It is much easier for the system to gain convictions for public acts to which the police officer can bear witness.[29] Since the group that Packer calls the "socialized" or "law-abiding" are the same group that have by definition the greatest remoteness from detection and conviction, it is uncertain whether deterrence has had this indirect, socializing effect on their behavior.

All of this is not to deny that punishment is demanded of those people who are caught or that the demand for "greater deterrence" (i.e., more severe sanctions) is currently popular in the United States. The belief that persons caught and convicted of crime should be punished is real and widespread, as is the belief that the criminal law deters and would do so more completely if it were more efficient in catching offenders and more severe in penalizing them. But these beliefs should be analyzed in the context of the situations in which they arise *and* in terms of the payoff (or function) of merely holding these beliefs.

One of the most incisive analyses of the functions of believing that a given social institution works is Bernard Beck's examinations of public welfare in the United States.[30] The notion that welfare recipients have moral deficiencies or lack industriousness, according to Beck, is functional for the existing economic system because it allows persons who are not on welfare to maintain that the American system really does provide equal opportunity to everyone who has sufficient pluck and determination to "achieve." The contrary view—that welfare is built into the American capitalist system—would require rejection of many dominant values and beliefs. Likewise, belief in deterrence may be functional to those who believe that accepted means of achievement are accessible to all, regardless of whether threats of punishment indeed deter. Deterrence theory is based upon the "All-American" belief that individuals have legitimate choices concerning the means by which to achieve.

The missing concepts in Packer's discussion of deterrence and retribution concern community and organization. Recent theories of public organization would suggest not that deterrence and retribution (as Packer defines them) work, but that beliefs in them "work," or perform significant functions in maintaining certain community structures and processes.[31]

These structures and processes will be examined in detail in the second half of this book. Suffice it to say for now that Packer's approach to the criminal sanction has two major deficiencies that are related to his inattention to the filtering and distortion that occur between conceptions of deterrence on a legislative (or pure theoretical) level and the impact of deterrence on persons. The effectiveness of deterrence not only depends upon but is determined by the public organizations that implement the law and by the interconnections among criminal justice agencies and other community level systems. Obtaining evidence of efficacy independent of variations in organizational behavior and community structure is not possible, even when the organizations are "telling the truth" rather than lying with statistics.

PACKER'S TWO MODELS OF THE CRIMINAL PROCESS

"Two Models of the Criminal Process," first published in 1964,[32] was later expanded to form the middle part of *The Limits of the Criminal Sanction*. Many believe that this section is by far the most valuable and novel portion of the book.[33] Packer proposes to examine the behavior that occurs in the criminal process as a by-product of competing value systems. The purpose of this examination during a discourse on the limits of the criminal sanction is quite practical. "The kind of criminal process we have is an important determinant of the kind of behavior content that the criminal law ought rationally to comprise."[34]

Packer suggests that two value clusters underlie all the operations of the criminal justice system—the "Crime Control Model" and the "Due Process Model." He suggests that neither model is dominant; that both affect the operations of all agencies of justice; and that it is through an understanding of the operational compromises of these two competing ideologies that we can understand why the system behaves as it does.

The different characteristics of the two belief systems are contrasted in Table 2.1.

While Packer discusses these two poles as different models, John Griffiths's major article, dealing with the same area, argues that Packer was really describing one model in which value systems compete. The model, said Griffiths, is one of battle because whether one upholds due process or crime control tactics, the goal of the process is conviction rather than correction.[35] Due Process adherents would make the road to exile a difficult one to travel, while the Crime Control proponents are more in favor of a major highway. But, in either case, the interest in the *guilty* party stops at conviction. Packer is very clear on this point, in terms of the fairness

Table 2.1. A Summary of Characteristics of Packer's Two Models of the Criminal Process

Crime Control	Due Process
1. Criminal justice process is positive guarantee of social freedom.	Criminal process is most severe social sanction to be used on free citizens.
2. Criminal acts are major threat to social order.	Investigation and prosecution of crimes can lead to severe constriction of social freedoms.
3. To ensure social order we need high rates of apprehension and conviction.	To ensure freedom we need to guarantee that procedures of apprehension and conviction are of high quality.
4. To achieve high rates we need a system that can routinely process cases with speed and finality of outcome.	To ensure minimal abuse of coercive sanctions we must have a highly visible decision process and means for review and challenge of outcomes.
5. Speed can be gained through uniformity of procedures for all cases, and finality can be achieved through an informal, administrative decisionmaking process.	To ensure visibility and care we must emphasize individuality of cases and high formality with a judicial decision-making process.
6. The best way of implementing above needs is through an "administrative" assembly line structure.	The best way of implementing above safeguards is through adversary process, with continual checks and balances to provide obstacle course to flow of cases.
7. Successful conclusion is achieved by an early screening out of people who are innocent or unlikely to be convicted, and gaining quick and inexpensive convictions of the rest, with little opportunity for challenge.	Successful conclusion is full application of rights in adversary proceeding that is concerned with determining the criminal responsibility of the accused.
8. This conclusion rests on a presumption of guilt, which is a prediction of likely outcome of the case.	This conclusion rests on a "presumption of innocence," which is a directive about how to proceed regardless of the probable outcome.
9. Focal point of process is the guilty plea, which holds need for judicial fact-finding to a minimum.	Focal point is the trial, because adjudicative fact-finding is most accurate and fair.
10. Reliability of the process is assured through high efficiency—processing cases as quickly and cheaply as possible, screening out weak cases prior to prosecution.	Reliability of the process is through quality control on each case; more efficiency can be oppressive in individual instance.
11. Correction of errors through administrative controls; criminals should never be released because of mistaken procedure by officials.	Correction of errors through appeal; "self-corrective" mechanism applied on a case-by-case basis; release of offenders, as correction, deters official misbehavior in the future.
12. There is basic confidence in the agency action and in the representativeness of the government that structured the executive agencies.	There is basic doubt about the efficacy of punishment applied through formal governmental mechanisms.

Table 2.1 *(Continued)*

	Crime Control	Due Process
13.	The validating authority in this process is legislative and statutory, where directives for action are set.	The validating authority of this process is judicial and constitutional, where limits to allowable action are set.

Source: **David Duffee and Robert Fitch,** *An Introduction to Corrections, A Policy and Systems Approach* (Santa Monica, Calif.: Goodyear, 1976).

that the Due Process model would extend to the defendant who is very probably guilty. He argues that the reason for treating such a man to all the rights and privileges of the innocent is not that even a guilty man is due such considerations, but, on the contrary, that even such a defendant, in the Due Proces model, has a realistic legal chance of being proven legally (rather than factually) not guilty. Thus, *every* man, no matter how weighty the facts arrayed against him, is due all considerations until the pronouncement of the judicial determination of guilt. Both Griffiths and Packer would agree that, regardless of its name, the strategy of battle is so dominant in the preconviction system, and in the general citizens' understanding of the preconviction system, that the consequences of this ideology permeate all criminal justice operations.

PACKER'S LIMITS

Packer sets out to find limiting criteria for the criminal sanction, based on the assumptions that its purposes are ambiguous and that the criminal process is a difficult and costly operation that is easily strained by an overload of cases or behaviors to control. Packer does not claim to have devised a complete list of limiting criteria, nor did he try to identify all the behaviors against which the sanction should be applied. But he does list six criteria, or characteristics of conduct, that should be present if a criminal statute and its enforcement should be a means of control.

1. The conduct is prominent in most people's view of socially threatening behavior, and is not condoned by any significant segment of society.
2. Subjecting it to the criminal sanction is not inconsistent with the goals of punishment.
3. Suppressing it will not inhibit socially desirable conduct.

4. It may be dealt with through even-handed and nondiscriminatory enforcement.
5. Controlling it through the criminal process will not expose that process to severe qualitative or quantitative strains.
6. There are no reasonable alternatives to the criminal sanction for dealing with it.[36]

Examples of current criminal laws that would falter under these criteria are fairly obvious. Packer discusses morals offenses, abortion, gambling, drunkenness, and some business crimes as behaviors that fail to meet some or all of these criteria. He cautions that unless earnest steps are taken to limit the sanction to those types of conduct that it is competent to deal with (under these criteria), the criminal sanction and the criminal process will become increasingly less effective in dealing with the types of conduct for which it is the only feasible control.

Packer's limits are seriously intended and adherence to them, even in a few instances, would certainly make significant changes both in the criminal justice system (for the persons who have been committing those types of behaviors) and for the communities that might then seek other ways of controlling that behavior (if the behavior was still determined to be undesirable). Packer assumes that the results of taking these limits seriously will include the system's ability to allocate a greater proportion of resources to "serious criminal conduct" and greater confidence and respect by citizens for the system and the criminal sanction. These are fairly common assumptions behind drives for legislative reform, but they are relatively myopic unless we have fairly certain answers about why these limits have not been adopted in the past. This is not to suggest that the purposes served by the present "overreach" of the criminal law are necessarily positive. On the contrary, it is quite possible that they have been generally detrimental, as in the case of the growing disrespect for the criminal law, as Packer proposes.

The problem is that there is nothing in Packer's discussion that would allow us to guess, and in absence of data one way or the other, it is unclear why there should be more caution in the application of the criminal sanction than there should be in its limitation. While Packer believes that these criteria, if applied, would make the criminal law less socially divisive, the opposite effect also seems quite possible, *if* the criteria are to be interpreted and applied as Packer intends them.

If read in the intended fashion, the net result *could* be a limitation of the criminal sanction to deal with behaviors found *most visibly* among the lower classes, minorities, and in cities. Stated in another way, Packer could limit the criminal sanction to behaviors known as "traditional street crime."[37] Packer's examples of conducts most appropriately subject to the

the criminal sanction are the F.B.I.'s "index crimes" of murder, rape, robbery, and aggravated assault. According to Packer, "no one would dispute the view that these offenses are the most threatening and the most strongly condemned in the entire criminal calendar."[38] His reliance on "threat" and "condemnation" in this statement is troublesome, since throughout the remainder of Part 3 he insists that the sanction should be reserved to deal with real social "harms" rather than to satisfy moral predispositions or ulterior political aims.

In effect, what Packer actually makes clear is the evanescence of the term "objective social harm," even when applied to crimes known as *mala in se*. If there actually were an *objective* determination of harm, then the system might be better directed against drunken driving, consumer fraud, organized and white-collar crime, all of which are more damaging excesses in terms of life and property than the ones he mentions. Packer rejects these crimes as most important because they are not the most visible, or are too complicated for people to see clearly as crimes, or do not raise the sharpest demand for retribution, or for similar reasons. However, by Packer's own criteria, then, his limits are contradictory. If the operational definition of important crime turns out in reality to mean the crime that the system most frequently concentrates on, then the morals crimes and drunkenness and the other minor crimes that Packer would purge from the criminal law must be just as important as those crimes that he cites, since the system expends tremendous energy on them.[39]

Throughout Part III of his book, Packer adopts the stance that the criminal sanction should be limited to those types of conduct where its use will provide a clear and direct utility in the control of the specific behavior described in the prohibition. Indeed, he suggests that the criminal sanction is best applied "in situations where both deterrence and incapacitation are effective: where people are relatively likely to be deflected by the possibility of being caught *and* where punishment is likely to prevent the commission of further crimes."[40] But, much earlier in Part I, Packer suggested that the most important impact of punishment was not on the offender, or the prospective offender, but on the law-abiding, as a reinforcement of their sense of values. If the sanction is most important for its indirect socializing, symbolic, and dramaturgical effects, the limiting criteria should not be based upon the direct effects, in terms of the conduct of groups that are the explicit objects of the sanction.

To demonstrate the shortcomings of Packer's suggested limitations on the use of the criminal sanction, one can extrapolate his six guidelines in terms of their potential consequences for the criminal justice system as it operates. Six of these implications, paralleling his six guidelines, are as follows:

1. If the criminal sanction is limited to behavior that is prominently

threatening, the sanction and the investigative resources of the system will not be applied in cases of conduct that is highly sophisticated and in which the damage is diffused or not immediately evident. This emphasis will operationally constrain use of the criminal sanction against the increasing number of crimes that employ complex technologies or are committed in the course of conducting legally approved business.

2. The criminal sanction, if it is to be applied in accordance with dominant or pervasive values, will not or cannot be utilized in order to educate or guide the dominant group in instances where common (or normative) behavior is socially harmful, or is contrary to other important values.

3. The criminal sanction should not be employed in events where its application inhibits "normal" behavior. Hence, by principle, the criminal sanction might be inapplicable to cases where normal behavior is itself criminal, as in the case of much price-fixing and consumer fraud. While there may indeed be better ways to handle such behavior than punishing it criminally, not doing so leaves the criminal sanction open to challenges that its officials are biased toward certain classes or establishments. In effect, it can limit the use of the sanction even more than is now the case to instances where the offender is *not* seen as a valuable contributing member of society. In too many cases, this will be the offender who is unemployed, on welfare, or in other ways isolated from the "valuable" behaviors of the American culture.

4. The criminal sanction must be open to even-handed and nondiscriminatory enforcement. This limit will in many ways reduce the current level of snooping, electronic surveillance, use of informers, entrapment, etc. But this limit also pressures the system's agents to be primarily concerned with behavior in public places rather than with the behavior of persons who can afford privacy. If the distributive justice system is itself unfair, the criminal system following this limit can only reproduce or reinforce this unfairness. In contrast, persons who favor affirmative action strategies might argue that the system should provide deprived persons a "break," either by being stricter with those who can afford privacy, or being more lenient with those who cannot.

5. The sanction is not to be used in ways that generate severe qualitative or quantitative strains on the system. This limit is intended to reduce the "punishment as a revolving door" policy, such as is the case with chronic drunks in large cities. But this guide may produce severe quantitative strains on other systems. Also, it might prevent prosecution in cases where the defendant had the resources to fight a just prosecution. Even now, prosecutors balance the expensive prosecution of one offender against several prosecutions of petty offenders who have more meager means of protecting themselves from intervention.

6. The sanction is to be used when there are no reasonable alternatives

for dealing with the behavior in question. This limit, taken seriously, could bring the system to a halt. There are many critics of criminal justice who believe there are always alternatives to punishment. For example, Korn believes that the criminal sanction is used primarily against the poor because it is they who cannot gain access to the existing alternatives.[41]

It is doubtful that Packer had these implications in mind, but these consequences *could* occur, based on information on the differential impact of public organizations upon persons in the United States who are differentially situated. The possibility that limiting the criminal sanction could have such results suggests two possible alternatives to Packer's assumptions about the criminal law and criminal process. One alternative is that the criminal law by its very nature is a means of discrimination or divisiveness. Its function is not to bring people together, but to keep them apart: to maintain the authority of those in power and to maintain the subordination of those who are out of power. This assumption could lead to communism or radicalism, or some other anticapitalist stance, but not necessarily. It could also lead to Van den Haag's position (which we shall review momentarily) that the criminal law is meant to maintain the current social structure by controlling coercively those whom the social system deprives of its benefits (and that it *should* do that because discrimination or deprivation of somebody is inevitable).

The second possible alternative assumption is that the criminal law can simply be limited out of existence because reasonable alternatives to its application always exist. This assumption may lead to anarchism, but not necessarily. It can also lead to the impetus for more subtle and less obviously coercive means of social control, alternatives that many authors have summarized as the coming of the welfare state.

RETRIBUTION: VAN DEN HAAG'S CHOCOLATE-COATED BULLET

For Herbert Packer, the criminal sanction seems an unpleasant device that he could imagine himself suffering for behaviors he cannot imagine himself doing. It is a plea to treat "those people" nicely on the way to the slaughter, so that should they escape, they will remember the fair escort and be kind, rather than remember the intended objective and be angry.

In contrast, for Van den Haag, the criminal sanction is the very same means of controlling "those people" as he would expect that they would use on him. He only recommends some steps to strengthen its controlling capacity so that he will not need to suffer his own recommendations.

Like Packer's works, Van den Haag's is also divided into three parts, but their focus is considerably different from Packer's. Part I, "The Institution of Punishment," defines terms, contrasts criminal or penal justice with distributive justice, and criticizes the viewpoint that punishment is unnecessary. Part II, "Controlling Crime," tackles many of the common explanations for crime and some of the commonly favored "alternatives to punishment." Part III begins with the assumption that punishment has now been defined and justified and goes on to describe a few types of punishment with suggestions on how they might be better used.

One of Van den Haag's major objectives in *Punishing Criminals* is to set the record straight on two key relationships which, in his belief, have been dangerously confused and confounded in the twentieth century. One is the relationship between criminal punishment and the variety of other means of social control available in a given society. The other is the relationship between crime and its supposed causes, and consequently, with the relationship between crime and punishment as a means of control.

In his opening pages, Van den Haag states that criminal laws prohibit activities called crimes by the threat and implementation of penalties, or punishment. In other words, criminal justice for Van den Haag is very narrowly limited to decisions concerning what to call crimes, decisions on the type and severity of penalties, and decisions on how these penalties can be most effectively administered. Criminal justice is not concerned with something he calls "social justice," or "distributive justice," the institutions for distributing (equitably or not) the things that are valued in a particular culture. Van den Haag asserts that the importance of criminal justice has risen because the proportion of crimes that are punished is low, the crime rate is "high," and perceptions of public safety are therefore threatened. He finds that the fundamental problem with criminal justice as presently instituted is doubt about the moral legitimacy of using punishment to control behavior.

Van den Haag then proposes to take a realistic, objective look at both punishment and its administration (as well as some alternatives) in an effort to determine whether criminal justice can be improved.[42] He begins with the simple statement that punishment is a deprivation or a pain imposed by law. "Suffering may be said to be punitive only when it is court-imposed retribution for violating laws."[43]

Like Packer, Van den Haag clearly identifies retribution and criminal punishment. However, he is very careful to distinguish retribution from revenge or vengeance, unlike the social psychologists, Ross and Bernard. Van den Haag argues that vengeance serves only the perpetrator, not the state or society, and that vengeance ungoverned by rules is generally not in proportion to the wrong committed. He finds retribution quite different because:

1. it is only imposed by a court after trial or a guilty plea;
2. it is only done to an offender found guilty of a crime;
3. the behavior punished is proscribed in advance;
4. the penalty is in proportion to the offense, and is published in advance;
5. it is inflicted as a means of enforcing the law and justifying legally imposed order, not to vindicate an individual.[44]

It is interesting, if somewhat troublesome, that Van den Haag characterizes the legal order as "objective." While it is clearly different from an individual's subjective desire for revenge, the order imposed through written rules is the product of the subjective desires of legislators, judges who interpret and apply rules in particular cases, and police who decide whether any particular behavior is included in the rules, and, even if it is, whether the rules should be enforced in that case. Van den Haag says that retribution, or maintenance of this objective order, will control subjective urges. He suggests that if retribution were dropped, revenge would become much more frequent, in the activity of vigilantes. Van den Haag may be confusing lack of legal order with lack of any order, or equating absence of law and law enforcement with disorder. This equation would be clearly unfounded, in that many stateless or lawless societies clearly have an objective order and do not rely heavily upon revenge (or find other non-legal means of maintaining order. At any rate, Van den Haag apparently places a great deal of subjective, personal value upon the particular type of order represented by the law.

Much like Packer, Van den Haag attaches much significance to the present and future effects of retribution. He is quite correct to insist that retribution is not a worthless (or impossible) attempt to correct the past. He argues that retribution is *not* aimed at some magical fixing of a past event, but rather is undertaken to restore order in the present. He also suggests that retribution—or the implementation of promised punishment—can affect the future by assuring persons that rules will be enforced, or promises of punishment kept.[45] Not only does retribution fulfill a promise to the offender, it also fulfills a promise to those who did not break the law. Van den Haag argues that those who did obey the law under threat of punishment will have been fooled (or fools) if the punishment is not exacted from offenders. He clearly makes the assumptions that the law-abiding: (1) were threatened and influenced by the threat, and (2) would have wanted to engage in the proscribed behavior, except for the threat.[46] Based on these assumptions, he argues that the criminal law does have a deterrent function because the crime rate would be somewhat higher without than with the threat of punishment.

Two important observations should be made regarding these assumptions. The first is that, much like Packer, Van den Haag is willing to state hypotheses and assumptions as if they were demonstrated fact (e.g., that the crime rate would be higher without threatened punishment, because *somebody* must have been deterred). Second, Van den Haag apparently makes a greater distinction between retribution and deterrence than did Packer: he feels that the threat of punishment has a significant, direct deterrent impact on the action of individuals, while Packer, at least in Part I of *Limits*, claims that the greatest impact of the criminal sanction is probably the indirect, cultural, or symbolic influence during the socialization process.[47]

Van den Haag suggests that the major distinction between the deterrent (or utilitarian) function of the criminal sanction and the retributive (or justice) function is one of time. He claims that utility is the main purpose in making laws and prescribing punishments, while retribution or justice must be the prevailing purpose in the judicial phases—in the distribution of penalties to individual offenders. Sanctions, or more precisely, criminal sanctions, are necessary because some people want to do what is prohibited. Van den Haag implies a "conflict model" of society in this discussion, although he finds the conflict either inevitable or good, and the criminal sanction either a necessary means of control or one that limits the scope of the conflict and guards or maintains the positive outcomes of this conflict. "What the laws prohibit because disadvantageous to society can be advantageous to some individuals; or they may think it is. Society must try to make prohibited acts clearly disadvantageous to all if its laws are to be heeded."[48]

While Van den Haag admits that conformity to legal prescriptions stands to benefit some persons more than others, he is quite ambiguous on the issue of who determines what is advantageous for society, and how. There is an apparent oversimplification, again, of the relationship between "individuals" and "society." In the above quotation, it sounds as though the legal proscriptions guard an "objective social order" (or are advantageous to society), whereas crimes are committed by individuals in conflict with the entire society. On the other hand, if conformity to the legal order clearly benefits some people more than others, a differential that Van den Haag admits, then it is hard to distinguish the benefit or advantage to society from the benefit or advantage to particular groups within society, specifically those whose social position increases their share in the distributive justice system through noncriminal methods. The criminal sanction then becomes a means of defending or perpetuating a particular class order or social structure in order to provide longevity to the incumbency of those with advantageous social positions. Van den Haag seems to admit the truth of this conclusion also: "However just in applying its rules, retributive justice cannot be ultimately just unless distributive justice is. For retributive justice necessarily defends and sanctions the distributive order in its major political and economic aspects."[49] However, Van den Haag counters two arguments usually associated with this admission that the criminal sanction perpetuates an unequal distribution of social resources. Some would say that crime is caused by relative deprivation and therefore that punishment is an immoral as well as an ineffective means of coping with crime. Van den Haag replies that not all equally deprived persons commit crimes, and that those deprived persons who do commit crimes should not then be excused. And some argue that the deprived do not commit more crimes than the well-to-do, but commit different kinds of crimes and are caught and punished more frequently. While Van den Haag doubts this possibility, he suggests that the correction of this condition, if it exists, is not to let the deprived go free also, but rather to be more effective in apprehending the well-to-do.[50]

Because Van den Haag is willing, specifically at least, to admit that some conflict will be inherent in the utilization of the criminal law as a means of social control, the contradictions in his rationale for deterrence and retribution are subtle. The argument that Van den Haag apparently wants his readers to accept is this: (1) the criminal law is far from a perfect vehicle for the maintenance of social order, but one necessary in societies governed by states; (2) modern, industrialized, urbanized societies apparently employ state structures as a means of social control, as substitutes or functional equivalents of the less formal and less bureaucratic social controls found in simpler societies; (3) distribution of social rewards in the social structure of this state society is discriminatory, or uneven, and the temptation to deviate from normative or legal behavior in order to obtain culturally valued objectives or life conditions will fall disproportionately upon the lower economic classes; (4) the criminal law and criminal penalties are imposed more frequently on those most frequently tempted, and therefore the criminal law is invoked against the lower economic classes most frequently; (5) the current social structure, however, is equally discriminatory and less invidious in its discriminations than the conceivable options, such as communism or fascism, and because our present distributive system is more flexible than those options, it holds out more benefits for more people, in relation to its disadvantages, than is true of other distributive systems; (6) the current distributive system is, therefore, worth preserving and the criminal justice system is one necessary means of preserving that order, but (7) the criminal justice system as currently operated has taken on sufficiently mixed purposes that the influence of retribution and deterrence are currently being lost; and (8) steps can be taken to strengthen these influences and, therefore, to maintain more effectively our current distributive system.[51]

Van den Haag places his values—primarily his commitment to our current social structure, means of government, and economic system—so squarely on the line that apparently he would have us challenge these values rather than his analysis of why and how retribution and deterrence function within that system and why and how his suggested improvements would be effective. It would seem, then, that he is counting on the probability that most readers will have similar values (which is, of course, a very safe bet) and, therefore, that his facts and predictions will be taken as accurate and his arguments seen as rational.

The weak point in Van den Haag's argument is found in his notion of social order and the criminal sanction as a means of preserving it. He states that it is to *society's* advantage to punish certain behavior, while it is more advantageous to *some individuals* than to others to behave in the ways forbidden. In other words, he seems to argue that enforcement of the criminal law benefits an abstract social order, rather than particular individuals or groups, while admitting that breaking the law benefits particular individuals and groups more than others. It is evidently very important to him to find some fiction or abstraction ("*the* social order") that benefits from the punishment of some groups more than others in order to make this mechanism of social control seem ethical or fair. If he admitted that "the social order" happens only to be one particular social order enjoyed by particular groups or individuals who stand to benefit from its maintenance, then the justice in retribution and the utility of deterrence would seem far more questionable.

He admits that the distributive system is discriminatory, but simply states that he values this set of discriminations over those inherent in other conceivable distributive systems. These admissions make it apparent that there is no functional or empirical difference between the notion of "the social order" and a social order that those in power define and seek to maintain. (This situation, of course, is identical to the definition of "social will" that McConnell justified on the grounds that the social elite had demonstrated their evolutionary superiority.) The *assumption* that this social order is the most advantageous to everyone in society is an assumption that will be held by, and will benefit, those persons in power in this system.

By recognizing that the criminal law is utilized as a means of control only, or most often, against outsiders, or against persons whom the distributive system has discriminated against, Van den Haag has implied that the criminal law cannot deter the most serious or damaging social acts because the persons who have the opportunity to commit them will do so using the same tools or means that are used to commit what are seen as socially desirable acts. The criminal law will be implemented most frequently and most severely against those persons who have only illegal opportunities to choose from and will be used less frequently and less severely against persons who have both legitimate and illegitimate opportunities in their goal-achieving arsenal.

Van den Haag's rather cavalier disregard for the relationship between social class and crime is particularly evident in his suggestions for handling "psychopaths" or "exceptional people." He suggests that irrational crimes, or those committed without normal, middle-class motives could be controlled by incapacitating all such people.[52] He is suggesting here that most crimes are committed by rational people, but that some crimes are the products of irrational people whose crimes either do not help them to achieve their personal objectives or who commit crimes against irrational odds (a negative cost-benefit ratio). For example, he suggests that the incarceration of all psychopaths would rid us of all crimes that psychopaths commit. Not only is this argument silly because it is circular, but it suggests that Van den Haag is completely naive about the effects of his valued distributive system upon the socially disturbing acts that he wants to control. If he is seriously suggesting that there is no relationship between incidence of mental illness (exceptional people) and social structure, he is ignoring almost all empirical investigations of mental illness from those of Durkheim[53] to the present.[54] Finally, he suggests that while the possibilities for effective incapacitation, intimidation, or rehabilitation are very limited, this is not important since the main penal objectives of retribution and deterrence do not depend at all on the individual offender. Again, he is making artificial distinctions between the individual and the social system that are empirically impossible to verify and logically damaging to his own arguments. He is maintaining that the ineffectiveness of the criminal law in controlling the behavior of the offender is totally irrelevant to its control of behavior in others. If this point were indeed true it would totally contradict his belief that crime is deterrable because it is usually committed by rational people. If offenders are like nonoffenders in the sense that most members of both groups are rational, how can it be that the criminal sanction having little if any effect on the one group can be expected to have a great effect on the other? Or, if he is suggesting that most offenders are the irrational or poorly skilled criminals (i.e., his exceptional people) why would he suggest that the criminal sanction, employed against the irrational criminal, will affect the behavior of the rational, unapprehended criminal? Surely the rational criminal, if he is capable of calculating the cost-benefit ratio of a particular crime, is also capable of discerning the difference between the exceptional persons who are punished and himself.

Van den Haag's irrational distinction between the impact of the criminal sanction on the offender and the nonoffender is even more evident in his explanation of why retribution and deterrence are weaker now than perhaps they were in some previous time: "By reducing the stigmatizing effect of punishment, mobility also reduces its deterrent effect; both are likely to be weaker in the less close-knit and stable community in which the punishment occurs and the more easily the punished person can leave his stigma behind by moving into circles where he is not known."[55] He suggests that deterrence and retribution will be less effective in a highly mobile, urban society than in a less complex one because of the relative anonymity under which people operate and the lack of mutual interdependence and normative consensus (close-knit and stable) among the people involved. While many persons make this observation about modern society, the conclusions Van den Haag draws from it are illogical. If modern social structure allows persons to escape retribution (reduced stigma) and the reduced stigma reduces the felt threat of the law (reduced deterrence), he cannot assume that the offender feels this reduction any more than the potential or the unapprehended offender.

> By definition, punishment could not deter at all, if actual and potential offenders alike were not deterrable. Incapacitation and reform would become society's main protection, for punishment is useless if the population falls into two separate groups: potential or actual offenders who are not deterrable, and others who are not potential offenders and need not be deterred.[56]

Arguing that both retribution and deterrance are less effective in our social structure than in that of simpler societies, he has successfully established that the criminal sanction is not an effective means of maintaining the social order, given our type of social structure. He has, in effect, stated that to the extent that offenders and nonoffenders are alike (except for their social station), the criminal law is a poor or ineffective substitute for the informal social controls that were utilized in more close-knit and stable societies. The criminal law is not a viable social control mechanism where there are few informal social sanctions available to support the values implied in the criminal law. Stated in another way, the criminal law or negative, punitive responses to deviance are not effective in a turbulent, rapidly changing social system that is morally and socially fragmented. Under these conditions, the criminal law will only serve to separate more completely those holding the formal mechanisms of control from those people against whom these mechanisms are used.

"Unquestionably, it is morally preferable, and less costly, to create conditions that reduce provocations to law breaking (than to enforce unfair laws). Enforcement is easier when laws are accepted and people feel morally obligated to obey them."[57]

As charitable and wise as this conclusion from Van den Haag may sound, the recommendation rings hollow. He has stated previously that this social system (and any other he can imagine) is inherently discriminatory and that the criminal law is a means of protecting that system of discrimination.

If this is true, it is difficult to see how he can conceive of a criminal law system that all persons will feel morally obligated to follow. The conclusion itself, however, is probably false. It is probably more accurate to say that the criminal sanction is a coercive alternative to reducing the disparities in the social structure. It is possible that our type of social structure requires the use of the criminal sanction. On the other hand, it is possible that alternative means of social control would achieve more effectively than the criminal law the control of undesirable or costly social behavior and yet allow us to retain many of the perceived advantages of our type of distributive justice. Van den Haag's commitment to the maintenance of the criminal sanctioning system is likely both to reduce the energies available to exploring these control options as well as to increase the inherent instability in the social structure that he seems to value so much.

What we should explore then are the manner in which our unstable and complex social structure mediates and changes both legal norms and informal ones and the extent to which workable options to the criminal law exist in complex, heterogeneous social systems. The next chapter begins this examination, in a small way, by examining the positions of Karl Menninger and Ramsey Clark concerning the criminal justice system.

Chapter 3

Social Welfare and Criminal Justice in Search of a Theory

A very different attitude toward criminal justice is provided by a group of scholars and critics represented here by Karl Menninger and Ramsey Clark. While far too divergent in thinking and training to be called a school, this group of criminal justice experts concentrates primarily on "social welfare" and the best means of achieving it, rather than on the social morality to be imposed by deterrence and retribution.

Perhaps the greatest distinction between the social moralists and the social welfare group is that the former assumes that the coercive threat of the criminal sanction is to be used against some (large or small) groups of people in order to maintain the morality or normative structure of society, while the latter group assumes that a moralistic approach to deviance not only lacks utility, but, in effect, is unethical because it promotes suffering and impedes advancing the welfare of all citizens. The social welfare group takes a complex but generally nonlegal stance toward the criminal justice system. Although there are many different approaches within this group, there is one common characteristic: the insistence that the criminal justice system must be evaluated in terms of its ability to improve the conditions as well as the behavior of the people against whom it directly intervenes. Relative to the social moralists, this group focuses far more on the offender. They would insist that the offender should not be sacrificed to the moral comfort of others, and that the welfare of offenders is inextricably bound to the welfare of the rest of society. Many of their arguments are seen as either naively "good-hearted" or irrationally biased toward criminals by the retributionists, who insist that the welfare group has ignored the unavoidable fact that the criminal law is basically and fundamentally a punitive device aimed at protecting the nonoffender. The Welfare group, in general, has two replies. First, they would disagree that nonoffenders are better served by punishing offenders than by finding alternatives to punishment. Second, they would argue that the primary goals of the criminal justice system have themselves changed from ones of retribution and deterrence to ones of treatment, rehabilitation, and/or social change.

Perhaps it is over the question of whether the criminal justice system is actually good for anything that the major rift in the Welfare group occurs. Some suggest that while the general goals of the criminal justice system have shifted from retribution to treatment and rehabilitation, the organizational changes necessary to implement these new goals have not evolved. These persons might argue that criminal justice's basic problems are the internal ones of revamping organizational technologies and structures so that they can accomplish the tasks of social welfare. Another segment of this group would argue that promotion of general social welfare has become a societal goal, but that antiquated institutions such as the criminal justice system retard our ability to implement this societal priority. For these persons, the primary problems are political: how to dismantle an ancient and well-established system and promote the building of other social institutions better suited to the goals at hand.

Two of the social welfare proponents' most difficult problems concern the same variables that the social moralists tended to ignore. One problem is that the Welfare group usually places too much faith in the known alternatives to criminal justice. In their eagerness to criticize criminal justice, they frequently ignore problems of organizational ineffectiveness in the other institutions of social welfare. A second problem is that they generally are incapable of explaining why the criminal justice system and the demand for retribution are so difficult to change or abolish, if their social utility is indeed obsolete. In other words, they have difficulty explaining, and in some cases totally ignore, the question of why modern American communities tend to handle social disturbances through coercive, group-dividing means. Without more detailed and theoretically guided attention to organization and community structure, many social welfare arguments become more incomplete and contradictory than the social moralist approaches.

THE EVOLUTION OF THE WELFARE APPROACH

Unlike the Moralists' justifications for the criminal law, which have been fairly static over time, the Welfare approach has shown some marked change since 1900, as the confidence in social science has waned and as the complexity of social problems has increased.

In 1912, McConnell could argue confidently that science could determine the specific cause of specific crimes and that each offender could then be treated accordingly.[1] This early belief that science could, and soon would, offer a cure for every problem was very strong, and probably influenced the lack of respect granted the law as a means of dealing with social problems. "Scientific approaches were seen as rational, and legal ones as prescientific and irrational. Moreover, scientific findings, as outcomes of rational enterprise, were supposedly things that everyone could accept and agree upon, while the law was perceived as a means of controlling conflict when the scientific means of resolving it had not yet become available. The law was rejected as slow, clumsy, and unsophisticated. Ross cautioned that "Often the very society that unweariedly works out its law into detail, and provides redress in more and more cases, is itself an organization of injustice."[2] A generation later, L. L. Bernard discounted the role of law in social control with the observation that "law is after all a somewhat clumsy instrument for the promotion of social welfare. It is all too frequently used as a cudgel with which to repress bad behavior instead of as an incentive to better conduct."[3] Bernard continued his criticism that the law is unpredictable in results and ineffective because it is dependent upon its enforceability as well as upon social approval and understanding to be effective.[4] Lastly, wrote Bernard, the law is extremely costly because its use is limited to those cases where social disruption can be analyzed in terms of proven fact about who was responsible for a particular problem.[5] A skeptic might ask whether any other means of social control is any less dependent upon social approval and understanding, less costly, or less dependent upon implementation through complex, bureaucratic structures.

Writing at about the same time as Bernard, Landis made the positive case for the social welfare movement, rather than the negative case against the legal system. He claimed that we had finally (in 1932) recognized poverty and other social problems as characteristics of social structure rather than characteristics of individuals.[6] The recognition that deviance of various sorts was a social rather than a moral problem was, he claimed, beginning to have effects on the societal response to deviance.

> Certain articles of social legislation, the growth of secondary group charity, the humanized attitudes toward juvenile delinquency and crime, which place upon the community its rightful share of responsibility—these and many similar gestures... suggest that a new type of thinking in terms of general "social welfare" may have reached at least the embryonic stage of development.[7]

In 1933, George Dession entered in the *Yale Law Journal* some classic observations on the influence of the general social welfare trend upon criminal justice. Using the term "psychiatry" to refer to the general efforts to change people through the utilization of professional and scientific knowledge, Dession proposed that the influx of psychiatry into criminal justice administration brought with it for the first time the idea that the criminal disposition could fail, because for the first time the punishment was supposed to rehabilitate.[8] He saw the interest in behavior changing theretofore absent in the administration of penalties and requiring a far greater sensitivity and sophistication than possessed by the organizations of criminal justice. Dession went on to argue, unlike many of his colleagues, that there was no basic incompatibility between modern behavioral science and the substantive criminal law. Rather, he thought that the real conflict was observable in getting the community to assume the costs of dispositional alternatives consistent with the technologies and organizational structures required by behavioral science. He suggested that psychiatrists and other treaters preferred to rail against the antiquated language of the criminal law or to work within the inadequate existing institutions rather than work for change in the economic and political conditions that militated against the effective implementation of ameliorative social technologies. He claimed that the optimistic promises of treatment on the one hand and the existence of inferior staffs and facilities on the other represented behavior so inconsistent that its occurrence in individuals would be labeled psychopathic.[9] While Dession certainly raised some red flags over the ameliorative uses of criminal justice, he still held out rather confidently the promise that social science, if provided with proper resources, can itself provide effective behavioral change.

A more recent, sociological view of the contradiction between treatment, or welfare goals, and actual organizational outcomes stresses the operating constraints on all "humane institutions," not just those on the criminal justice system. This point of view stresses that "humane," public institutions are inevitably inefficient and ineffective because of their relation to the political process.[10] High ideal goals are set for these institutions by humanitarians during the legislative process because of the reward or value that they perceive to be gained simply by setting such goals. The goal setters, however, do not have to implement the organizations that result from their enabling legislation. These organizations lack the technologies to achieve the goals. About all that such public institutions can really offer, at best, is some practical help or suggestions on how to survive and, most often, merely the management of internal organizational conflict and the avoidance of routine human disasters. But neither the staff nor the clients of such organizations are able to settle for practical help and management rather than cures, the staff because they are evaluated by the public failures at cure (e.g., new crimes), and the clients because their lives are frequently controlled by the public belief that cure is possible.¹¹ This analysis raises doubts that ameliorative or remedial social welfare is possible in the first place, or at least suggests that the political process surrounding public organizations makes its achievement very difficult. And yet Clark, Menninger, and others claim that Welfare goals for criminal justice hold far more value than the alternative of retributive reactions to social disturbance.

RAMSEY CLARK'S *CRIME IN AMERICA*

Crime in America is an intense, emotional statement about crime (or certain types of crime), its causes (or at least its correlates), about the way it is handled, and about what should happen in the future as a response to crime. *Crime in America* is not an unlearned book, but it is written for the uninformed if interested layman, not for the scholar or expert. It is not a scientific book, but it frequently calls upon scientific theory and empirical study, although it does so in a selective and careless manner. Most of all, it is not an impartial, unemotional book. It is a call to action or at least a call to conscience. It is perhaps best understood as a poetic book, or a rhetorical book in the old sense—it means to persuade, not to reason. Segments of the work are as emotionally charged and as stirringly written as any other writing about crime and criminal justice today. It is also, very importantly, a political book, written to have impact upon the valuation of alternatives in the political decisionmaking process. It is not a dispassionate discourse aimed to impress scholars and professionals with its innovation, logic, or empirical discoveries. Hence, this work is quite unlike that of Packer or Van den Haag, both of whom claim to give values a backseat to logic, objectivity, and (occasionally) to empirical inquiry. We have seen that despite those claims, the other two works do not escape value preferences and ideological flag-waving. Clark is different in that he implies from the start that the basic decisions in criminal justice are not guided (and cannot be guided) by a rational process. His primary objective, then, is to influence readers to make decisions as he would want them to, to convince readers that change in the criminal justice system is necessary, and that these changes need to go in the direction of improving the lives of those the system touches.

Coincidentally, Clark's work, like the other two, is divided into three parts. The first deals with the causes of crime, the second with the processes of criminal justice, and the third with what he calls the false conflict between liberty and security. Thus in many ways Clark's structure closely parallels the structure of Packer's book.

The work begins with a now frequently quoted paragraph:

"Crime reflects the character of a people. This is a painful fact we do not want to face. Other premises are easier to accept. Other causes easier to control. There is no simple reform for defective character. It is as stubborn, durable and as strong as ourselves. It is ourselves."[12]

Exactly what such a statement might mean is perhaps irrelevant. The words sound forceful, calling us to consider crime very important to our way of life, and to our understanding of ourselves. In some ways, it may be reminiscent of Packer's observation about the rehabilitative purpose of criminal sanctions: if such purpose were to be effective, it would entail remaking the whole society. For that reason, Packer rejects rehabilitation; for that reason, Clark seems to accept it. Central to his argument seems to be the notion that society has to be remade "or else." It is rather unclear from his approach whether this vast undertaking must be made so that crime can be avoided, or because crime is symptomatic of so many other facets of the American character, and that these other problems, along with crime, must be eradicated. Thus, beginning on the opposite side of the fence from Packer, Clark also explicitly conflicts with Van den Haag. While the latter believes that our present society is better than any imaginable alternative, Clark apparently sees the current American "character" as in need of a great deal of work.

His belief that a vast overhaul of society must be undertaken is founded on some other assumptions. After reviewing what he terms the "fountainheads" of crime, such as filth, disease, poverty, and the other problems of the urban ghetto, he avows that for the government to act only to "keep the poor in their place" will assure violence in the future.[13] He objects strongly to plans of social control that rely heavily upon more frequent and obtrusive surveillance, and swifter and more severe penalties for crime. Labeling the strategies of deterrence and retribution as "repression," he argues that such maneuvers on the part of the government against people who commit crime will only lead to deeper divisions among the American people.

The alternative, he feels, is the creation of a wholesome environment: "Healthy people in a just and concerned society will not commit significant crime."[14] Exactly what "healthy" means in this context is uncertain. The word is used in an obviously broad sense, to encompass both physical and mental well-being, but seems to imply as well that only unhealthy or sick (in some sense) people commit crimes. It is this belief in the irrationality of crime that seems to undergird all of his urgings. The argument, loosely coupled as it is, seems to go that terrible social conditions create sick people and sick people commit crime. Given these assumptions, Clark's relatively easy dismissal of retribution and deterrence can be understood. Sick people, by definition, cannot be deterred; their course of action is determined by their condition. Likewise, retribution makes little sense, since crimes are irrational and the culprits are not deserving of punishment: "Riots, muggings, robbery and rape are loathsome not only because they are inherently irrational and inhumane but because they and their causes are so foreign to the experience of people with power that they are incomprehensible."[15] In addition to the explicit feeling that only irrational people commit these crimes is the feeling that only certain groups of people, the powerless, experience the conditions that give rise to that irrationality. Accepting these kinds of assumptions as proven fact, or at least as scientific theory, Clark argues that the use of the criminal sanction against criminals is an antiquated response by people who now should know better.

Like the other authors we have discussed, Clark's apparent concern is with "street" crime: rape, robbery, assault, and so on. Unlike Packer and Van den Haag, however, Clark accepts the belief that such crimes are obviously caused by the conditions of powerlessness and therefore that the "fault" and the cure of crime lie squarely in the hands of the people in power. Who, exactly, the "power" people are is never made specific. At times, Clark speaks as if the government, probably the federal government, is in power. At other times, the term "in power" seems to refer to anyone who lives in comfortable conditions.

While Clark begins by sounding as if the people in power are distinctly different from the powerless, either because they have power or because they are not subjected to criminogenic conditions, he soon reverses himself. "Society cannot hope to control violent and irrational anti-social conduct while cunning predatory crime by people in power continues unabated."[16] It is unclear if the predatory crime of the powerful is somehow different in origin than urban street crime, or if it too is determined by environmental factors. Apparently, the rich and powerful are not to be excused for their wrongdoings, perhaps because their crime, while cunning and predatory, is rational. This is troublesome enough by itself, but Clark follows this statement with the assertion that seven out of eight lower-class crimes are economic in nature. If they can be economic and still irrational, we have a very strange situation indeed.

The remainder of the book, like the first two chapters, continues with rampant illogic, absence of definition, and bald assertion without any attempt at documentation. Surprisingly, the problems occur not only when the lawyer is discussing social problems, but continue when Clark turns to more legal concepts. At one point, he speaks of the major crimes in the country being the ones of "unequal protection" and "deprivation." While these may be deplorable practices or conditions, it is hard to understand why a lawyer would allow himself to speak of them as crimes, except that Clark seems to reject legal distinctions and legal remedies altogether.

It would appear that the remaking of the American character that Clark has in mind would include the broadening of our conceptions of illegal conduct to include all sorts of other injustices. This sounds more convincing in his words than in these, precisely because his words hide the major questions implicit in the kinds of changes he seems to imply. Clark argues that we should be concerned with the welfare of all the people, and create conditions that promote everyone's health. But it is exactly by legislating the morals and the welfare of the American citizenry that we have experienced disasters such as Prohibition and the cruelty and inhumanity of the current juvenile justice system. If something about the people in power has generated, or is responsible for, street crime, one might also worry about the powerful people who would engineer welfare or healthy conditions, rather than punish criminals. But Clark seems oblivious to the excesses of human zeal unless they are committed within the criminal justice system, in terms of criminal punishments.

Clark believes that some form of welfare-oriented alternative to criminal justice is both possible and necessary if we are to reduce crime and reshape our society. He never defines rehabilitation, but it apparently operates on two levels. First, there is rehabilitation of individuals who have committed crime: 80% of all serious crime is committed by people convicted of crime before . . . we know that for most of them rehabilitation is possible.[17] The statistical fallacies in this statement not excluded, the most startling part of it is the utter faith in some sort of character change for individuals, which he seems to think is quite effective. But for Clark, rehabilitation of the individual is paralleled, on a broader front, by rehabilitation of society itself. Just as crime demonstrates defects in individual and social character, there are apparently changes that can cure both the defects in single human beings and the defects in the social order.

It is over this dual concept of rehabilitation that he is perhaps at his most illogical. He argues simultaneously that the rehabilitation of the individual is highly important to the safety of society, because so many crimes are committed by persons who have already been caught for one crime, but also that the criminal justice apparatus cannot deal with the causes of crime, and can do little to prevent or reduce it. If the criminal justice system or the punishment of one individual for his crime cannot deal with causes, or effectively reduce and prevent crime, there is large reason to doubt that any strategy of intervention aimed at the individual can be effective at reduction and prevention. Perhaps part of the problem is that Clark can find no reasonable suggestion, within his flailing critique of the entire structure of things as they stand, for what to do with the individuals who commit crime but should remain, within his framework, undamaged by a punitive response to their behavior. Since he has argued that criminal punishment is morally wrong and ineffective for the criminal (or the powerless criminal), he might have to argue that they should be set free. But obviously, while excusing their conduct as determined by the unhealthy world they live in, the behavior of criminals must be controlled. One cannot condone freeing irrational and inhumane people to commit more rapes, muggings, and robberies. Thus Clark must invent a fiction, namely that these people can be treated or rehabilitated. This presumably would be morally supportable, since it would not be punishment. But of course, it is an old argument, the same one by which the Illinois Juvenile Court was established in 1899. It is also much the same argument by which one incarcerates people in mental hospitals or institutions for drug addiction, rather than punishing the illegal behavior.

Clark's arguments for rehabilitating society are not much more startling. Indeed, he never really takes a stab at suggesting any sort of societal overhaul. What he actually recommends is a rehabilitation, or refurbishing, of the present criminal justice system. He suggests that more money should be spent on the police, and that the state correctional systems should be perfected. His orientation toward the refurbishing of the separate justice agencies is strangely inconsistent. At one point, he argues that the police must remain a local agency so that the people retain a hand in deciding police operation. On the other side, he feels that correctional systems should be under the aegis of a strong centralized government. But it is doubtful both that a local police can avoid the ills that plague other local services, which Clark deplores, and that a state correctional system can have much impact upon the home environments of the persons punished within them, or be attentive to the desires of local people in the administration of the bureaucracies that serve them.

The naivete in his belief about curing ghetto ills continues as he addresses the relationship of the governmental bureaucracies to the powerless people: "The disorganization of society in ghetto areas is so complete that merely a place to complain releases tension and skillfully done creates understanding."[18] Such a statement not only is patronizing and insulting to the demands and needs of ghetto dwellers, but completely ignores the entire history of urban social reform during the 1960s. Marris and Rein[19] and Stephen Rose,[20] among others, have skillfully demonstrated that the urban reform projects undertaken while Clark was Attorney General were structured to provide precisely those places to complain, and other similar "cooling off" activities, and that the end result was continuing, increasing bitterness and continuing neglect for the social conditions of the poor.

In balance, I would have to say that there are more problems with this approach than with the one of retribution and deterrence. Clark is obviously committed to social change, and he obviously feels that the abuses and unfairness in the American system of resource distribution give rise to crime and to the mechanisms that respond to crime. But his illogic, ignorance of fact, and lack of any firm suggestions, either for individuals or for the system, can only provide impetus for the reformers who believe that retribution and deterrence are more appropriate. Moreover, Clark's orientation to a welfare replacement for criminal punishment is based upon poorer understanding of the organizations that administer services than his understanding of the organizations that administer punishment.

MENNINGER'S PUNISHMENT FOR THE PUNISHERS

If one could excuse Clark's inability to treat rehabilitation logically or completely because of his layman's approach to its practice and problems, one cannot be so lenient with Menninger, a practicing psychiatrist who writes as if the only credential one needs to solve the crime problem is that of being a famous psychiatrist. Claiming major responsibility for the reform of mental health institutions in Kansas, Menninger insists that similar action can revitalize the correctional system. That the mental health system can provide the criminal justice system with a model for reform is a weak argument because significant differences exist between the two systems and because it is doubtful that the mental health system really has been reformed to the extent that Menninger claims.

Like Clark, Menninger has difficulty dealing with crime as a legal and social fact. He refers to the criminal process, or to the kinds of things that happen to defendants and convicts, as the "crimes against criminals" (and thereby derives the title for his book, *The Crime of Punishment*: "I suspect that all the crimes committed by all the jailed criminals do not equal in total social damage of the crimes committed against them."[21] It is apparent from his context that Menninger is not speaking literally of crimes committed by officials or other offenders against jailed offenders, but metaphorically of an irrational, inefficient, and ineffective criminal process. Even if the process is indeed poorly run, to speak of it as a crime can scarcely help the reform process.

Menninger refuses to deal with crimes as defined legally because, like many other psychiatrists, he perceives the legal definition of behavior as itself a fiction and an outmoded one at that. For example, he argues that justice is an unhelpful word when we are attempting to deal with the problems of crime. To Menninger justice is simply a codeword for doing what we like to people we like and doing damage to those we don't like. The administration of justice, he feels, is more an attempt to correct injustices than it is to achieve anything positive.[22] Thus, refusing to deal with the term, he ignores important questions such as whether a social group have the right to harm those they do not like, if the reasons for that dislike are defined in an orderly way. Furthermore, one might wonder how to control a group's proclivities to do as they like to people they like and the reverse to people they do not, if controls such as those posed by the concept of justice and its administration were devalued. Menninger's answers to these questions are at least implied throughout his book: doctors and other trained rehabilitation agents have the power and expertise to do what people need done to them, meaning that antiquated control systems such as criminal justice should therefore give way to the discipline applied by the medical and related professions.

Treatment of the criminal, unlike punishment, he argues, is morally correct because it can be effective, and will improve individuals and protect society, while justice as a control device is merely a form of organized vengeance that neither does the offender good nor provides safety to the public.[23]

Menninger, like Clark, runs into a roadblock when he tries to describe how offenders should be handled for their crimes. Curiously, he decides that they should incur "penalties," which he attempts to distinguish from "punishment."

> Penalty is a predetermined price levied automatically, invariably, and categorically in direct relation to a violation or infraction of a pre-set rule or "law". . . . But the element of punishment is an adventitious and indefensible *additional* penalty; it corrupts the legal principle of *quid pro quo* with a 'moral' surcharge.[24]

He goes on to admit that setting proper penalties would be very difficult, but that they would serve to make things equitable, in contrast to punishment which is pain inflicted out of all proportion to the offense.

His evidence that we now have, in his terms, a "punitive" rather than penalty-levying system, is rather meager. He argues that severe penalties for crimes "which most of us feel little temptation to commit"[25] provides some evidence for his position. This argument, of course, would lead to the conclusion that stiff penalties for traffic violations are not punitive, but that stiff penalties for murder are, since more people are tempted to commit the former than the latter. Even if this position were logical, it would seem a dangerous one from which to build an equitable system of penalties. His other argument for the punitive nature of the current criminal system is that punishments are differentially assigned. While there is strong consensus that much inequality exists in the sentencing system in the United States, this evidence does not help us to separate penalties from "punitiveness." We need evidence that bears on the severity of the punishment to the offense. Many recent sentencing reforms provide reasonable suggestions for controlling the inequality in judicial sentencing discretion, but none of these reforms can answer the question of how much punishment is an equal payment for the crime committed.[26]

The most obvious problem, of course, is that a preference for penalties rather than punitiveness does not help us in the least to determine what should be done to offenders. Packer and Van den Haag make it very clear that what Menninger calls a penalty they call a punishment, and they take great pains to distinguish the criminal punishment, or penalty, from vengeance or other nonlegal concepts that do not provide for controls on the response to the offense in question.

If Menninger's suggestion for penalties rather than punishments means anything in terms of policy change, it would imply more equitable and certain administration of criminal punishments, or sentences. There is nothing in this argument that allows us to distinguish penalty from punishment on the basis of the *content* of the processes in question. Would equitable distribution of the death sentence be penalizing rather than punitive, and unequal administration of psychiatric sessions be punitive? Clearly, this is not what Menninger has in mind. Instead, he takes the position that anything done to an offender on the basis of the act he has committed is punitive, because the rational and effective response would be aimed at the reasons for his behavior. In other words, Menninger seeks to replace a retributive system with one of rehabilitation. How this substitution will allow us to determine a schedule of penalties is, of course, totally unclear. Most scholars would argue that it was the introduction of rehabilitative intent into the criminal process that pushed the system toward inequality in punishments, because rehabilitating an individual requires attention to *his* problems and needs rather than to the relationship of his behavior to some predetermined schedule of penalties.[27] Perhaps the most consistent way to read Menninger on this point is merely to assume that he feels a fair criminal system is impossible to achieve (that is, that penalties cannot be created), and that therefore a criminal punishment or penalty system should be abandoned.

Rather than treat the offender for the crime committed, Menninger would argue for treatment of the offender's "problems." He runs into difficulties here because, writing in the middle sixties, he is cognizant that equating crime with sickness is no longer a popular ideological stance, let alone an adequate description of criminal behavior. But Menninger finds no way to skirt the danger. Admitting that crime is not a disease, in the sense that it is not caused by malfunctioning of bodily processes or presence of outside negative agents, he decides that criminal behavior is an "illness" that can be treated: "The prisoner, like the doctor's other patients, should emerge from his treatment experience a different person, differently equipped, differently functioning, and headed in different direction from when he began treatment."[28]

This approach does not define treatment by process, but by outcome, and is therefore no guide in determinations of how, where, and by whom the criminal should be treated for his illness. If a prisoner having served a ten-year sentence emerged in appearance as Menninger describes above, would treatment have taken place? The book provides no answer. Instead, Menninger asks us to believe that such outcomes are possible and that it is a crime not to allow them to predominate. He says that the criminal can be cured and sent home by use of the same techniques used to cure and release mental patients. What these techniques are, and whether they really work in mental health a majority of the time, is quite questionable.[29] More doubtful still is his feeling that offenders would seek such help for their illness. He claims, contrary to the great majority of penological experts, that offenders volunteer for treatment applications, although they know this will not shorten their sentence. One can only question his knowledge of the correctional system, in which offenders routinely "volunteer" for rehabilitative programs in order to receive earlier parole.[30]

While ignoring all evidence of the well-known "time game" or con game between the keepers and kept in our prisons, Menninger recognizes some of the problems of correctional institutions as they currently operate. He feels that the conflict within prisons between reformation and punishment is divisive to staff and confusing to the public. He goes on to point out that the twenty-two principles laid down by the American Correctional Association in 1870 still have not been implemented, and that reformation of the individual has not replaced vindictive suffering as the operational principle of prisons.

Most critics of Menninger's position attack his defense of rehabilitation by pointing out merely that it has not worked, or that it cannot work. Both criticisms may be true, but both really miss the weakest position in Menninger's argument. Whether a "treatment" institution could have worked, or would work in the future, were it not for the confounding element of punishment, is really a futile question. Menninger, and others who take his rehabilitation approach, simply can't deal with the question of *why* the principles of rehabilitation have not been instituted. Merely to state that confounding or conflicting principles have been used in the past is not enough. Through what forces, by what arguments, and with what organization will consistent principles be implemented in the future? This question is also likely to haunt Van den Haag, Packer, and others who would take the reverse of Menninger's position. Those in favor of retribution–deterrence state also that rehabilitation has not worked because of its conflict with the other motives and goals involved. But, rather than opt for a consistently rehabilitative system, they do the opposite, and argue for a consistently implemented retributive system. It may prove as difficult to rid the criminal justice apparatus of its welfare tendencies as it is to rid it of its retributive tendencies. But neither side has sought yet to address such questions.

About as close as Menninger comes to trying to analyze the reasons for the conflicting trends in the system are a few statements, peppered throughout the book, about society's self-destructive tendencies. He criticizes society for being confused about the whole question and for leaving the important problem of punishment in the hands of a few professional "avengers."[31] He states somewhat later that "society" sees the crime problem as a dramatization of good versus evil that is resolved with criminal convictions. Finally, he concludes that "society secretly *wants* crime, *needs* crime and gains definite satisfactions from the present mishandling of it! We condemn crime, we punish offenders for it; but we need it. The crime and punishment ritual is part of our lives."[32] One might ask that if the situation is such, might not it be destructive to society to eliminate punishment?

Menninger's position on change is unsystematic. He seems to rely upon the belief that professional treaters, left to do their work, could make a much better system. His evidence for their ability is anecdotal material that relates the great progress made by some of his friends in isolated instances.[33] Finally he suggests that correctional organizations should establish facilities and programs akin to mental health centers, "in direct communication and in a working relationship with all the people of the area—not just the sick ones."[34] He expands upon this to suggest some form of "public safety centers" that would prevent crime rather than catch criminals. He cautions, however, that neither of these programs nor similar improvements would be possible unless the public changes its attitude about punishment.

The chances of consistent policy and program emerging from these kinds of recommendations are doubtful. Why should correctional departments duplicate the functions of mental health agencies, since punishment is to be abolished in the first place? Who will fund the relatively high cost of treating offenders? Who will define public safety? Will any external controls be imposed upon the professional cadres that implement treatments, or are their decisions supreme? If the democratic processes that have established our current criminal justice system are not competent to change public attitudes, or rid them of self-destructive elements, by what processes will public attitudes be controlled or changed? Are the costs of these changes worth paying for the gains, if any, in the handling of the criminal offender?

Since the beginning of the seventies, most criminal justice experts, liberal and conservative alike, have rejected with surprising unanimity the prescriptions for change, such as they are, by critics such as Menninger and Clark. Their arguments, only a few short years ago recognized as the epitomy of liberal thinking, are now seen as poorly disguised and poorly thought out attempts to keep professional helpers on top of the criminal justice power heap, rather than as serious attempts to improve the conditions of the people handled by the system or the conditions of the people who feel threatened by crime and offenders. Indeed, one would probably conclude that the current popularity of the reforms suggested by Van den Haag, Packer, and others in favor of deterrence and retribution might be due as much to the weaknesses of the opposing argument as it is to the strength of the Moralist position.

But it would be incorrect to assume that the Welfare group has lost the war. Indeed, from some perspectives, one could argue that they have won it. Many of the retributive-deterrent reforms now in vogue effectively provide other public agency systems with more power, more resources, and more "clients," thereby reserving the criminal justice system and the criminal sanction for limited use against "important" or "serious" crime. The resolution of the age-old punishment-treatment conflict for criminal justice may do little more than change the locus of such ideological conflict from one that once occurred *inside* the system to one that will occur *between* systems.

Chapter 4

Assumptions and Implications about Society in Welfare and Moralist Approaches

There is one level not as immediately evident as the others, on which the social reformers such as Clark and Menninger or the adherents to social order such as Packer and Van den Haag conflict. The crux of this disagreement concerns the separate frames of reference upon which the Welfare and the Moralist groups build their arguments and select and organize their facts. Admitting that the present system is inequitable, Van den Haag proclaims both that all imaginable systems are likely to be so and that the present social structure is preferable to disorder. Clark and Menninger seem to begin from quite a different position. They perceive the continuation of a unified, effective system of threats— the means of controlling strain in an inequitable system—as automatically reducing social attention to the inequitable distribution of resources. (Van den Haag does not directly address this point, but implicitly, at least, does not agree with it.) Moreover, the Welfare group perceives the alternatives to strengthening the criminal sanction (or reliance on retribution and deterrence) not as *disorder* but as a different and more desirable order.

Perhaps the old joke about Switzerland is appropriate here as a means of highlighting the prelogical, prefactual disagreements. Van den Haag suggests that crime is both inevitable and a necessary cost of creativity, technological advance, physical comfort, and the other perceived advantages of twentieth century America. Likewise, the war- and disease-torn nations of Italy, France, and Germany produced the Renaissance, the democratic revolution, and our greatest philosophy. Switzerland, free of most of the strife of its neighbors, goes the story, produced only the cuckoo clock! Indeed, some of our greatest cultural masterpieces and political ideas may have been shaped out of suffering, but to place a higher value on the "net results" of strained social structures than upon the possibility of social harmony is not a necessary conclusion nor a logical justification for the kind of social control system that Van den Haag recommends. Some people may well prefer the social system that produces a cuckoo clock, and the political peace of Geneva to which the "culturally advanced" powers retreat in order to negotiate their temporary treaties!

One could dispense with the Moralist-Welfare conflict with a frustrated sigh saying that it's all a matter of perspective or it's all a matter of taste. Yes and no. It may all be a matter of taste or of perspective. But, even if this is true, enterprises of the greatest social import have been waged on no more initially solid ground than this. Matters of taste and frames of reference are not idiosyncratic or unique; they are themselves socially patterned. Frames of reference for the analysis of social problems are built both on the analyst's understanding of the present situation and on his conception of desirable future states or more preferable outcomes. But the analysis of existing states and projection of future situations are not separate activities.

A person's idea of the future (or his purpose) is likely to influence the lens utilized to condense the present into understandable statements. Stated another way, the analysis of any particular system (or ordered set of elements) is partially determined by the analyst's identification of the system or upon his decision on the location of its boundaries.

None of the four authors discussed above frequently utilizes system terminology. They have bounded quite differently, however, their systems of (different) interest. Van den Haag (and to a lesser extent, Packer) begin with the assumption that the social order achievable as a partial consequence of the criminal law and its administration would have advantages for the majority of a state's population that would far outweigh the disadvantages for the majority of that state's population. And, they are willing to admit that criminal deviance is inevitable. They also posit that such deviance can be kept to an agreed-upon minimum, far below the level of frequency with which it now occurs. The key problems, they both suggest, exist in the implementation of the penal sanction, with the two fundamental questions being: (1) the proper scope of the criminal sanction; and (2) the proper means of apprehending, prosecuting and (in Van den Haag's system) carrying out the penal sanction.

In contrast, Clark and Menninger seem to begin with the assumption that the American social system is in a state of rapid flux, in which new and old institutions of control and welfare overlap and conflict. Moreover, they perceive the eventual withering away of legal institutions as inevitable, but also as a process that should be planned and facilitated. They feel that concerted social action taken to buttress the old foundations of social order will not only confuse the process of social change but make it a process of disorder, violence, and potential societal destruction.

Apparently, there are implicit assumptions operating here that form the basis for the explicit assumptions. The Moralists might argue that the type of society to which we could move (through proper criminal law administration) is not unlike our present society, except that the incidence of crime would be less. Another would seem to be that the criminal law function (as described in their theoretical elaborations) has operated more effectively at other times, or in other places.

Likewise, the Welfare group bases its explicit argument upon some less specified beliefs about the way in which the current systems of justice and welfare operate and about how a social welfare system could operate in the future. The basis for these beliefs are the existence of nonpunitive and rehabilitative systems (such as mental health, perhaps), and the existence of cultures where the criminal law is not used as a predominant deterrent, and where living conditions and group processes are healthier and happier for all involved.

Highlighting the underlying frames of reference of the Moralist and Welfare positions would be quite helpful at this point. It would help us see whether their disagreements about the actual and ideal functions of the criminal justice system are necessary and inevitable, or whether part of the conflict that we have described in the last two chapters is based upon avoidable misunderstandings of what criminal justice is actually all about.

Van den Haag, Packer, Clark, and Menninger, however, do not help us much in the task of comparing their basic assumptions. None of them take the time and trouble to describe their view of the entire criminal justice system, or the way that system fits into their view of the larger social structure. And none of them are explicit about the future societies they want to create. Both sides are so convinced that the reader will see things their way that many basic questions about society, social structure, and social change and control are ignored. This chapter will attempt to construct, or reconstruct, the conceptions of the present and of the future that are implied in the Moralist and Welfare positions.

THE SOCIAL MORALIST CONCEPTION OF THE PRESENT

It must be emphasized that in many respects, sociological and social system analysis is outside the scope of the task that the Moralists assign themselves, so it would be unfair to criticize them for not providing a complete picture of social structure, culture, and political dynamics in the United States. Most of them imply that they are not competent to attempt such a task. Nevertheless, one can ask that their notions of the criminal law, of the administration of the criminal sanction, and of normative and deviant behavior, all of which are central to their discussion, be grounded in some basic framework.

Van den Haag and Packer, and others who write in the same mode, usually speak of "society" in a rather simplistic vein, but one which has a long tradition behind it in jurisprudential scholarship.[1] Basically, "society" is used synonomously with "social system," the "populace," the "people," the "social group," "civilized society," "American society," occasionally the "state," and so on, to represent all of the people in the United States as they are ordered in their public or social relationships and as they are imbued with particular cultural attributes characteristic of "American" civilization. While this is undoubtedly a vague term, it is quite important to Moralist arguments for criminal law and their understanding of social control.

Packer and Van den Haag acknowledge a considerable amount of disagreement, conflict, enmity, dissension, and disorder within the "society." Packer, for example, places in the middle part of his book the exposition of the "two models" of the criminal process, the interplay of which represents for him one of the basic cultural conflicts in American society. Van den Haag cites Packer only three times (each time favorably), deterrence being the subject on all three occasions. Yet there is an apparent congruity between the types of society that both see, and similarity in the problems of the society that they feel are significant. Van den Haag recognizes somewhat fleetingly the existence of the value conflict that Packer describes in detail. The primary reason for the difference in emphasis is that Van den Haag goes to considerable lengths to attack the due process position, arguing that it has eroded to some extent the strength of the law. Hence, he does not give equal weight to his presentation of this type of cultural or value conflict.

Van den Haag is far more explicit about structural and economic conflicts. In contrast, Packer's references to this structural conflict are indirect. He mentions that deterrent threats are ineffective against desperate people who have "lost" (or who have never had) the social advantages the means to which are controlled by the law. Later, in dealing with the two models of the criminal process, Packer implies that the due process position is partially based upon the need to balance the power of the individual against the power of the state, and that special precautions are necessary in cases of the poor and uneducated. Another reading of this might also suggest that the due process model partially levels class or structural differentials, vis-à-vis state interventions against particular class members, but this might be pushing Packer too far. Suffice it to say that both writers recognize that social structure does not give everyone in the United States equal opportunity, or equal comfort and social advantage.

On the question of where the law "comes from" and what it is used for, the Moralist position is fairly clear, although, again, basic concepts are not. Packer and Van den Haag see the law, and specifically the criminal law, as an expression of cultural values, the most formalized expression that exists in society. They are not very specific about the processes by which the law is developed or legislated, although they apparently do not intend to be. They both make the fundamental distinction between "the law" as explicit, written values and "laws" as specific, written rules, some of which conflict and not all of which represent well either the "intent" of the law or basic cultural norms. They would both agree that "laws" need revision, while "the law" as a basic system of social proceeding needs to be protected.

While we need not reiterate their stance on the deterrent and retributive functions of law, it is crucial to try to summarize what their stance on these functions implies for their view of the underlying system of law as a means by which society expresses its values, tries to maintain its values, and seeks to control, if not resolve, conflicts in value and disputes about behavior. Risking oversimplification of their views, one could argue that they believe that the "society," or the American social system, is a real entity, a social fact rather than an abstract concept, which, with difficulty, can be described. Moreover, this description would be basically the same, regardless of the source. In fact, they might argue that criminals would describe the same kind of society as noncriminals would and that whether noncriminal or not, most people have basically the same values, seek the same objectives, and agree about the legitimate means to reach these objectives.

More important, perhaps, is their position on *access* to the criminal law system. It would seem important, if the law is to function as an expression of value and as a means of maintaining normative behavior, that most persons in "society" have adequate means of affecting what laws are written and how they are enforced. While some social theorists have seen a deficiency of access within the current American system,[2] the question of access gives the social moralists little trouble. They believe that the criminal law represents the underlying American culture so effectively that there is little need to examine exactly how this process takes place. One or the other of the following processes is alleged to take place: either the kind of law development system we have makes satisfactory compromises among the various values and views of American groups, in the long run, or persons who now feel inadequately represented in the legal system *could* obtain representation if they desired to do so.

This is not to say that the Moralists feel no mistakes are made. This group basically agrees that the "overreach" of the criminal law can be a problem and that there are limits to the kinds of behaviors that can be effectively proscribed or punished. They may disagree on the precise scope of the criminal law, but agree essentially on the notion that overly prescriptive legislation can make the system inefficient. In other words, they recognize some limit to the resources that can be expended for law enforcement, and feel that some behaviors are more damaging than others. More importantly, beneath the superficial disagreements on the location of the outer reach of the law and on how limited the government should be in trying to enforce law, there is a subterreanean assertion tht the law fundamentally protects all the citizens of the "society," or that there is a coterminality between the "society" and the welfare of all the various groups within it.

Other social analysts have termed this assertion the belief in the basic integration of society: that beneath its various strains and conflicts there is one fundamental whole or single unit to which the various groups belong.[3] This assertion is akin to the demographic theory of a "melting pot America," in which the variety of different groups, beliefs, behaviors, and the like are eventually assimilated. Or, more precisely, regardless of the different starting points of the various groups in American society, the end point is, or will be, not a harmonious aggregate but a single, unified cultural entity.

To the social moralists, the criminal law and the system of its administration produces societal integration. The law, of course, is recognized as an artificial, human device, and therefore considerably more fallible than the natural laws of physics or even the social traditions that govern less complex and more homogeneous societies. But, the law remains one of the major institutional supports that assures the continuation of assimilation or integration. The law delimits how conflict will take place and how disagreements will be resolved. It is in this way, perhaps, that Packer sees the criminal sanction as "regrettable but necessary." Less complex stews in smaller pots might not need to resort to such a rough and ready device, but the American melting pot requires such reinforcing means so that the underlying social processes can be maintained. Van den Haag's position is similar, although it is less optimistic than Packer's. Van den Haag believes that the criminal sanction and the current means of its administration have been sufficiently devalued that maintenance of the current trends in this system will threaten the assimilation/integration process. It is unclear whether Van den Haag's more pessimistic stance could be interpreted as recognition that the assimilation/integration process is breaking down or that it was perhaps never an adequate description of American society. He does state, however, that our "system" is to him a good one, and should be maintained through the institution of a stronger deterrent/retribution system.

THE SOCIAL MORALIST CONCEPTION OF THE FUTURE

Where Van den Haag and Packer intend to take us with their deterrence/retribution system is implicit in the above description of what they think we now "have." They see American society as a complicated, messy, inefficient collection of people whose contrasting and conflicting positions, beliefs, values, and behaviors are fundamentally reconcilable. They want to lead us to a more perfect version of what we now have, that is, the American "ideal" of popular and populist American tradition. Other recent works on the criminal sanction and criminal justice that fall very much in the same tradition are Fogel's ". . . *We Are the Living Proof . . . ,*" Morris's *The Future of Imprisonment*, von Hirsch's *Doing Justice*, and Wilson's *Thinking About Crime*.[4]

Few, if any, of these men believe, or state they believe, that some final democratic millennium is coming. None of them are utopians. They pride themselves on being realists, and realistic about the great difficulties inherent in trying to keep the American "society" together—or in getting it together. None of them proclaim an "end state," or a final unchanging product, a finished version of American "society." It is probably for that reason alone that it is so difficult to piece together their conception of the future.

Rather than a utopian model of distinctly different and immutable future, these men, or their mode of analysis, hold out a maintenance of process by which the American "society" can endure. The outcome is either inessential or impossible to determine. It is more accurate to speak of *outcomes* at an infinite variety of points in time, all such outcomes circumscribed, or limited, by the democratic legal process that the authors believe in. This group thus believes in change, but not in fundamental change, or perhaps more precisely their stance toward fundamental change in American society takes one of two forms: (1) Some might state that several significant or fundamental changes in the structure of American life are possible, but avoidable, if we pay increasing attention to the strains in the system and to the need for specific and sequential and incremental changes, (2) Others, notably Van den Haag, intellectually scoff at the notion that any conceivable alternative to the current society is really fundamentally different—meaning that communist or autocratic legal processes would impose controls on human behavior just as the current system does, that resources and rewards would still be differentially distributed, and that these other versions of society (while not fundamentally different), simply are not as preferable as our own.[5]

THE SOCIAL WELFARE CONCEPTION OF THE PRESENT

The social welfare conception of the present social system is even more difficult to piece together than that of the Moralists. As is true of the first group, it is not the intention of Menninger, Clark, and other writers in this tradition to explain in detail the social underpinnings of criminal "illness," of the law, or, for that matter, of the alternative approaches, such as rehabilitation, that they find more reasonable.[6] Nevertheless, their view of the social system is decidedly more complex; stated more accurately, they perceive that society is too complex to be controlled adequately by a mechanism as "simple" as the criminal law and its administration. They would seem to imply that the legal approach to social order ignores important facets of social organization, such as group processes, value formation, socialization, subcultures, alienation, and to some extent urbanization and bureaucratization.

It is not true, however, that the Welfare group provides a more coherent and complete description of the greater social complexity to which they allude. It would be more accurate to say that they attribute many social problems to these facets of social structure and that they argue that the criminal law and its implementtion cannot control, let alone solve, some of these problems because the law does not affect the underlying social processes that give rise to the problems. By and large, however, the Welfare group concentrates on social problems such as crime, deviance, mental illness, disease, and poverty, rather than explicating the structural elements that generate these problems. In addition, one problem they spend the least time examining, despite their perception of it as crucial, is the society's tendency to depend upon ineffective problem-solving mechanisms, such as the law, in order to handle its social problems. Given the importance they place on the disutility of the criminal law, one might expect that the Welfare group would recommend changes in the social processes that reinforce its use. Instead, they concentrate on crime and alternative ways of dealing with it.

If the Moralist group view of society focuses on the "individual" and upon a broad, vague, encompassing "society," the Welfare group generally has a more middle-range vision that deals with communities, usually cities, smaller social groups, such as the gang, the family, neighborhoods of alienated people, and so on. The Welfare group does focus, like the other, on a constructed version on the individual personality: the Moralists use a "rational" man construct, the Welfare groups a "healthy" man construct. Neither of these "models" of man are, in fact, models of the internal biological and/or psychological processes and structures of a human being. On the contrary, both the "rational" and the "healthy" man are reflections of the two groups' initial perceptions of society. The rational man is a microcosm of the legally ordered "society," while the healthy man is a microcosm of the society free of social problems.

The "healthy" individual is no more an objective empirical referent than the "rational" man is. As Etzioni pointed out in his major thesis concerning the choice of basic units for social analysis, the "individual human being" is as much an analytic category as is the "social system":

> Groups and personalities are equally analytic; both are conceptual abstractions from sense data about behavior.... Viewing a person as an abstraction runs counter to commonsense notions that associate personality with the biological individual and, hence, view a person as more concrete than a group .... [But] we do not encounter an "individual"; we meet only segments of persons ....[7]

To focus upon the individual human being as a basic unit of analysis (and of social planning) is a long-standing Western convention, but a convention nonetheless. Various diseases may have technological definitions, but concepts of health are culturally structured, as are any concepts of ill health that refer to deviance rather than physical sickness. Thus, it is possible to approach the reconstruction of the Welfare version of society by treating their version of the "healthy" individual as an anthropomorphic rendition of their view of society.

From this starting point, the piecemeal Welfare version of society is as follows. American society is a hodgepodge collection of social groups that are not currently related to each other in a fashion that yields a coherent, unified entity. Nevertheless, society as fashioned has functioned reasonably well for the majority of the groups and persons who live within it. The function of society is to produce an acceptable, and perhaps an expanding, condition of welfare for all the people within it, in the sense that biological needs are fulfilled, safety and security are provided, and a variety of social needs, such as recognition, material comfort, freedom, and upward mobility are present. These needs are met through basic social institutions, such as education, work, political representation, the family and so on. The consequence of the simultaneous functioning of these institutions is the healthy individual who is satisfied with himself, relates well to others, and is in a position of sufficient strength to facilitate the well-being of other individuals.

American society, however, has achieved this state of well-being for all its various members in significantly varying degrees; moreover the level of varying well-being has reached a plateau at which the relative deprivation of some groups is likely to threaten the well-being of other groups and is morally reprehensible in and of itself. The capacity of the groups with adequate well-being to continue to allow the ill health of the minority signals two problems with the current society. First, the "powerless" (in

Clark's words) or the ill (in Menninger's) have such limited means by which to try to achieve a better condition of welfare for themselves that these attempts injure themselves, those they are in immediate contact with (i.e., victims), and indirectly the majority of society, who must pay exorbitantly for the damaging means that the ill use to survive. Second, the unwillingness of the majority of society to take any firm and effective steps to increase the welfare of the deprived indicates that the functioning of society for all its members is faulty, since one of the basic indicators of the "healthy" individual is his ability and his willingness to aid or pull up those who are below him in terms of social living conditions. The prolonged exposure of the deprived to the conditions of ill health has rendered them, on an individual level, pathological, and the willingness of the majority to countenance this prolonged exposure has, or will, render them equally pathological. In the not too distant future, perhaps in the short run, this dual situation will yield a "sick" society.'

Nevertheless, the means to correct the problems are at hand: the technological competence and the economic resources exist by which to correct the deficiencies suffered by the ill, powerless, and deprived, and this technology and these resources, once applied, will provide the minority with sufficient social skills to enter the social system on the same level of functioning, and to enjoy the same rewards, as the now complacent society.

Beneath this assumption is a necessary additional one: that American society is basically an open system, or an inclusionary system, in which any properly functioning or healthy individual can find his place. The level of welfare enjoyed by the majority is decidedly not limited to those who already enjoy it; it can expand to meet the needs of new members who enter.

If so, what has blocked the "uplifting" process so that the deprived have become stuck, as it were, in their own subsociety, beneath or out of touch with the welfare-providing institutions that serve the majority of the population? This question is an extremely difficult one to answer within the welfare framework. Again risking oversimplification, it would seem that the basic answer is "communication." For example, both Menninger and Clark emphasize that the criminal sanction, as a reaction to the pathological survival patterns of the deprived, is primarily irrational, meaning a response that is based on a misunderstanding of the behavior that is observed, and of the goals that the deprived are attempting to achieve with that behavior. If the majority understood that the deprived wanted only what the majority itself enjoys (and takes for granted), then it would not punish such behavior and attempt to isolate minority individuals within institutions.

Reasons for the communication breakdown are somewhat ambiguous. Perhaps it is likely that the communication difficulty is based upon the differential rate at which the various groups in American society have reached the level of welfare adequacy. Some groups have reached, or have had all along, such material and social benefit that they have extreme difficulty empathizing with those who are in drastically different social situations. The people "on the bottom" look and act differently, speak different languages, and it is difficult to believe that they want merely to gain the same physical and social conditions as the majority. Hence, the majority reacts with punishment, which in turn reinforces the notion that the ill and powerless are outsiders, rather than members of the same society.

But, of course, the ill *are* ill—the social conditions they have experienced have made them that, and one cannot simply open the door to social well-being and bid them enjoy. Thus, one has to alter the conceptual understanding of the majority, to make them willing to use the technological and economic resources at their disposal, and one must alter the behavior of the minority so that they can take advantage of the healthful conditions provided through the social institutions of society.

The stance of the Welfare group on the technological means of rehabilitation has been examined in the last chapter. Whatever the deficiencies in the Welfare group's presentation of these technologies, it is important to their position that these means of behavior change are assumed—or claimed—to exist. Thus, the more fundamental change is with the communication channels to and from the majority. As Menninger has stated, majority attitudes about crime and punishment must be changed. Again, we hit the question of how this should be done, or more importantly, why the understanding has not yet been gained, why the majority are willing to rely upon law and punishment. But again, the Welfare group refuse to address the functions of law and punishment. They merely assert that these social processes militate against the end objective, the creation of a greater level of social welfare.

Dealing with this roadblock—the function of law and punishment for the welfare of American society—from the point of view of the Welfare group, we can complete their picture of American society. Clark and Menninger and others of this group do not deal explicitly with this question, because they apparently do not see it as a problem. Law and punishment serve no function; the criminal justice system is simply an outmoded social institution, one that might have served a purpose before welfare for all members of society was a goal or a possibility, but that serves no useful purpose now. Thus, the Welfare group does not have to stand back and analyze law and punishment objectively; rather, they need to communicate: (1) its disutility for welfare; (2) the "scientific" explanations of the pathological behavior of the deprived; and (3) the *existence* (not the specific practices) of the technologies that will end that pathology. Achieving those three goals of communication, the majority will cease its reliance on law and punishment and release the economic resources to the technologists who can change behavior. This three-pronged improvement in communication, then, is the basis for their writing, and the explanation for the rhetorical, poetic urgency of the tone they adopt. The books themselves serve the purpose of improving communication. The books themselves are the necessary call to conscience (and provision of information about the feasibility of behavior change) that will tip American society off its current dangerous plateau and get the system of welfare operating on a new upswing.

This analysis leads to three final assumptions about American society, as seen by the Welfare group: (1) American society exhibits a rational political order that reacts on the basis of its receipt of scientific information; (2) the greatest welfare for all is the fundamental principle of American society; and (3) the minority, or currently disadvantaged, will trust the majority, and the technological agents of that society, who will be instrumental in uplifting them to the conditions of welfare offered within the American system.

THE SOCIAL WELFARE CONCEPTION OF THE FUTURE

Unlike the Moralist group, the social welfare group comes much closer to subscribing to a social end state, a society that would be the perfect realization implied in the potential of the current American society, as they see it. Thus, this group is far more optimistic about the goals of American society than Packer and Van den Haag, who offer to control crime, not end it. Consequently, the Welfare group is far more urgent and excited about the problems they perceive in the current society, since those problems not only threaten an American process of living, but threaten as well a very valuable and achievable future society, which will have no social problems, no illness, and no deprivation.

The Welfare group is not convinced that crime, filth, mental illness, poverty, and the like, are inevitable; rather, they have faith in the American social institutions as not only fundamentally sound but ultimately perfectable. But this faith in the American social institutions and in American society, if it should get unclogged and moving again, ironically provides the Welfare group with an idea of the future that is not *too* far removed from the idea of the future proposed by the Moralist group. There are significant differences, to be sure, differences that probably seem more significant as they are more fully explicated. Nevertheless, the place to which the Welfare groups want to take us, or American society, is similar to the Moralist future in that it, too, is quite "familiar." No basic tenets of

American culture will be lost, the basic social institutions will remain the same, and the assumed rational political process will be even more so. Thus, if one were to extract from the two sides merely their abstract ideas for the form of American society some fifty years from now, the forms would be very much the same. The key difference is the context within which those abstract ideas of American future take shape, and the means used to arrive there. The Moralists do not promise that the ideal American society will be reached or concretized, but only that it should remain the image that the legal process continually attempts to embody. The Welfare group holds out some hope of realizing that ideal.

What might be some of the core characteristics in the American society of the future, as seen by the Welfare group? Most of the characteristics revolve around the use of the ideal image of society as realizable, for if realization is to take place, there will be *some* differences between that society and the one we now experience. The primary distinguishing feature might be that equality of opportunity will have been achieved. American society will be meritocratic, the skills of each person, coupled with his objectives, determining the type of work he will undertake and the rewards earned. But underneath the merit system, there would apparently be some membership baseline for welfare so that persons with lesser or different skills would not be deprived of material well-being and social standing. Everyone would have access to facilities of equal capacity and competence for dealing with education, health, infirmity, guidance, and so on.

Society would apparently be guided by scientists, or by politicians who had adequate and powerful scientific staffs whose recommendations would be given full weight. The ambiguities about political and societal leadership are primarily caused by unanswered questions about the processes that will achieve the welfare state. A significantly greater level of guidance by scientists and professionals is necessary to get the current American social system moving toward the welfare future. But it is unclear whether the social engineering role of the technological group is to remain an overarching social characteristic once the present problems have been dealt with. Thus, the "on top or on tap" question about science is still open.

The economic base of society in the future is relatively unclear. (Neither the Moralists nor the Welfare group spend much time in analyzing economic questions about the current system or projecting the economic structure of the future.) The American society of the future, for the Welfare group, probably exhibits a disjuncture between the economic contribution of individuals to the social system and the economic reward obtained from the system by individuals. In other words, persons may be guaranteed work based upon their skills, but the relationship between the quality and amount of labor and the return of monetary payment, or direct social resources, will be different. That is, in the welfare society of the future, all citizens will *deserve* the same conditions of welfare, regardless of economic role. The equality of welfare conditions might be achieved in one of two ways (either of which are only guesses at questions unanswered by the Welfare group). Either the social amenities and necessities will be socialized (housing, clothing, food, whatever, given to people as they need it), or those persons who receive the greatest income will pay heavily in taxes to subsidize the welfare conditions of the less skillful or less productive members of the economy.[8]

The other unclear point in the Welfare future society has to do with the differences among social groups, the variations in culture, value, belief, and the like, that have supposedly fragmented the current society. It is not clear from the implications in the work of Clark and Menninger whether these social differences will continue to exist, or whether there will be no subsocieties. If distinct social groups continue to be recognizable, these distinctions will no longer be associated with different levels of well-being. However, it might be thought that equal opportunity, meritocracy, scientific guidance, and so on, will level out most social group distinctions. It seems likely that the Welfare group would admit that differences in ethnicity, color, and social roles will remain, but that these differences will be insignificant to the prediction of an individual's welfare conditions or to the choice of values and personal objectives. Instead, the key social groupings will center on distinctions of choice, that persons will associate in accordance with the work they perform (and want to perform) and in accordance with personal affinities for other people. Moreover, within this society, such choices could be made several times within a person's lifetime.

Hence, the social welfare version of the future is ambiguous and hazy, but has some identifiable characteristics. The society will be open, equally supportive of the welfare needs of all, and organized around the ability of people to choose their own objectives and achieve them.

Chapter 5

Systems Analysis and Criminal Justice

THE PROBLEM OF GETTING FROM "HERE" TO "THERE"

The foregoing discussion attempted to clarify two opposing sets of beliefs about the current social system and about a future social system. Persons who favor retributive-deterrent purposes for the criminal sanction tend to see the current social system as a more or less stable entity. The prime characteristic of this social system, for this group, is the process of function by rule or law. This group's prime objective, implied in their recommendations for change, in their conception of the way American society could be, is to maintain the democratic process for rule formation, and to achieve social objectives in terms of the continuing process of rule formation, implementation, enforcement, and revision. Persons who favor rehabilitation of deviant individuals, and welfare-oriented revision in American institutions, tend to see the current American social system as a rather unstable entity, one torn between traditional means of obtaining and maintaining order and feasible new social objectives, the pursuit of which would require doing away with legal punishment systems and replacing these with more recent behavior control technologies. The prime characteristic of society, for this group, is the split between American social reform capacity, or potential, and the reality of inertia and divisiveness about the American future. This group's prime objectives are to alter some of the major social institutions in America, such as the criminal process, and to create a new set of social responses to social conflict and deviance.

Both groups assume that the various factions of American society that now frequently conflict are ultimately reconcilable. The Moralists assume that a consistently implemented retribution-deterrence system will enable the American democratic process to proceed in a more orderly fashion. The Welfare group assumes that replacement of the criminal punishment system with a welfare alternative would reduce many of the current conflicts.

It is obvious that the Welfare group and the Moralist group are not too far apart on their goals for American society. Their models of the future are not necessarily the same, but major aspects are quite similar. They are also not widely apart on starting points: they agree that a reasonably high level of conflict exists in the current society, that this conflict is reconcilable, that the current criminal justice system is inefficient and ineffective whatever its goals, and that the criminal justice system or some substitute system for controlling or responding to deviant acts may help to instill or restore order.

Their sharpest point of contention involves a selection of means by which to travel from where we are to a specified system of the future. Hence, the major *apparent* disagreement emanates from a conception of control in social systems. "Apparent" is emphasized as a warning. Control of and in social systems is a complex problem, and no conception of control of social interaction can stand independently of the related ideas that we have just reviewed. Getting a social system to move from its present state to some future desired state is a task that entails: (1) some accuracy concerning the conception of the present system; (2) some accuracy or some demonstrable feasibility about the nature of the future system; and (3) a reasonable connection between the two through planned guidance, control, or intervention.[1]

At least three sources of error might enter into the criminal justice reform efforts that we have discussed. It is possible that either or both groups have faulty conceptions of the current social system. It is also possible that their idea of the future is not a feasible one, given the structure and dynamics of American society. Finally, the strategy of intervention that they prescribe might not present a means of making the current social system develop into the system they desire.[2]

It should also be noted that possibly more than one strategy is necessary to guide the social system. Perhaps not one, but several groups of planned social reforms must be introduced in order to make the future approximate our conception of it. Thus, it might turn out that the apparent source of contention between these groups can be reconciled. Instead of choosing deterrence/retribution over welfare, or vice versa, perhaps both types of control or intervention systems are necessary. Homans argued, relevant to control of deviance in small groups, that effective control required activation of several simultaneous responses to that same deviant incident.[3] Hence, rather than end up with an either/or choice of a single control strategy, it might be more appropriate to consider how both punitive and welfare controls can be applied to the same social problem.

When one examines these suggested reforms in some detail, it becomes clear that the deterrence/retribution movement of the 1970s does not attempt to abolish the welfare-oriented control strategies. For example, Morris believes his prescriptions for a future prison based on retribution will strengthen the effectiveness of simultaneous or subsequent treatment efforts with offenders, because his guidelines will remove the coercive edge and the manipulation that accompanies the current treatment/punishment combination.[4]

Finally, we must also be open to the possibility that both the Welfare and the Moralist groups are right! Perhaps neither of them have erred in either their portrayals of the social system nor in their choice of control strategies. How is this possible? Human systems have a characteristic of many other open systems, that of equifinality, that implies that different system processes may arrive at the same end point. In other words, distinct methods may be equally functional in reaching a specified end state.[5] Football teams with very distinct talents and strategies may be equally successful in winning football games. Communal, extended family, and nuclear family arrangements may be equally final processes for raising and socializing children. Similarly, it is possible that retribution/deterrence and welfare controls are equifinal relative to achieving the American future system that both groups desire. If this possibility were true, then settling the dispute between the groups may not be a rational or an empirical effort. If both processes of control can achieve the same results, it may be a political and/or a value choice as to whether one should prefer punishment to treatment. Of course, even if both strategies were to prove possible, or functional, their level of feasibility may differ. Perhaps one is more cost-effective than the other, or perhaps we will have the kinds of manpower to man one system while the other system would require a major reshuffling of expertise, and so on.

It is my belief that the two groups are inaccurate on all three counts mentioned above. That is, I think that their descriptions of the current social system are inaccurate, that their ideas of the future are not feasible, given the current trends in American society, and that neither the retribution nor the welfare control strategies, if implemented, would produce the results they expect. The major focus here will be upon the nature of the criminal justice system, and whether and to what extent it does or can function as a control or guidance system by which to get us from point A to point B. In order to look at this problem, however, it is necessary to be far more specific about criminal justice operations and structure than either the Welfare or the Moralist groups think necessary. If the criminal justice system or some type of substitute system is to function to "change" society or to guide it toward some more desirable future, we must examine the current system within the context of its relationship to other subsystems of the society, the extent to which it can change or alter those systems, and the extent to which it is changed by those other systems.

THE CONCEPT OF CONTROL

The science of control, or cybernetics, is "the science of communication and control in the animal and the machine . . . . cybernetics studies the flow of information round a system, and the way in which that information is used by the system as a means of controlling itself."[6] The study of control, as a science, is much younger than the study of social control. The mathematician, Norbert Winer, coined the term cybernetics in 1947,[7] while E. A. Ross was writing of social control in 1901.[8] While many of the models and techniques of cybernetics have now been applied to social systems, as well as to machines and biological systems,[9] the attempt to introduce a cybernetic approach to the examination of change in societies as social systems is rare. Beer's classic work on control in systems devotes only one chapter to cybernetics in government, and even that chapter tends to downplay the difficulty of gaining the kinds of measurements necessary in order for societal-level systems to control themselves.[10]

Etzioni's major attempt to develop the conceptual basis for a cybernetic society, which he calls the "active society," really fails to delineate the types of control that would be necessary to govern societal-level decisions and is even less specific and convincing about how societal goals will be selected.[11] Ackoff and Emery also treat social systems as purposeful systems, or guided systems, but their approach falls off short of analyzing societal-level organization.[12] Furthermore, their definitions of purposeful social systems are built upon constructs derived from the individual as a psychological system.[13] Many macrosociologists today insist that models of systems sufficient to the examination of individual and small group behavior are insufficient or even distortive and inaccurate when applied to social systems that are larger than a single complex organization.[14] Social policy analysts, examining social reform programs designed to guide or control societal processes in specified directions, have generally concluded that the programs have failed to achieve their objectives because the control devices employed were not sufficient to the task. The control programs implemented in the 1960s invariably focused on individuals who needed remediation rather than on changing power relationships or economic relationships in the entire system.[15]

Examinations of systems that are larger and more complex than single complex organizations, or bureaucracies, is a relatively new effort. Interorganizational theory, as opposed to theories that explain intraorganizational relationships, only became widely popular during the 1960s.[16] Of course, there were many broad-scale efforts to build theories of society and social systems prior to that, from Marx's economically based analysis to Parsons's value-based analysis. More recent societal analysis, however, which has grown up after concerted work on interorganizational theory began, criticizes the earlier social-system analysis on one of two grounds.

Classical Marxian analysis has failed to predict the current social system structure, in which a socialist revolution has not emerged. Marx downplayed the growth and pivotal character of complex organizations and interorganizational networks in controlling and constraining conflict between classes.[17] Parsons's work, based on analogies between biological systems and social systems, is faulted because it implies an integrative coherence to macrolevel systems that does not now exist, and may not be feasible in the future.[18] In general, there would seem to be a consensus among analysts of society in the United States that certain natural controls are apparent within the American social system, in the sense that programs and policies that ignore basic constraints on interorganizational interaction will fail, or conversely, that certain "natural" tendencies are nearly irreversible.[19] On the other hand, many analysts conclude that the probability is very low of somehow organizing interorganizational entities in order to guide society toward proposed goals in a planned manner.[20]

Equilibrium and Control

If, indeed, there is a break, both in theory and in fact, between the types of controls or guides that may be imposed upon social systems the size of complex organizations or smaller and the types of controls that can be imposed upon social systems interorganizational or larger, the nature of this break would be crucial to discussions of criminal justice for the following reason. Both the Welfare and the Moralist groups admit to two types of control—guidance or redirection—that the criminal justice network, or a substitute, is supposed to provide. On the one hand, they perceive that interventions, of either a punitive or a treatment nature, might change the behavior of individual human beings. One can examine the processes and outcomes of arrest, prosecution, conviction, and imprisonment or field supervision of offenders. One can do the same for educational or remedial counseling, behavior modification, and other treatment programs that are supposed to change the conditions of the individual or conditions inside the individual. But, neither the Moralists nor the Welfare group is *primarily* concerned with this level of "control" as provided by criminal justice or a substitute. The Moralists focus primarily upon the societal impact of retributive symbols and deterrent threats. The major focus of the Welfare groups is change in societal conditions that give rise to individual deviance.

Thus, both groups seek to employ as a societal level control some network of agencies, an interorganizational system, which would function to control or guide the social system, in order to take us from our current social state to a more desirable future. One can reasonably ask what the criminal justice or welfare system would have to look like and what it would have to do in order to perform this function. Can criminal justice or a welfare system provide societal-level control? Now, neither group is naive enough to stipulate that its preferred control system, by itself, is sufficient to the task. The more accurate question is then to what extent, if at all, can a criminal justice or welfare alternative *contribute* to societal-level control? Even though this second version of the question implies a much lower level of expectation about the control system in question (i.e., it is not expected to do the whole job), this question is much more complex than the first one. We could probably say *a priori* that criminal justice/welfare cannot provide societal control. It cannot possibly provide the requisite variety to control all the possible deviations and elaborations that can occur in economic, political, and cultural institutions. But, whether it can *contribute* to societal control is less obviously false, and empirically more difficult to investigate.

To answer this question, we need to know what criminal justice/welfare does, what it can do if revised, how it connects now and would later link with other components of the societal control network, whether this link is compatible or detrimental to other control efforts, and so on.

Perhaps the simplest place to begin this series of questions is with a relatively abstract question regarding the mode of control relative to the type of system in which the control is imbedded. What kinds of controls can control what kinds of systems? A full elaboration of this question is cybernetics itself, and well beyond the scope of this book. We must limit our inquiry to: (1) What type of system the American social system is, and (2) what type of control or controls would be sufficient to guide it. But again, these questions are important but too vast in scope and too complex to be answered, or even properly addressed here. Then, where is there a beginning simple enough that we have some chance of establishing a firm starting point?

Obviously, a simple beginning point will require considerable slighting of detail, and we must expect that this beginning will require considerable revision as theory development continues. Nevertheless, the amount of detail actually required is much less than we might expect at first. Our focus should be upon the *a priori* soundness of the current notions of criminal justice as a control network, and then upon reexamination of how this network of agencies is articulated with other elements of the social system. We have seen thus far how the Moralist and Welfare group expect that the system of criminal justice agencies should and does act. The rest of this chapter is devoted to the examination of how these expectations for the system came about, and the extent to which these expectations reflect accurately the basic structures and operations of control systems in general. The second half of the book will then attempt to reexamine the operations of the criminal justice agencies in the American society, concentrating upon their articulation with other elements of American social structure. Again, our basic intent is not to set up a new set of suggestions for criminal justice reform, or a new ideology for how offenders should be handled, but merely to begin an empirically grounded and testable theory of criminal justice operation or administration.

Social systems, according to Buckley, may be divided into those that are goal-oriented and those that are goal-directed.[21] Directed systems can choose goals and then select behaviors in order to reach those objectives. For example, the social-technical system that resulted in placing men on the moon was a directed system. Goal-oriented systems have less complex information. While subgroups or individuals in goal-oriented systems may achieve their own goals, the behavior of the various subunits cannot be called goal seeking. The Parsonian model of society, in which the various core values and the social institutions that represent them operate to constrain each other, is a goal-oriented system.[22] Geoffrey Vickers also stresses the goal-oriented nature of modern urban (particularly British) society. The various political and economic institutions produce trends in society by the manner of their interaction, but the direction supplied by this interaction is not planned. For example, management and unions may each have goals to seek at the bargaining table, but within the current economy, the conflicts between union and management do not result in a resolution within the system of management and labor. The byproduct of this two-party goal seeking is an orientation of the entire economic system toward ever-increasing inflation, continued problems for the consumer, greater demands by labor, and the meeting of those demands by management in a way that continues the inflation spiral. One cannot say that the public economy is goal-directed, but only that it is oriented toward some unchosen goals (or outcomes) because of the structure of the system.[23]

Clearly, a notion that a control apparatus can lead a system from one point to another, at least when the future point is specified now, requires the creation of a goal-directed system, one in which all the goal seeking of the subunits of the system are consistent, in result, with the direction one chooses for the system as a whole.[24] Thus, one might question whether, or in what ways, a criminal justice system can function as a means of making the goals of subunits of the social system congruent, and, if this is possible, whether the direction or redirection supplied by the criminal justice system is or can be tied into a goal selecting and monitoring system for the entire social system.

At least, these questions would be relevant to the type of social direction implied in the welfare notions of the future American social state—an end point—about which there is an alleged consensus from the American people. While the Welfare group may be relatively ignorant or naive about the sophistication and complexity of the leadership patterns, the authority structure, and the institutional matrix that would allow this type of direction to occur, I think that this type of "massive-society-as-one-complex-organization" is implied in their beliefs about treatment, and in their exhortations that the American people should work in unified fashion. I also think that this type of social direction is the foundation of their implicit trust in social technology, or in a technological elite who should lead us toward that end state.

The Moralist group, in contrast, have a somewhat lesser view of the directional capacity that must be built into the American social system. Because they do not hold out a specified goal toward which society as an organization must be directed, the type of control network they require is also less grand and complex. In effect, the social system they desire to produce is not a goal-directed system, but a goal-oriented one, in which the democratic processes are maintained. Thus they wish to produce stability (if Van den Haag is correct), or to maintain a state of equilibrium (if Packer is more correct).

The concept of equilibrium in social systems has always been a difficult one to conceptualize. Physical systems are in equilibrium when all the system's energy is equally distributed, and activity stops. Social systems are said to be in equilibrium, in contrast, only by rough analogy, since social systems are not maintained when the activity of their subunits ceases, but when a constant state of activity is feasible.[25] Within an open, social system, such a state is achieved through the constant importation of energy and resources, the transformation of that input, and the exportation of products. But, in addition, the import and export levels and values must be balanced, so that there is a constant trade-off between the system in question and its environment.[26] This relationship between social systems can produce what is called a homeostatic state, a condition in which the communication between systems is mutually satisfying or mutually functional and thus allows the internal-external dynamic to continue.

The notion of control in an homeostatic system is at this point relatively familiar and simple. For example, self-controlling mechanical systems, such as the heating system of a house, or the water-level maintaining system in the household toilet, both employ the basic homeostatic feedback loop. In the heating example, a thermostat coupled to the ignition of the heating plant can maintain a rather homeostatic temperature level by reading the air temperature and comparing it to a predetermined level. A specified deviation between the heat in the room and the specified temperature level in the thermostat will kick on the furnace until the control device and the heat in the room again approximate equality.[27] Homans writes that social systems are, in general, "in equilibrium and control is effective when the state of the elements that enter the system and of the mutual relationship between them is such that any small change in one of the elements will be followed by changes in the other elements tending to reduce the amount of that change."[28] Such control requires that obedience to the sanctions applied produces the greatest possible satisfaction for all the units in question and that disobedience of those sanctions results in a decrease in satisfaction for all groups concerned.[29] According to this model, one cannot specify that a certain action, as a responce to deviance, is a control, unless its application results in a return to a homeostatic relationship.

The above presentation does not enable us to judge whether the Moralist or Welfare conceptions of the criminal justice function are or are not appropriate. It only outlines the system behavior that would have to be observable if the criminal sanction can be used as a homeostatic control. If the application of the criminal sanction now produces the centrifugal tendencies of homeostatic control, or could be made to do so with some modifications in the system, then the criminal justice system might be a viable contributor to an orderly American society of the type specified by Packer and Van den Haag.

The Response to Deviance as a Control

One of the most helpful papers in trying to conceptualize the place of criminal justice in social control is a 1959 discussion by Theodore Mills.[30] Mills begins by positing that most theoretical discussions of crime and its control do not take into account whether the type of control applied to the deviant act is appropriate to the type of system in which the deviance is observed. He suggests that most discussions of delinquency control assume that the behavior in question is imbedded in "a simple system." The simple system, according to Mills, has three characteristics, in relation to response to deviance, that together make the application of an equilibrium model appropriate:

1. In a simple system, the extent of the demand domain behind the deviant behavior is matched by the range of legitimate control.
2. Simple systems question the value of the deviance prior to the application of controls.
3. In simple systems, the sanctions available to the control agents penetrate beyond symptoms to the demand problems.[31]

If these characteristics are not manifest in the system responding to deviance within it, startling results may occur: "When, contrary to the conditions in the simple system, demands underlying deviance are beyond the scope of legitimate control, we may expect either routine application of sanctions, which by definition cannot reach the demands or application of more effective but illegitimate sanctions."[32]

Mills goes on to suggest that in complex rather than simple systems: (1) there is no evaluation of the adaptive value of the deviance before sanctions are applied; (2) there may be no match between the control repertoire of officials and the problem or demand domain of the deviants (that is, the demands are inaccessible or unknown); and (3) there may be several controlling units responding to the same behavior in conflicting ways. One could add, then, that control in simple systems results in the inclusion of the deviant in the original group through the exclusion of or constraint on any behavior that is beyond the tolerance of that group. Such deviant controlling processes are widely observable in small groups and small towns, and in general, in human systems that are relatively homogenous and information-rich.[33]

In contrast, the application of simple controls in complex systems produces opposite results: the deviant is identified with the behavior that produced the reaction, the deviant is isolated from the group whose norms were violated, the deviant tends to value the deviant behavior and make it normative, and is then controlled (within the deviant group) by his ability to reproduce that kind of behavior and by his ability to elicit negative reactions to it from the outside (original) group. As a consequence, continued application by the officials of the original group of negative sanctions to the deviant's behavior becomes positively reinforcing and the deviance, as well as the distance between the original group and the deviant, is amplified.[34]

The Criminal Justice System as a Control

We have then several questions before us in terms of the function of the criminal justice system as a control. From the Welfare group perspective, criminal justice is thought to be a simple control applied within a complex system (or their comments can be interpreted as such). The emphasis on the need to rehabilitate—or to deal with the "root causes" of crime—rather than punish or penalize can be viewed as recognition that the demand domain (to use Mills's terminology) must be addressed if control is to be successful. The primary fault with the Welfare approach to control, it would seem, is not their ragged attack on the criminal sanction but with the nature of the substitute controls that they would impose. There is little evidence to muster for the rehabilitative response to deviance and crime as being any more complex or more coterminous with the demand domain behind deviance than would be the criminal sanction.[35] In effect, the Welfare group merely propose another simple control to apply, inappropriately, to a complex situation.

From the perspective of the Moralist group, criminal justice can function as a societal control if: (1) the present social system is simple and a negative feedback model of control is therefore appropriate; (2) if the social system is currently complex and the criminal sanction is also complex; (3) or if the reforms of the criminal justice system that they propose would yield the appropriate match between controls and social system characteristics.

That the current social system is not simple, but one with complex interdependence and conflicts, can almost be answered out of hand. Critics such as Dahrendorf, who document the conflict model of society, would certainly oppose the suggestion that simple controls can be effective. Dahrendorf, Bell, and others suggest that the only type of social control currently observable is the unguided opposition among conflicting elements in the social system. That is, they think that complexity itself produces its own control since each social unit is too greatly locked to other units for deviance to be too great in any direction before it will be checked.[36] But even those analysts who see society as an integrated unit, such as Talcott Parsons, see the criminal sanction as irrelevant to social control. Parsons believes that the punitive response to deviance only amplifies deviance.[37] Thus, both those theorists who begin with a conflict model of society as well as those theorists who begin with an integrated model of society believe that deviance within the social system is too complex a phenomenon to be controlled through the appliction of "simple controls." Stated in other terms, this means that deviation from societal norms cannot be controlled effectively through the use of a simple feedback model.

For the conflict theorists, negative feedback controls are inappropriate because the deviating units are not believed to have the same goals or the same information processing systems as the units in charge of implementing the negative feedback. (For instance, the gang leader might take it as a positive reinforcement that the policeman sees him as a troublemaker and tries to exert official sanctions). For the integrative theorists, negative feedback might work, but the sanctioning alternatives available to the officials of the criminal system do not provide such feedback. The reason, according to Parsons, is identical to the theoretical discussion presented by Mills: formal punitive sanctions do not answer the problem situation or the ego motivation behind the deviant behavior.

I think it is essentially accurate that most Moralist conceptions of the criminal justice system *do* start with the twin assumptions that: (1) the social system is a single integrated system, and (2) the criminal sanction does provide the appropriate negative feedback. If this is so, proposals for the utility of the criminal sanction should probably be rejected at this point. However, we can provide the moralist argument with the benefit of the doubt, if only to follow through with the other options covered by Mills's model. To reiterate, perhaps (1) the criminal sanction does apply to a complex social system because its operation provides more or different control than the feedback model would supply, or (2) the reforms suggested by Packer, Van den Haag, or others would have the effect of changing the social system structure, the function of the criminal sanction, or both, so that a match would be obtained between the sanctioning repertoire and deviance generated in the social structure.

Let us examine the second option, that both the social system and the criminal controls are equally complex. Mills and Wilkins provide us with a guide in explicating this possibility. They caution that one should not confuse the simplicity of social structure with the simplicity of a control network. A simple or homogeneous social system often has complex and extensive information systems (in layman's parlance, everyone knows everyone else's business). This means that the roles and functions of the various groups and individuals in society tightly interlock so that no one has a wide range of roles from which to choose.[38] (For instance, the banker in a small town cannot escape his role, nor the town drunk the role expectations held about him.) A wide range of behavior may be tolerated within such a social system, but only from the "appropriate" persons. Thus, the deviant is included rather than excluded because his behavior, while not condoned, is encapsulated and tolerated to the extent that the deviant performs the deviant role in the places and the ways that are structured for it into the system. Mills summarizes this type of social structure by stating that complex information-sharing, via well-known roles and role expectations, simplifies the control required. Informal controls are almost always sufficient and can be applied by almost anyone in the social system.[39]

In contrast, complex social structures are often less clearly articulated. One of the classic analyses of a complex social system, the modern urban area, suggests that the high density of many diverse people performing many various functions almost precludes the type of informal information loops that control behavior in simple systems. In order for the conflicting elements of an urban center to function simultaneously, the system, as an ecological area, tends to diversify, specialize, and become fragmented. Certain behaviors are recognized as appropriate to certain areas of the region. Persons are no longer controlled; instead there is ecological regulation of where particular behaviors will take place. Thus, while the simple system asks for, or pressures for, the internalization of norms and values appropriate to the entire group, the complex system only manages to control the places where behaviors are to occur. This type of control system by its very nature cannot address the social problems to which deviance may be a response; it can only manage the occurrence of deviance within very rough limits.[40]

Mills argues that the multi-organizational arrangements for the processing of criminal deviants manifest very clearly the urban, bureaucratic characteristics of specialization and fragmentation, with the result that the discrepancy between the deviant demand domain and the targets of controls widens: "One consequence of acknowledging a demand as a cause of deviance is to extend the responsibility of controlling agents to cover the demand. Unless the resources are unlimited in this respect, and in order to avoid negligence, groups tend to define, to limit, and to protect their realms of responsibility."[41] Theoretically, this parceling out portions of the "deviance problem" to specialized agencies will reinforce the tendency of the control network to remain complex so that the various units within the network operate to optimize their own sphere of responsibility.[42]

Several empirical validations of this reinforced complexity are available in criminal justice research. One of the most directly relevant observations of criminal justice interorganizational behavior is Reiss and Black's presentation on police agency reaction to the due process rulings of the appellate court system. They begin by pointing out that "the major means any subsystem has for controlling others in the legal system is through its own operating organization. . . ."[43] Because the Supreme Court of the United States has no direct control (in terms of a single unified line of authority) over any particular police department, the police can find means to subvert the goals of the Court and still achieve the territorial control they wish to exert in their areas of authority.[44] Applied to our simple feedback control model, these observations would suggest that the various units of the criminal process cannot even control each other vis-à-vis a system of target definition, means elaboration, evaluation, and feedback, because they do not have the same organizational reactions to the same events. Hence, it is relatively unrealistic to expect them to be able to provide a unified, coherent system of signals to the deviant that might steer the offender toward the desired behavior, even if the offender did have the same goals as the political groups that underwrite the criminal justice apparatus. Because the agencies that operate the criminal process and formulate policy about crime prevention and control do not provide or contain an overall "last answer" control center, there is little chance that the system of criminal justice can adopt and implement a concerted strategy for crime reduction, punishment of offenders, support of dominant culture norms, rehabilitation, or other overarching goals that might be selected.

This situation must be taken as the basic state of the art upon which any understanding of criminal justice operations and any proposals for effective reform must start. The existence of this state of conflicting complexity not only means that single objectives for the criminal sanction are unlikely to be interpreted and implemented uniformly, but also that it is unlikely that many parts of the system operate as if the implementation of the criminal sanction itself is the only or even the predominant objective of all the separate and relatively autonomous units within the network.

If the Moralists believe that the criminal justice system offers a complex control response to a complex social structure, the above analysis leads to the rejection of that belief on the following grounds. One, it is unlikely that the criminal sanction as conceived within the deterrence-retribution framework can be effectively implemented by the current criminal justice network. Second, the complex, fragmented, and conflicting system of local police, county courts, and local and state correctional organizations may well form some portion of a control system for the social structure, but the controls it offers are unlikely to be ones associated with meeting the demand domain behind deviant actions. It is quite possible that the present state of criminal justice organization performs several political and economic functions for the communities and states in which the organizations are embedded. But, any conception of criminal justice operations as a set of coherent and well-articulated responses across the several organizations is not likely to help in trying to determine what those functions are or evaluate how well those functions are performed. Thus, of the second option for the Moralist position, we can conclude that the criminal justice system may or may not be a component in a control unit for society, *but* that the control functions it performs are probably not those of limiting rational choice to legal behavior.

In the third option for the Moralist position, we consider whether the reforms of the system proposed by Van den Haag, Packer, and others would in some way change the criminal justice system or change the amount of complexity in the social structure. That is, might the reform of the criminal justice system make it an effective control operation, even if it is not one now? This question is a difficult and dangerous one to consider, of course, when we have no satisfactory theory of the functions now performed by the system. Since neither the Welfare nor the Moralist positions attempt to suggest the purpose or function of the "undesirable" characteristics of the system, the notion of reform must remain incomplete at this point. We can only raise the issue briefly, with the caveat that *successful* reformation of the criminal justice system might produce more rather than less social disorder because all current rationales for reformative action begin with a normative position that the system should be (and is not) doing a particular thing. Changing the system in order to produce that particular thing might conceivably be effected. But, without consideration of what these changes will induce vis-à-vis dropping the *current* functions or operations, we have no way of predicting whether the particular objectives sought by the reformative program will in fact lead to the overall goal of social stability or will, in fact, produce greater rents in the social fabric.

Of change in social control itself, Mills writes that the most effective means of coping with deviance is to develop a *new* system, rather than to strengthen an old system.[45] This statement is a reformulation of well-established theorems about complex organizations. In organizations one finds that problems are usually not handled by retooling or redesigning a current organizational component, but by elaboration of new units. In other words, elaboration and expansion are generally the most effective way of handling problems.[46] It is possible, however, to consider the reforms proposed for limiting the criminal sanction and/or strengthening the deterrence/retribution function as in some ways the generation of a "new system." Any proposals that would couple the operations of police with those of the courts, or limit the operations of post-adjudicatory agencies to the implementation of punishment would be relatively new operations. One could raise many questions about the feasibility of these changes. But the more relevant questions probably involve the expected outcomes, should such a reform movement be successful.

The implementation of a system of agencies that could concentrate on deterring specified crimes and providing fair or just retribution to those who were not deterred would be highly dependent upon the existence of a particular social structure as well as upon the predominance of a particular culture. On the one hand, the social structure would have to provide an economic distribution of goods (a distribution of opportunity by which to achieve, and/or a distribution of resources independent of economic opportunity) such that it can be argued that rational consideration of behavioral outcomes can be expected to dissuade persons from commission of crimes. This is another way of saying tht a social structure must be created in which deviance is "marginal rather than institutional." Such systems do seem to exist, but most of them are subsistence economies or ones in which highly differential rewards are institutionalized (as in caste systems some years ago or in feudal economies). On the cultural side, the society would require a common set of norms and values that can provide legitimacy to laws and rules of procedure and thus the fairness required for retribution.

Most predictions of American social structure and culture do not suggest that these requirements are likely occurrences within any foreseeable future. For example, Bell argues that the culture increasingly bears anti-establishment antinomian characteristics, while the social structure will apparently provide widening gaps in ability, opportunity, and resource distribution.[47] If such predictions are accurate, the implementation of a coherent and unified criminal justice system may well reduce the system's sphere of legitimacy and applicability to the point where public policy can no longer support it. For example, Wilkins argues that a "more of the same" approach to crime control (meaning deterrence/retribution) will result in the dissolution of the legislative process and the cessation of the utilization of the criminal sanction altogether.[48]

WELFARE, MORALS, AND SOCIAL STABILITY

In summary, considering the criminal justice system as a control unit regulating the extent of societal deviations leads to several conclusions, none of which support either the Welfare or Moralist position. The Moralist group treats the law, the criminal sanction, and the sanction implemented through the criminal justice system as if the law were a statement of a unified cultural position and the sanction implemented provided regulation of the observance of cultural norms. The assumption is made that legitimacy exists for such regulation or can be obtained. The Welfare group treats the criminal law and its implementation as a result of a divisive social structure that in turn divides and increases conflict in the culture. The assumption is made that legitimacy for the system does not exist.

The Moralist position might apply accurately to a social structure that could be described in Parsonian terms of integration and strain. But the majority of sociological opinion severely challenges the accuracy of such a conception of society. The Welfare position tends to align somewhat better with the conflict theory of society elaborated by Dahrendorf and others. But the Welfare group, as it elaborates its alternatives to criminal justice, implies an elitist position for treaters or social changers, which is unlikely to be workable. Those persons who go further with a Welfare version of control suggest that major institutional revisions, rather than behavioral control of individual behavior, will become the predominant strategy by which to introduce or maintain stability in a complex system. In any case, visions of criminal justice reform or visions of welfare treatment substitutes for punishment do not seem to fare well. Indeed, what is perhaps more surprising (in terms of its unlikelihood) than the conservative and liberal versions of criminal justice are the recent Marxian arguments that the criminal justice agencies are a part of a larger, conspiratorial social-industrial complex. It just does not seem likely that support for the criminal justice system can bring about the degree of control that the Marxists impute to such a system.

THE DEVELOPMENT OF SYSTEMS ANALYSIS AND OUR CONCEPTION OF CRIMINAL JUSTICE

If the current frameworks for the understanding of criminal justice do not provide us with the tools by which to link the activities of that system with the structure and dynamics of the larger social system, they cannot provide us with useful guidelines for criminal justice reform or provide us with a basis for explaining why the criminal justice systems of one region and jurisdiction differ from those of another. Before we go on to consider some alternative frames of reference for the analysis of criminal justice, it would be helpful if we could derive some insight into why the predominant frameworks have been adopted so wholeheartedly.

Most commentators on public policy changes in the last twenty years have noted simultaneous shifts on several fronts that have served to increase significantly the rift in public organizations between the economic division of labor and the political bases of goal-setting and policymaking. Prior to an era beginning somewhere around 1955–60, public sector human service organizations had considerably less visibility than is now the case. Public organizations were seen as entities that dispensed services or products for which there was not a competitive market, or for which distribution of outputs was not to be limited by the recipient's ability to pay. Education, welfare, protection from harm, and collection of refuse were generally seen as necessary goods, access to which was governed by membership in the social group, rather than upon a recipient's ability or even willingness to shoulder the full burden for the cost of the product. However, social services were traditionally seen as political dynamite: unsatisfactory service could mean a potential loss at the polls, but politicians could do little to improve services.

Political leaders often sought to take credit for satisfactory service, but to avoid the blame for poor service by creating an aura of isolation for the political appointees that ran the various public organizations. Problems were the appointee's problem; solutions often amounted to little more than changing appointees.

While this game with public service is still common,[49] the rationalizing of organization, vast changes in planning and evaluation technology, and the increased access of the public to the inside machinations of public services have all limited the extent to which political success could hinge upon public statements and public ceremonies without minimal reflection of public promises in the actual practices and outputs of the organizations in question.

Part of the reason for this change in the accountability demands upon public organizations can be traced to the introduction in the last two generations of private corporation executives into major policy and executive positions in public service. These leaders have brought with them the idea that government can be run like business and have applied to public organization many of the decision criteria, planning technologies, and public relations methods that brought them success in private firms. Among the most significant of these importations has been the introduction of systems analysis to the problems of public service.[50]

These changes in terms of their consequences for public service organization are no more evident than in the comparison of the two national commissions charged with the examination of and recommendations about criminal justice. The National Commission on Law Enforcement Observance (The Wickersham Commission) reported on the full scope of criminal process activities for President Hoover in 1933. The topics covered in the more than dozen reports of the Wickersham Commission are surprisingly similar to the topics covered by the President's Commission On Law Enforcement and the Administration of Justice, reporting in 1967. Both commissions deal with drunkenness and public order crimes, organized crime, police, courts, corrections, and related topics. Many of the conclusions of the two commissions are also strikingly similar, given the span of years and the changes in practice between the two reporting periods. But there is one major difference: the Wickersham Commission plodded through each separate agency and issue in sequential and separate fashion, while the tone, plan of attack, and guarded optimism of the President's Commission are all directly attributable to its major innovation, the "invention of the criminal justice system" as the basic frame of reference within which to record the practices of police, court, and correctional agencies and from which to launch its myriad suggestions for change.

This is not to say that no one saw the several agencies interconnected by mutual influence and overlapping responsibility prior to 1967. However, the entire emphasis did change from one of approaching each agency of justice separately, within its own environment and beset with its own constraints, to one of approaching the outputs of the organizations as their mutual influences conjoined to form some "end products."

From a stranger's viewpoint, there may be no more valid reason to examine the police vis-à-vis the courts than there is to examine the police vis-à-vis the mayor, the school system, the class structure of a community, or the taxable resources in a jurisdiction. But the systems approach, as utilized in the 1967 reports, is focused predominantly on the articulation of the criminal process responsibilities of the criminal justice agencies.

Systems analysis, of course, is a neutral device. It is a method for interconnecting units and functions and relating those components to inputs and outputs. But *what* system is to be analyzed is not always clear, particularly in social rather than in biological or physical systems. That the President's Commission chose the criminal process interfaces as the *overriding* concern when describing and evaluating the agencies in question was itself a *political* rather than an *economic* decision. Based upon this major shift in emphasis, and not prior to that time, comes the belief that criminal justice, as a system, is a three component arrangement for processing individuals from investigation through punishment.[51] This choice of system boundaries is the primary reason that most analysis today presses for the examination of police-courts-corrections as if they could approach organizational unity and produce outcomes attributable to the coordinated effort of all of them.

THE CONSEQUENCES FOR CRIMINAL JUSTICE

General system theory, the closely related techniques of operations research, and the less formalized systems approach all had their infancy, if not their birth, in the climate of national urgency of World War II.[52] In the heat of that world crisis, the power and legitimacy of science and technology, as applied to social and political problems, took a quantum jump.[53]

While the application of the same science and technology to peacetime problems and nonmilitary endeavors took a while longer, their application has grown steadily. Whether fortuitously or not, the political benedictions over the "crime problem" as another "war" have probably hastened the application of systems analysis to criminal justice and made it unavoidable that the strategies of problem delineation and solution adopted by the President's Crime Commission in 1967 would emphasize operational research.[54]

The consequences for criminal justice, both as a public policy area and as a set of operating agencies have been several, significant, and perhaps unstoppable. Yet, it is important to understand that the war analogy applied to crime is but an analogy, if indeed it is more than a political catchphrase. Moreover, the analogy, while detailed in such a way that would make operations research and systems analysis fit the problem, would not even fit the military situations now confronting nations, let alone the social and political situations implied in the "crime problem." The most drastic difference between crime and the World War II type war (which, of course, ended with the technological innovations born in that war), is that the crime problem does not contain an outside enemy nor any rallying points external to the social system around which to achieve cohesion, legitimacy, and common goals. The elite scientific groups who worked for the country during World War II could probably safely assume that they worked for the "good of all," at least until the invention of the bomb. But, the elite scientific groups who form commission and foundation staffs and advisory boards in this decade, as they confront assignments of improving criminal justice, can assume that they work for the good of everyone only by the adoption of conventions and models of society that are barely supported by their own empirical evidence, let alone by political realities.

> The analogy of war on crime should break down because it is only when the enemies of society are perceived as outside that society that the concept of war . . . has any significance. Maybe the criminal is a social misfit, but who is misfitting what? The criminal and the deviant are part of our society until we *define* them as outside it. Society is not a configuration of independent dichotomies—criminal v. law abiding, good v. bad, truth v. falsity, black v. white, us v. them . . . . The model of warfare does not hold because society cannot be divided into 'friend' and 'foe.'[55]

More specifically, the consequences for criminal justice have been at least threefold. The application of systems analysis to criminal justice, as it has been applied so far, had led: (1) to the adoption of the integrative view of society; (2) the adoption of control objectives for criminal justice agencies; and (3) the adoption of the belief that the criminal justice agencies form a unitary system, or have in common a set of interfaces and goals that are functionally more important than any other interfaces that the separate agencies may have. Because we are dealing here with a system *within* society, and of society, the adoption of such beliefs has real effects upon the type of system we have and the type of society in which we live.

The adoption of the belief that society is an integrated entity is the most subtle and fundamental of these effects. I mean by the integrated model the notion that the various groups and interests represented within the borders of the United States have the same goal orientations and the same standards for evaluating progress and that the outcomes of a well-planned attack on a social problem will benefit one group as well as another. This belief is fundamental to both the Moralist and the Welfare positions on criminal justice. But, as is the case with both those groups, it is important to remember that actual demonstration of consensus about policy and outcome is not sought nor is achievement of it really expected. Instead, the belief functions as a portion of an ideology that allows policy, program design, and implementation to be undertaken in the present pattern, by groups and organizations who claim to speak for or act for the best interests of the "whole group." The actors and organizations who make the best claim about doing so, usually to each other, are the actors and organizations that will have the upper hand at any given time. The maintenance of the belief in the integrated society also allows us to approach criminals as persons to be punished and isolated from the group, or as misfits who are to be remediated to its expectations.

The adoption of the belief that the criminal justice agencies can provide control of persons and events, to reduce the frequency with which the group boundaries are crossed, is a direct result of the belief that there is a unitary group to be steered or maintained. Finally, the pressure to unify the criminal justice system becomes a logical extension, and requisite, of the control strategy.

Whether there are alternatives to this already institutionalized approach is our next question. Whether the alternatives, if they exist, are feasible for adoption or present policy and program implications is also unknown. It would seem to me that the need for alternatives is at least suggested by the premonition that the current set of operating assumptions have done more for the organizations that foster them than for the persons supposedly served by them. But, this is only premonition or contrasting belief and should fall or prosper upon the soundness of the competing explanation of criminal justice.

It would seem likely, at this juncture, that an alternative, if it is sound, will not be one that calls for a simpler approach or that utilizes less complex technology. The faults with the existing models of criminal justice are not so much the function of our analytical techniques, but the inability, thus far, to give the analytical and technological advances at our disposal an adequate idea space in which to operate. The faults, in other words, may not be with systems analysis but with the choice of systems for examination.

Chapter 6

Searching for the Context of Criminal Justice

I have argued so far that the predominant method for conceptualizing criminal justice concentrates upon the operations of a single unified system of agencies to which observers infer one or two predominant goals or purposes. In other words, most criminal justice analysis begins with a normative framework, a set of expectations or standards that the analyst expects of the system. When—and the instances are frequent—the system does not meet expectations or standards, the analyst is variously shocked, miffed, or self-congratulatory for providing evidence that the claptrap systems designed and operated by men do not achieve the goals idealized by men.

This method of conceptualizing criminal justice has its merits, for it is basically an optimistic and proactive venture in which the analyst seeks to bring a system of human activity to new heights of achievement. At the same time, this procedure is inherently frustrating, since human endeavors rarely meet the levels of expectation set for them. One is therefore frequently dissatisfied and spurred on to greater activity, new foundations for system structure and operations, and new attempts to reach the preestablished goals.

This method of analysis is common to operations research as frequently applied to business and defense problems. Goals are set deliberately, tasks undertaken in order to meet these goals, measurements of outcome taken, and the divergence of outcome from goal is utilized as the basis for retooling the operations. The organizations that use this procedure most profitably have no vested interest in the particular operations designed and implemented, except of course the cost sunk into the implementation. They would prefer that the first operation might accomplish the end result rather than the nth operation, because success at first application is cheaper. But the operation, whether an advertising campaign or a foray into enemy territory, can be discarded if it proves unsuccessful. The object, or the vested interest, is the goal upon which the operation is predicated.

The operations in these instances are very real, tangible, limited endeavors designed to accomplish specific goals. Frequently such operations can be conceived of and analyzed as projects, with starting and ending dates, milestones designated within these bounds, and critical tasks to be completed as specified if the project is to be successful.

In such instances, normative analysis of the operation is rational. The initiators know what they want to do, how to do it, and whether it is or can be accomplished. If project X does not work, it can be disassembled, workers reassigned, and resources reallocated. If the cost of project X has been extremely high, or if wild promises have been made and unfulfilled, a few heads may fly during disassembly. Edsels happen and are not excused lightly. But generally, the organization need not continue the operation *ad infinitum* beyond any prospect of returning a yield.

But the application of such normative analysis to criminal justice is premature, if not totally inappropriate. The system of criminal law and its administration is not a project, nor is it an event that occurs within an organization. Criminal justice is not constructed upon a narrow set of goals nor is it built to specifications established to increase the probability of a particular outcome or set of outcomes. Evaluating criminal justice against a set of goals to be accomplished and using empirical indicators to demonstrate outcomes fall short or wide of said goals is often merely an analytical exercise, valuable perhaps in establishing academic careers or in advancing a philosophy of punishment. But it is difficult to conceive of the findings of such analyses having the same relationship to criminal justice as such findings might have to an ad campaign, a television show, a new cosmetic or a new gadget in the arsenal of the Straegic Air Command.

Criminal justice, unlike a project or an operation, is a basic social institution. It may wither away as the extended family has done, or it may reflower as some say formal religion in America has done. But it is stretching analogies to say that the extended family was "disassembled" because it did not achieve its goals or that formal religion has become popular because it has demonstrably brought its followers closer to God. As a social institution, criminal justice is a minor one compared to the family, religion, or education. It involves far fewer people, costs less, and likely provides fewer social functions. It may be only a portion of the much larger political institution, but there is no doubt that it is a strongly embedded institutional social form. It has not been rationally constructed during a brief period of history as a means of accomplishing a few, clear-cut, specified goals. Asking that the criminal justice system achieve goals, such as deterring offenses or rehabilitating criminals, may seem logical, but it is unlikely that criminal justice has actually had to accomplish any particular goal to any particular degree in order to exist. Moreover, most of the goals against which outcomes of criminal justice are compared can and have been assigned to other social institutions as well. Familial, religious, and educational institutions might deter and deter with greater effectiveness than criminal justice. The same or other institutions may rehabilitate as well as or better than criminal justice.

Rather than ask what criminal justice hypothetically can do, we might gain more understanding about the system by asking what it does do, or why it exists within the American social system. Study upon study about what it specifically does not achieve does not enable us to cope with its endurance as a social institution. Since criminal justice is not a bounded organizational project, or even a set of endeavors geared to one set of specified objectives, the insistence of analyzing it as a unified system for the performance of specified objectives may inhibit our ability to understand how criminal justice operates in particular circumstances. Rather than idealize the system of "police-courts-corrections" and then expect real agencies to achieve some approximation of our ideal, it may be more productive, as a starting point, to examine criminal justice in the context of the milieu in which it is practiced.

Approaching criminal justice within a normative framework, or expecting the system to "do something," the analyst usually is forced to treat deviations from the ideal system as chance occurrences, or as evidence that certain actual systems need to be changed or upgraded in order to achieve expectations. We can approach the task of criminal justice analysis differently by examining criminal justice agencies in operation and by seeking to find the variables that explain the variation among agencies or constrain if not determine the operation of any single agency.

A wide variety of information is available that confirms that criminal justice is not a monolithic, commonly conceived, routine exercise. Criminal justice may well have different meanings in different places or behave differently under contrasting conditions. Before we attempt to change actual operating agencies to conform to a unitary conception of criminal justice, we may wish first to ask why such variations occur, whether these variations are functional equivalents, or whether the contrasting practices provide to the locality in which they are observed contributions to social order that might be lost if all criminal justice agencies everywhere behaved appropriately to the expectations of the analyst.

In this chapter, I will examine the three key assumptions about the criminal justice system as a societal control, in the context of the research data that detract from the validity of these notions. First, I shall argue that the criminal justice system is not a unitary system, or is not the same type of system in all places, and may serve different functions in different places. Second, I shall argue that any particular criminal justice system is rarely an integrated and coordinated system with all its separate agencies operating toward the same goals. The system is not integrated because while police, court, and correctional agencies allegedly serving one locality have some things in common, their organizational operations are often determined by the things they do not have in common: their differential relationships with other community systems. Third, I shall argue that criminal justice agencies do not actually exist within a social context where deterrence, or other negative sanctions, can actually be applied effectively, because it is not true that every group in a locality wants the same things, or has an equal hand in defining what is tolerable, desirable, or needed. Instead, criminal justice operations, based upon the faulty assumption that integration exists, can actually increase the divisions among various groups and limit the chances of deriving mutually acceptable standards of how persons should act toward each other.

CRIMINAL JUSTICE AS A UNITARY SYSTEM

I have argued that the perception of the "criminal justice system" as a unitary, coherent set of interagency operations is more likely a belief or desire brought to the analysis by the analyst, rather than a characteristic of the agencies and operations observed. All criminal analysts acknowledge that no "criminal justice system" actually exists, but instead many separate systems in many different jurisdictions. But most criminal justice analysts gloss over the observed differences in order to stress the commonalities, or underscore variation across systems as dysfunctional to some conception of social order. The emphasis remains upon the unitary, idealized conception of criminal justice.

To conservatives and liberals alike, deviations from the unitary system of criminal justice are usually occasions for criticism. Conservatives tend to favor swiftness and surety of punishment and thus the expected increase in deterrence that might appear without deviations. Liberals tend to focus on the inhumaneness in some of the deviations observed and stress that in unitary systems such excesses could be controlled. Radicals decry the inhumaneness and injustice in coherent, unitary systems of criminal justice, but they take the existence of such a coherent monolith as fact, perhaps reflecting upon the reform agendas of conservatives and liberals, rather than on actual observation of criminal justice agencies.

Criminal justice operations vary widely across areas of the country. Contrary to the suppositions of the unified model, there is a wide variety of evidence that criminal justice agencies relate to each other not only as determined by their roles in the criminal process, but also as determined by their roles in a community political context. Indeed, there may be more variation between, say, the police and the prosecutor in towns A and B than between the production and sales forces in companies C and D. In systems that have output indicators to which quality can be assessed, variation will be less likely than in human systems that cannot specify the quality of the operation. Since there are few, if any, universal agreements about "good" police work, the non–criminal justice factors influencing the police may determine how police and prosecutor interact as much or more so than does the law. But if sales and production can be assessed separately and together in terms of their contribution to profit, it is *less* likely that factors extraneous to the system will predominate in structuring the linkages.[1]

Frequent examples exist of rather significant variation in criminal justice practice and results across the myriad systems that actually exist. On a rather general level, Michael Banton's comparative observations of police in the United States and Scotland raises serious questions as to whether the police functions are the same in the two cultures. Banton argues that the Scottish officer is principally a symbol of community or social order and that beyond obeying and/or enjoying the ministerial quality of the police status, the Scottish officer has relatively little to do. In contrast, Banton finds the American policeman highly active and personal in the performance of his role. The American officer cannot defer to the general public regard for the police status. Instead, he needs to intervene actively in order to produce or maintain whatever semblance or level of order the officer personally feels to be appropriate to the instant situation.[2] Stated in other terms, we might say that there is a higher, or more rigid, degree of institutionalization in Scottish interaction patterns than in American. The Scottish officer needs less often to call upon personal authority than his American counterpart because most people in the Scottish village perceive the officer as a reminder or a reinforcement of norms that most of them hold in common. Banton constantly emphasizes that the Scottish officer defers to this consensus or common ground and usually obtains the expected result. In contrast, the American officer is likely to find less predictable the norms to which specific citizens adhere, and in addition is often confronted with a situation where citizens with different norms are in conflict. He cannot, in these situations, defer to a common, institutionalized understanding. Rather than function as a cultural reinforcement, a symbol of what is appropriate to all parties in a situation, the police officer in the United States more often functions as a means of resolving normative conflicts, or keeping such conflicts within bounds.

To the extent that such observations can be validated with more systematic empirical investigations, they would tend to detract not only from the global conception of the criminal justice system as a societal control but also from the application of Moralist or Welfare reforms. The control model and most reforms suggested by it would seem more applicable to the Scottish social context wherein the higher level of institutionalization provides a common set of behaviors or a consensually based public order to which the police symbol can serve as a referent.

The argument that police functions may differ between heterogeneous and homogeneous cultures is not limited to international comparisons. Banton, for example, is quick to comment on the marked variations among American police forces. He found much greater similarity across Great Britain than across the United States. At the same time, Banton, Wilkins, and others argue that the observed differences across nations can also be found *within* the United States. They suggest that the same high degree of density, interlocking roles, or institutionalization that accounts for the Scottish/Americn variation can account for many observed variations among different American communites.[3] More specifically, the village policeman, or the officer in a small, homogeneous community is more likely to act as a symbol of consensual order than is a police officer in a complex urban environment. The officer in the urban setting is more likely to invoke the law as a means of obtaining or restoring order whereas the village officer is more likely to rely upon informal or cultural controls. Compared to the village officer, the urban officer less frequently has sufficient information about the norms operating in the situation at hand and less frequently has complete information about the participants in any disturbing situation. The urban police therefore are pressed more frequently toward treating one, or all, of the parties to a disturbance within the statuses and roles available within the criminal law.

While Banton's comments upon this possibility remain relatively anecdotal and Wilkins's are highly theoretical, an empirical validation is available in the work of James Q. Wilson.[4] The major concern of Wilson's investigation was the extent to which community political and social variations constrained police department policy (written or unwritten) on the decisions of (1) when to intervene in a situation and (2) how to intervene. While Wilson's methodology was more appropriate to raising rather than testing hypotheses, his study examined police discretionary behavior in a large number of specific cities about which a wide variety of data were collected. Hence Wilson's work, while definitely requiring follow-up, provides a broader base for generalization than the more frequent two-culture or two-community comparisons.

Wilson's investigations led him to stipulate that in American cities, even in those of one legal code, there were at least three varieties of police behavior. Which type of behavior would emerge seemed highly dependent upon the local sociopolitical context. He found in Syracuse, New York, a "legalistic style" of policing, meaning that the police, on the average, tended to invoke a rule or enforce a law as the "solution" (or appropriate response) in a large number of disturbance situations. This style, which also appeared in Oakland, California, seemed contingent upon the emergence of a reform government in a relatively large city. Hence there had been recent political promises for greater activity on the part of public service organizations as well as promises that services would not be provided on politically discriminatory bases, but to all citizens equally.

In other cities, generally somewhat smaller in size, Wilson's investigations often encountered a "watchman style" police force. This type of organization, which was found in Albany, Amsterdam, and Newburg, New York, tended to stem from machine politics and patronage, low pay and low respect for public workers, and city governments that were dominated by one party, one ethnic group, or some other force that had collapsed or simplified the standards applicable to public behavior. "Watchman" police departments were unlikely to intervene frequently and unlikely to utilize the criminal sanction as the solution to disturbing situations. Instead, most discretionary police matters were handled informally, the object being to maintain order or contain the situation rather than arrest an offender.

Finally, Wilson observed a "service style" police department in other communities, usually those that were fairly homogeneous, fairly small, and relatively middle-class. In such communities Wilson observed that city government officials belonged to the same class as the majority of their constituents and that relatively high agreement existed that government was a civic duty and policing a public service. Hence, police were very often engaged in a variety of service efforts unrelated to law enforcement and were likely to respond to disturbing situations as occasions for counseling or rendering help rather than enforcing rules. Compared to legalistic departments, service departments did not intervene in a formal fashion, but compared to watchman departments they intervened fairly frequently.

Wilson tends to treat these three different patterns of policing as functional equivalents. That is, they are analyzed as three distinct means or processes for achieving the same end, the maintenance of public order. But an application of the Banton/Wilkins theory to the Wilson data would suggest that the ends achieved as well as the means used may have differed. That is, different functional domains were established for the police organization in the various cities. The function to be performed seemed dependent both upon the linkages between the police and the local political structure and upon the extent to which normative consensus existed in the community. In those instances when the police operated as a control, there was often little resort to the criminal sanction, as well as wide agreement across the community upon standards by which to judge behavior. In instances where there was low consensus, and the police acted "professionally," or within the confines, of enforcing the law, there was often much less agreement about public order, higher crime rates, and greater intergroup conflict. These data would tend to support Theodore Mills's contention, elaborated in Chapter 5, that criminal justice as a social control to deviance operates in simple rather than complex social systems, because the criteria of order that are prerequisites to the application of negative feedback are lacking in highly complex, urban systems.[5] If deterrence/retribution or social welfare assumptions hold at all, they would seem most likely to hold in smaller, homogeneous communities. These communities usually do not provide us with the impetus to reform the criminal justice system because the type and level of deviance recorded therein is not troublesome.

At the same time that we note significant differences in what the police and other agencies of justice do, relative to the type of community in which they operate, more specific linkages among justice and non–justice agencies also seem important. The emphasis on the control function of the justice system, and upon the coherent superordinate goals of the system, has resulted in downplay of the interorganizational linkages both across justice agencies and among any particular set of justice and non–justice agencies.[6] Consequently there is too great a tendency to perceive the criminal justice system as a single organization rather than as a loosely coupled string of agencies that are components in many other community systems as well.

Roland Warren and his colleagues argue that the functions performed by social service agencies are incomplete and inaccurately understood if we examine only the goals and internal operations of a single agency or even the exchanges between agency diads. More important to the analysis of community structure and process is the ability of the analyst to examine the consequences of "the interorganizational field," or the interactions among multiple agency sets.[7]

Skolnick and Woodworth take a step in this direction in their analysis of a morals detail in two western police departments. Their goal was to highlight the impact of bureaucratic linkages between organizations upon both the reported crime rate in an area and the means of response. Their choice of crimes, statutory rape, was chosen because it is a crime to which the police universally pay little attention and the community norms are ambivalent at best. In examining rates of arrest in two contiguous cities, the investigators discovered marked variation, regardless of the fact that neither police department gave high priority to enforcement and individual officers detested the assignment. The explanation of the differences in reported rape and arrest, then, had little to do with community value differences, incidence of the behavior, or police attitude toward the crime. In one city, the police department and the department of welfare pooled information, the welfare department refusing to pay support unless a paternity complaint was filed by the mother with the police department. In the other city, the police and welfare organizations operated separately. The first department made far more arrests and successful prosecutions.[8]

On the other end of the criminal process, McCleary reports that the ability of a parole agent to protect or to provide advocacy for his client is determined not simply by the nature of the parolee's behavior, but also by the status of the agent in a matrix of judicial, prosecutorial, state correctional, and local welfare organizations. Agents sacrifice some parolees to build their reputation and are able to act as service brokers for other clients to the extent that the agent's current reputation is untarnished.[9] Similarly, Duffee and Warner discovered that the rate with which halfway house residents were able to resolve similar reintegration problems was highly correlated with the status of the halfway house within the local social service agency field.[10]

Another point detracts from the notion that the criminal justice agencies share a common set of goals on the operational level, have the same standards for evaluating their activities, or indeed would behave as a unified system. Very simply, agency executives communicate with each other very infrequently, either across the criminal process, or within similar agencies. Patrick V. Murphy argues that various police departments do not do the same things because different police chiefs rarely find a common forum within which to share information, develop productivity standards, or define police roles.[11] The same has been said of correctional executives, who spend the greatest part of their time managing internal operations rather than developing common policies with executives in other agencies.[12] If this situation is seen as problematic in police and corrections, it has been labeled acute in the courts, in which each judge rules his own courtroom independent of other judges in the same court, let alone judges in other jurisdictions.[13] Lack of communication across the criminal process has also been cited as frequent and troublesome, although this form of "breakdown" may be more relevant to the next section, on integration of the system, than to the unitary nature of the system. Suffice it for now to say that agency executives in varying jurisdictions have not seen it as a high priority or as a feasible undertaking to reduce differences across jurisdictions.

The observations of differences across jurisdictions usually fall into two general types. First, there are a series of differences in process. For example, the American Bar Foundation field surveys do an admirable job of summarizing rather marked discrepancies across three states in the way in which arrests, decision to charge, guilty pleading, and sentencing may be handled.[14] Second, there are a series of differences in outcomes. For example, Murphy cites only a few of many instances in which police departments of equal size have highly different arrest rates, and cities of the same size have varying crime rates.[15]

The perception of process and outcome differences as extensive as exist might suggest that one cannot apply one idea of criminal justice to all the systems in question. Or, to take it one step further, one may not impose one notion of order on all localities that will satisfy all local conditions. But the idea that varying processes and outcomes may be evidence that different functions are being performed is rarely raised.

For example, the President's Commission on Law Enforcement and the Administration of Justice deplored the variations in judicial organization at the local level. On the one hand, the Commission was rigorous in decrying the "conditions of inequity, indignity, and ineffectiveness" that existed in the lower, as opposed to the felony, courts.[16] The Commission also deplored the rural justice of the peace courts when it compared the physical conditions, knowledge of the law, and observance of procedure in those, compared to city courts.[17] To the extent that all courts, low or high, rural or urban, have the *same tasks*, or perform the same functions, then the observed variations in process may be "deplorable." But the value placed on the variation is clearly a judgment based upon a particular purpose, framed within a particular set of guiding assumptions. But does a trial before a rural justice of the peace represent the same thing, socially and politically, as a trial before an urban magistrate? Does criminal deviance have the same scope, frequency, and antecedent conditions in rural and urban areas? Most investigations suggest not. But if not, then what will occur in the rural community if we import an urban set of processes?

CRIMINAL JUSTICE AS AN INTEGRATED SYSTEM

Variations across communities and jurisdictions may allow us to ask whether the criminal justice system has the same functions in all places. Variations across separate agencies within the same criminal justice system may allow us to ask whether the control model of the system is anywhere appropriate as a description. The presentation of criminal justice as a societal control would suggest that the system operates toward planned goals with planned methods.

But it is frequently observed that the interaction among the agencies of criminal justice is cumbersome and slow, and takes place without many rules: "Nowhere within the legal system is there formal provision for organizational subordination of one subsystem to the other so that decisions in any one subsystem can be directly and effectively enforced in others by administrative or other organizational sanctions. The law itself, rather than organizational implementation generally governs such relationships."[18] But to see this interagency characteristic as negative or deficient is not necessary, nor is it inherent in the nature of the processes involved. Homans writes, for example, that "much legal behavior is ritual" and that the criminal justice agencies are not structured to "have much effect on the law breaker."[19]

The observation of distinct goals for each agency, operations that have little coherence across agencies, and distinct ideological justifications for police, courts, and correctional organization could provide the basis for interesting research on the identification of agency interactions that are apparently more significant for the individual organizations than is their linkage in a "criminal justice system." To gain a more complete picture of actual agency activity, as well as to assess the potential capacities of criminal justice agencies to act together, it is necessary to examine more systematically and more deeply the influences of community structure and community norms upon agency actions. Simply stressing the constraints upon the criminal justice system by the "community" is not sufficient. We have seen both liberals and conservatives and Moralist and Welfare approaches assume that reforming the criminal justice apparatus so that it *could* formulate and implement goals is a beneficent or a functional undertaking. So far we have examined a variety of data that suggest that, at least presently, variations in the community context of criminal justice place a large number of constraints on the agencies. These constraints detract from the capacity of the criminal justice system to behave the same way in diverse places. These constraints also detract from the possibility of integrating the agencies in any particular system.

We must not forget that a variety of other factors independent of community variations may exist that also detract from the possibility of unification and integration. Some of these constraints have their roots within the nature of a complex organization itself. It is commonplace, for example, that organizations will rarely operate against their own interests. To create a criminal justice system that could implement planned goals of control or welfare may or may not be functional for some or all communities. In either case, for integration to occur, it would also have to be advantageous for the agencies involved.

The desirability of making a variety of agencies cooperate with each other is expressed today by many planners in criminal justice, welfare, health, and other fields. The justification for increased interagency cooperation is often stated as the higher level of benefit for clients because of increases in coherence and continuity of services and greater efficiency for the funding authorities.[20] Regardless of the validity of those justifications, many efforts at coordination fail. Speaking specifically of attempts to coordinate juvenile delinquency programs, William Reid comments that one of the reasons for coordination failure is that the justifications for it (or the perceived payoff) lie outside the agencies. Regardless of possible greater yield to clients or funding sources, many agencies may find the drain on resources (in terms of manpower and space and time) to be greater than the benefits.[21] Malcolm Feeley concurs with such observations but goes on to generalize about criminal justice as a system in which integration simply is not consistent with organizational structure. There are no organizational incentives to interorganizational cooperation.[22] Feeley concludes that "any far reaching discussion of reform and proposals for change in the administration within the American system of criminal justice would have to deal with this problem of the nature and distribution of compliance-inducing mechanisms."[23]

In the criminal justice system, the separate agencies have sufficient autonomy that their responses to each other are not very controllable, either by the other agency or by some generalized popular pressure for coordination and accountability.

> Open rejection is rarely the reaction to external pressure. Rather the organization stages a show of acceptance to mollify the external "threat" and, at the same time, rejects or modifies implementation so that it can continue to maintain its structure as well as previously negotiated coalitions, both internal and external.[24]

While the existing state of conflict or nonintegration among the various agencies may be perceived as a system deficiency vis-à-vis societal control objectives, we should expect that agencies will resist efforts toward their integration, for their own benefit, if not for the benefit of any other party. However, the organizational and the community factors that resist the pressures for integration are related to each other. The police, generally, are municipal agencies, and court agencies operate primarily on the county level, whereas correctional auspices are a mixture of county and state governments. Integration across the criminal process may be resisted because of goals internal to particular agencies. But we must not forget that this interagency conflict may also be a manifestation of strains between local, regional, and centralized governments and/or strains between separate communities. The problems of regionalizing police and jails may highlight the cross-community conflict. Resistance to centralizing court authority or correctional authority on the part of local courts and local jails highlights the conflict among levels of government.

Litwak and Hylton suggest that many interorganizational relationships, particularly in the public sphere, represent an institutionalization of conflict.[25] Many observers would add that this perceived pattern of interagency "inefficiency" and "ineffectiveness" is in reality the means by which local autonomy is maintained.[26] Gouldner would add that criminal justice reformers who seek to increase humaneness or effectiveness by pushing for integration of the system are, in effect, placing their weight behind the self-aggrandizement of national government and/or national organizations.[27]

REACTIONS TO PRESSURE FOR INTEGRATION

It seems quite likely that the feasibility of a control model of the criminal justice system may be thwarted by factors internal and external to the system. Explanations of some of these reactions are complex and will be reserved for the more detailed discussion of community structure in the next chapter. Here it might be sufficient to enumerate a variety of these reactions and draw from them some implications concerning present functions of criminal justice agencies. In general we could say that criminal justice agencies, as well as the set of them taken as a system, react in the "wrong" way toward the various mechanisms that can be applied to achieve integration or to prioritize and rationalize their goals.

If a set of organizations are to be structured in such a way that they can perform societal control functions, or even to control individuals, they need to be in a position to apply to the target of control certain sanctions that will constrain the deviations in the target's behavior, or to keep the distribution of target behavior constricted to some normal or tolerated range. The variety of sanctions available are not limitless, and the range in criminal justice is usually restricted to negative sanctions. Regardless of the relative effectiveness of this limitation in the sanctioning arsenal, the application of the available controls to targets depends upon the availability of a similar sanctioning repertoire by which to limit or govern behavior in the control system itself. For example, a father will not be effective in controlling the behavior of his children if the criteria he uses to invoke control are inconsistent, or if his ability to monitor their behavior is sporadic. Effectiveness of discipline may be affected not only by the behavior of the target, but also by the behavior of the control. If, perhaps, the father is extremely unhappy at work, fighting constantly with his wife, away too frequently on extended business trips (for example), control of children may be less than adequate. But in these instances, correction of the situation requires changes in the controls on the father's behavior before or instead of changes of controls on the children.

Viewing the objectives of the criminal justice system as ones of control, for the sake of argument, we can observe many deficiencies in the means available to control the system. As an opening caveat, one could say that the shortcomings of criminal justice controls vis-à-vis their targets are recycled at the higher level, or that the agencies in the system respond to sanction applications toward themselves in a manner quite similar to the way that control targets respond to the application of criminal justice sanctions.[28]

For whatever reason, it is typical for there to be a basic similarity between the range of sanctions available to the control units for application to the target and the range of sanctions available to apply to the behavior of the control units. The cultural and political restrictions on the criminal justice system, its limitation to the application of only negative sanctions, will therefore tend to make available only negative sanctions for control of the criminal justice system.[29] The basic characteristic of such systems is that they focus only on negatively evaluated variance in the situation that is to be controlled. Rewards for doing the appropriate thing are uncertain and probable, while punishments for doing the wrong thing are relatively certain. This limitation in the control repertoire tends to produce threat and generate conditions for dishonesty, rather than to create conditions that will change the negative behavior. In addition, punitively oriented control systems, because they ascribe purpose and intent to the wrong action, create a situation in which the undesired behavior is attributed to the individual actor rather than to the structure of the situation.[30]

The utilization of negative sanctions as a means to control offender behavior has often been criticized as ineffective. But the application of negative sanctions to offenders is only one form of the general control framework in criminal justice. The same general pattern applies to the control of staff within an agency or to the control of one agency by another. Management scientists claim that such forms of organizational control produce the primary motivation of escaping the punishment rather than achieving goals,[31] and exacerbating claims of inequality in the system because those who receive the extrinsic and negative sanctions typically do not grant legitimacy to either the sanction appliers or to the goals allegedly supported by the sanctions.[32] "The generalization that emerges is that [negative sanction systems] have a strong tendency to generate and accentuate the very behavior they seek to prevent: non-compliance."[33]

Instead of achieving the goals implied in the negative sanctions, their application is usually highly correlated on the individual level with cynicism, goldbricking, and defensive, rigid behaviors, and on the organizational level with covert operations, resistance to outside inspection, and scapegoating. In addition, the organizational members who are subjected to control through external and negative sanctions "seem to feel justified in feeding systems invalid data when they are being evaluated . . . ."[34] Hence, not only do the organizational operations often continue to diverge from goals, but the divergence of achievement from objectives can widen dramatically as the agencies tend to distort information in order to avoid additional occasions for sanctioning.

In this kind of situation, behaviors that would theoretically lead to achievement of control goals (either the ends of deterrent or rehabilitative efforts) are abandoned by the organization and cannot serve as predictors of either organizational processes or outcomes of organizational decisions. For example, McCleary relates that parolees "will be abandoned or even sacrificed when the situation, the parole officer's perception, and the parole officer's reputation demand it."[35] Search for effective police deterrent measures will be abandoned to the immediate need for political success, to the retrenchment of established programs, and to the belief that increased productivity at control efforts will decrease job security.[36] Prosecutors will abandon decision criteria representative of deterrence, retribution, or fairness in favor of criteria based on efficiency and speed.[37]

In general, the claims of prevention and deterrence tend to exist as popular myths to which the various agencies beckon when they cannot explain to outsiders why agency practices are what they are. As Goldstein says of the police, "the preventive function tends to receive attention only when personnel are not otherwise occupied."[38] But the control goals espoused in deterrent/retribution or welfare reforms will not be reflected in organizational behavior.

THE ASSUMED INTEGRATION OF SOCIETY

The control model of criminal justice requires not only that the various systems of criminal justice in the United States operate in the same way and that the various components of the system can act as an integrated system. The validity of this model also requires, at least to some degree, that the American society behave as if it were an integrated entity, with all of its groups oriented, if not directed, toward the same goals. The integrated model of society *must* be valid if the control model of the criminal justice system is to have any efficacy. Without this integrated society, the criminal justice system would lack the single notion of social order to compare to actual societal activity.

The control model of criminal justice would assume that the criminal justice system has unitary and predominant goals, such as those stated by Andenaes: "By general prevention we mean the ability of criminal law and its enforcement to make citizens law-abiding. If general prevention were 100 percent effective there would be no crime at all."[39] Andenaes states that the three effects of general prevention are different, but congruent and reinforcing. The criminal justice system can (1) perform as a deterrent; (2) strengthen moral inhibitions; and (3) stimulate habitual law-abiding conduct.[40]

These objectives of criminal justice assume either that the social structure has one dominant culture (as may be the case in Andenaes's Norway), or that the social structure can accommodate all persons in society who come to desire the same cultural objectives, and moreover that the operation of the social system does not continually separate persons into distinct groups with conflicting aims and objectives. Stated another way, for the criminal justice system to operate under a single umbrella-like goal such as general prevention, the social structure must assure that the general prevention pressures exerted by the justice system will have similar impacts on most, if not all, of the people in the social system.

Two of the people who have investigated deterrence most thoroughly raise serious doubts about general prevention as defined by Andenaes. First, they suggest that "in regard to any particular form of serious criminal activity, the proportion of the population that can be realistically regarded as potential offenders will, at least in periods of relative stability, be limited."[41] Second, Zimring and Hawkins argue that relative to the propensity to commit a crime, the American population is stratified into significantly different groups or classes so that the ability of the law and its enforcement to "stimulate habitual law-abiding conduct" is distinctly discriminating. Only the group "who are objectively on the margin of a particular form of criminal behavior or in other words, the class of persons 'next most likely' to engage in the criminal behavior in question" are likely to be swayed by the punishment applied to those who do engage in the criminal behavior.[42] Third, Zimring and Hawkins suggest that if we divide a population into the criminal, the marginal, and the noncriminal, relative to any particular offense, the patterns of response to be expected from the criminal and marginal groups to deterrent threats will be, or can be, quite different than the pattern of response observed in the noncriminal or normal population.[43]

Evidence that there are different classes of persons in the United States whose probability of offending and whose reactions to deterrent threat are class-related would suggest that there is insufficient similarity among groups to justify a consistent and coherent approach to crime control. The assumption of such similarity among groups is frequently characteristic of those with agency power: "The practice of working from the top down, from an *a priori* statement of macro-goals and objectives, predetermines a consensual view of the social system."[44] However, there may be little that the criminal justice system can do to promote societal integration, and at the same time much that it can do to increase the fragmentation of the social structure. For example, the operation of the criminal justice system, including its impact on images of societal solidarity, can give the appearance of social unity where there is actually little unity.[45] The maintenance of the criminal justice apparatus, with the *appearance* of deterrence and retribution fulfilled, can often provide explanations of social deviance that center upon individual malfunctioning or individual ill will, rather than upon the structural antecedents to conflict. Wilkins argues that the criminal justice system is one mechanism by which we divert attention from the social system to scapegoated "sinners."[46]

In summary, this chapter takes us one step further from unblinking acceptance in the normal procedures for describing criminal justice, listing its problems, and delineating its reforms. Research reviewed herein provides, in itself, no alternative explanations, but does suggest some questions that few criminal justice studies take seriously. Are the social functions of policing, judging, and correcting different in community X than community Y? Are the linkages of police to courts or correctional agencies more explanative of agency behavior than linkages between these agencies and other units of community activity? Are at least some communities so radically different in structure from that assumed by criminal justice planners, managers, and critics that application of typical "improvements" may create less rather than more order in those communities?

The implications of these questions are sufficiently contraindicative to current criminal justice policy trends that they require more complete explication and investigation. The common link among all such questions is that there has been an inadequate search for the context of criminal justice. We are either very ignorant of, or quite willing to hide from ourselves, the actual implications of current criminal justice policy, unless we are willing to examine more specifically and concretely the relationships among a variety of criminal justice practices and a variety of alternative community structures, or versions of human order.

We can proceed with this investigation in several ways. Some persons would simply strike out for one set of human living arrangements as correct or proper, to the exclusion of others. For example, liberals and conservatives might suggest that even if their versions of society are not accurate, deliberate forcing of reality to expectation might bring their desires about. That is, they might argue that all communities should be constructed in the fashion to which their criminal justice reforms would lead us. Others might suggest that any activity by the "state" is antithetical to the nature of human beings, that somehow we must destroy or repudiate this penchant for structuring human action through conformity to standards enforced by complex organizations.

I would proceed more slowly. I am not sure that liberal/conservative ideas inevitably lead us to more benign (or despotic) totalitarian situations. But I am also not sure that rejection of complex organization and state regulation is either feasible or desirable.

Instead, I would be more confident in the benefits of uncertainty than the comforts of belief. Let us examine the varieties of order that exist, in the sense of the variations in community that are observable now, before we determine where, and when, and what kinds of social orders are best.

In this context, the next chapter examines three versions of community order that again challenge any single and simple answers to whither and whether criminal justice.

Chapter 7

Problems with Definition of Social Order, or Models of Community Conflict

So far I have argued that the most common approaches to the study of criminal justice are normative. In other words, criminal justice analysts are predisposed to believe that the "criminal justice system" should serve a few rational purposes. The principle purposes elucidated by a variety of writers fall into what I call Moralist and Welfare positions. While most analysts of either position believe there are a great many problems with current criminal justice operations, they also believe that by firmly defining criminal justice goals and by properly reforming the criminal justice system, a better American society is achievable. The Welfare and Moralist groups, therefore, both seek to treat the criminal justice system as a societal control unit.

I have spent some time (principally in Chapter 5) trying to describe the characteristics of societal control organizations—both those that seem to work in relatively homogeneous and simple collectivities and those that seem to work in relatively heterogeneous and complex social systems. It is my conclusion that the criminal justice systems as described by Moralists and Welfarists simply do not possess the characteristics that would enable the system—as it is or as it would be reformed—to operate as a societal control.

In the last chapter I went on to challenge some basic assumptions about criminal justice. These basic assumptions are held in common by the

Welfare and Moralist groups, even though they differ on other matters. To reiterate, those assumptions are: (1) that criminal justice has a unified or common purpose, wherever it is found; (2) that in fact an integrated, coherent system of criminal justice exists—or that the administration of the criminal process is the overriding concern of criminal justice agencies; and (3) that existence of an integrated, consensual version of the social system justifies the existence of a monolithic, integrated criminal justice system. I find little substantial evidence to support these assumptions, and considerable evidence to the contrary. Based on this evidence, I would conclude that attempts to clean up or rationalize criminal justice goals and to integrate more completely criminal justice agencies would not benefit all people in society or society itself, although such reforms might conceivably benefit particular groups in society to the detriment of others. Maintaining a belief in a consensual, melting pot America provides a strong ideological basis for the reform of the criminal justice system, specifically for increasing unification, standardization, and centralization. These trends, in essence, stress the need to increase the "efficiency" of the criminal justice system. Despite the debates about goals, there is really no attempt to examine effectiveness. The reforms are based on the assumption that a more efficient criminal justice system would be effective as a societal control.

I have no doubt that these kinds of reform efforts may be effective for some purposes. That is, such reforms are indeed likely to have payoffs for some groups. But little attention is usually paid to the payoffs or benefits of the many, fragmented, and differentiated criminal justice systems that now operate in various parts of this country. Beginning in this chapter and continuing through Chapter 10, I want to examine some of the more important variations in criminal justice operations from area to area and to build a case for the variety of functions, or consequences, that these different operations may serve to bring about.

In this chapter, the primary objective is a presentation of three alternative versions of social order—or more accurately of "social orders." These versions of social interaction in the United States are *not* attempts to present a complete description of an American social system. In fact, the variety of studies reviewed in this chapter provides the foundation for the hypothesis that there is no *one* coherent social system but instead a number of different, perhaps conflicting, kinds of social interaction, each one resulting in a somewhat different kind of social order.

This is not to say that there is no political and economic "superstructure," and it is not to say that the dynamics of this superstructure do not affect the various more localized kinds of social order that exist. I do intend to demonstrate, however, that particular mixes of both formal and informal social groups obtain some ecological identity of their own—or that these "subunits" of the superstructure have substantial autonomy from national, centralized forces, when it comes to defining what is proper or orderly and when it comes to determining how human needs will be met.

A systematic statement about these various, decentralized versions of social interaction and social order is set out in Chapter 8. The present chapter examines some of the processes of decisionmaking, resource distribution, and group identity that give rise to such social differentiation.

GOAL POLARITY WITHIN COMMUNITIES

The Moralist and Welfare discussions of criminal justice, which are by far the most frequent and politically powerful, do recognize considerable conflict in both society and the criminal justice system. But both groups treat such conflict as if it were resolvable. Furthermore, the models for the reform of the criminal justice system that argue for the use of the system as a societal control insist that (1) the criminal justice system can and must be used to reduce and resolve such conflict, or (2) that the government must find the means to reduce or resolve conflict so that the criminal justice system can operate effectively. Were the criminal justice reformers more sophisticated, their recommendations for reform might smack considerably more of Orwells's *1984*, since the utilization of a criminal justice system in relation to control could provide us with blueprints for massive political indoctrination and cultural homogenation. Most reform strategies do not conjure up such pictures because they concentrate upon the steps that could be taken to make the criminal justice system a coherent and consistent system, rather than upon the alterations in the social system that would have to occur before the criminal justice reforms could take place.

Nevertheless, the literature is replete with recognition of value and goal conflict, ambiguity, and ambivalence that provides us with some measure of the constraints within which the criminal justice system must operate. As early as 1914, E. A. Ross noted that the system of criminal penalties operated in a "double-bind": "But the severity of the penal system as a whole is limited by the social situation . . . . While punishment must be harsh enough to terrorize most of the evil-disposed, they must not outrun the approval of the community."[1]

Considerably later, Andenaes discussed the potential conflict between the needs of specific prevention on the one hand and general prevention on the other. Admitting that humanization, dominance of treatment programs, and the relaxation of conflict between offenders and criminal justice staff might improve the ability of the system to control individuals, Andenaes adds that the orientation of the system toward offender control may be in direct conflict with the orientation of the system toward satisfaction of the nonoffender with the level of conformity symbolized in the sanctioning process.[2]

Toby disagrees with Andenaes on the societal implications of the treatment-punishment controversy, but Toby's analysis identifies perhaps a second source of conflict that must be considered. He suggests that the rise of treatment within the penal system has been the means by which the correctional organizations have attempted to defend themselves from the full impact of cultural conflict. He suggests that many persons, particularly those in face-to-face contact with the offender, have severe doubts that most offenders are really "bad," or deserve punishment for willful wrongdoing. The diagnosis of offenders as sick rather than bad, then, may reduce cognitive dissonance of staff, since the labeling of offenders as sick rather than bad similarly confirms that the offender "has not gotten away with it."[3] In other words, Toby argues that the rise of treatment as an ideology for correctional organization is unrelated to the effectiveness of treatment in altering the behavior of offenders. It is instead related to the ability of the treatment ideology to insulate better the persons responsible for correctional supervision from the stigma, and the doubts, about the validity of punishment.

Banton's study of comparative police behavior led him to suggest that the views of appropriate police roles are predetermined by the cultural predisposition to base social situation on either force or cooperation. Repressive police strategies may be associated with the beliefs that (1) man needs restraint, or (2) that the organization of society is faulty and that the police preserve the predominating power structure. Preventive police strategies are associated with beliefs that the police (1) ameliorate dysfunctional aspects of the social organism, or (2) that the police preserve contracts between individuals.[4] The repressive strategies would seem reminiscent of police functions as presented by Moralists and radicals, while the preventive functions are reminiscent of functions propounded by adherents to the Welfare model.

While these theoretical considerations provide a broad framework for the examination of conflict about punishment and punishing, they are limited. If indeed the cultural topography in America can constrain criminal justice practice, we should know more about public opinion. But as Korn has lamented, public opinion is a sacred cow often invoked but rarely consulted.[5] Most discussions of conflict tend to assume that public opinion is accurately described in terms a continuum, in which the poles are "treatment" and "custody,"[6] or "due process and crime control,"[7] or "punishment vs. treatment,"[8] or "concern for the offender balanced against concerns for the community,"[9] or surveillance and service,[10] or assistance and control.[11] But in the criminal justice field, most of these descriptions of goal conflict in the American culture turn out in reality to be a description of (1) *what criminal justice executives perceive* as public ambivalence, or (2) the conflicting constraints that these executives themselves attempt to accommodate with their action. There is little evidence that would suggest that these executives and researchers have obtained a valid picture of the community orientation toward the issue of punishment. We know only that criminal justice staff enunciate, and researchers validate or reinforce, a perceived public polarity between easy and harsh, punitive and therapeutic measures.

The public surveys of which I am aware, while they leave room for considerable elaboration, would suggest that public values, as opposed to agency-head values, concerning punishment are too complex to be described as an operative tension between poles, or as a single dimension or continuum. McIntyre's analysis of public values concerning policing found two sets of values, distinguished by the specificity of the question or issue at hand. There was general public concern about law enforcement on a symbolic level, with the public split on preventive or repressive techniques as a means to control the incidence of crime. At another level, McIntyre found a concern over individual rights, which operated independently of the concern for punishment.[12] McIntyre also found that the same individuals views of what should be done, and of what values were to be supported by official actions, varied when questions shifted from "general strategies" to decisions about specific offenders. That is, even a respondent in favor of strong repressive police measures could opt for leniency applied in specified circumstances. (On the reverse side of the coin, other researchers have found that the public might generally favor community correctional programs, but resists suggestions that such programs should operate in their neighborhoods).[13]

A survey conducted in Pennsylvania in 1973 lends further support to the proposition that community attitudes about criminal justice and crime are both complex and little understood. Cluster analysis of responses to survey questions concerning alternative correctional programs demonstrated two *separate* value dimensions underlying public opinion. The researchers found that respondents could be weak or strong on the issue of retribution and *independently* weak or strong on the issue of rehabilitation. Moreover, the structure of public value on these two dimensions became more confusing if class variables were introduced. Middle-class respondents in general were overwhelmingly opposed *both* to strategies of correction that were associated with retribution and to strategies associated with rehabilitation. On the other hand, lower-class communities were strongly in favor of both sets of strategies.[14] These data might suggest that middle-class persons, at least in Pennsylvania, are too removed from the actual experience of crime and criminal justice to be highly concerned about the issues, while lower-class communities feel the effects of both victimization and punishment on a more personal level. Whatever the explanation, these data and McIntyre's would indicate three possible value clusters—those of retribution, rehabilitation, and civil rights—that must be analyzed and accommodated simultaneously. If such data could be confirmed in larger surveys, it would indicate that criminal justice policy and operations cannot be simplified and streamlined by resolving the supposed conflict between punishment and treatment or between deterrence/retribution and welfare.

Current debates on criminal justice policy in general, and on purposes of sentencing in particular, do not seem to accommodate or even to acknowledge the potential complexity of the goal and value structure in the social system. To the extent that goal conflict is recognized, the typical response is that the legislatures should determine the purposes of sentencing and then provide for the appropriate type of sentencing structure.[15] This kind of approach to the problem implies that social structure can be engineered, so that operations and agencies can be rationally matched to chosen goals. But there is no evidence that we can as yet engineer social structure. Indeed, most commentators suggest that sentencing must be structured to reflect the goals and values of a given culture. But if so, then we cannot alter that set of goals and values in order to provide a rational and coherent punishment system. Stated in another way, the usual approaches to criminal justice reform, based upon the presumption that society is ultimately rational and unified, cannot deal with any indications that the social structure itself is inherently conflicting, giving rise to several sets of goals and values that cannot be assigned priority and integrated.[16]

If inherent conflict indeed exists in criminal justice goals because inherent conflict exists in basic social structure, what is the nature of some of those basic conflicts or dilemmas within which the system must operate? While both theoretical and empirical studies are ambivalent on this question, there would seem to be some agreement about the existence of a dilemma between the objectives of controlling damage or harm, objectively measured, and the symbolic functions of punishment. Arnold's seminal analysis stresses that " . . . we must recognize that there are two very distinct problems in Criminal Administration: (1) the keeping of order in the community, and (2) the dramatization of the moral notions in the community."[17] Arnold goes on to argue that were we simply concerned in the criminal process with the reduction of relative social damage, the criminal system would look decidedly different than it does. Criminal investigation would stress organizational and white collar crime, for example, rather than control of street crime. For that matter, were only controlling harm important, the issue of guilt itself would be of little importance. But within the criminal punishment system, we are concerned with more than, or other things as well as, extent of damage done or the seriousness of the future danger involved. Arnold states that the system is also one key forum for the dramatization of community values, and is on that level more visible and powerful when a traditional criminal and a traditional crime are involved. Hence regardless of relative damage, the traditional criminal will be processed while the middle-class criminal will be ignored.[18]

McIntyre's previously cited survey of attitudes toward the police would tend to validate Arnold's theoretical position. She observes that incidence of victimization and therefore of extended public contact with the criminal justice system is far too limited to influence public attitudes about punishment, or to affect public policy. Most public attitudes about punishment and about crime are formed from vicarious sources.[19] In other words, it will be primarily on the level of symbolic content that criminal justice can influence public attitude and belief, and, vice versa, it will be over the symbolic messages of the criminal process that public attitude will affect public policy.

This process, in and of itself, does not lead directly to conflicts in public value. It is at least possible to conceive of a system of punishment unrelated to the control of actual social damages in the punishment process, that totally satisfied public demand, convincing the public that laws were upheld and it was protected, regardless of how much crime itself escalated. That there is conflict between processes geared to control of harm and processes geared to satisfaction of "moral notions" seems, however, relatively evident. The impetus of much current criminal justice reform is the concern with making the operations more effective in controlling harm and recognition that the system has done very little of that in the past.

Kirchway argued that the conflict has become evident only in the twentieth century because it is not until 1900 that the consequences of punishing were considered in determinations of punishment strategies. He stated that public opinion has always influenced the law and the forms of punishment used but that only in the modern era has the study of penal consequences (i.e., recidivism) influenced the law.[20] Stated in another way, it has only been in the twentieth century that informational feedback loops have become complex enough to promote the conflict between the rational pursuits of controlling harms (by matching organizational processes to future behavioral consequences) and the cultural pursuits of reinforcing norms (by using punishment symbolically).

Meyer and Rowan comment on this heightened conflict in all modern organizations, especially in public service organizations:

> Institutionalized products, services, techniques, policies, and programs function as powerful myths, and many organizations adopt them ceremonially. But conformity to institutionalized rules often conflicts sharply with efficiency criteria and, conversely, to coordinate and control activity in order to promote

efficiency undermines an organization's ceremonial conformity and sacrifices its support and legitimacy.[21]

Within the criminal justice system, the conflict between the steps an organization must take for institutional conformity and the steps it must take for technical rationality, or efficiency, would seem to underlie many of the perceived conflicts in criminal justice policies and programs. The system must be concerned not only with the processing of the offender as a symbol, in the drama of a public statement about norms, but it must also be concerned with the processing of the offender as an individual. The operations upon him that may satisfy the symbolic function may not be compatible with the operations necessary to reduce the negative consequences of his future behavior. Criminal justice organization faces the problem of simultaneously meeting separate tests of its practices.[22]

Multiple and conflicting tests of organizational action, observes Herbert Simon, is a common condition in complex organizations. He argues that the term "organizational goal" must be reserved for the course of action adopted by the organization as the most satisfactory response to multiple tests or multiple constraints:

> . . . It is doubtful whether the decisions are generally directed toward achieving *a* goal. It is easier, and clearer, to view the decisions as being concerned with discovering courses of action that satisfy a whole set of constraints. It is this set, and not any one of its members, that is most accurately viewed as the goal of the action.[23]

Parson's major work on social structure posits that most institutionalized roles emerge from the combination of two sets of "pattern variables." He suggests that there is a basic polarity within each set, for example, a cultural polarity between universalism or particularism and a motivational polarity between ascription and achievement.[24] While Parsons, no doubt correctly, would assert that a predominant combination of these variable sets generally exists in any particular society, it may also be argued that these pattern variables are differentially distributed over segments of a nation, as in different regions or different communities. At any rate, we would expect these variable sets to influence in varying proportions separate parts of the criminal process, and separate components of the same organization at any point in the process. A stress on universalistic ascription can be perceived in revisions of penal law. All persons convicted of the same offense should be punished to the same extent. But a stress toward particularistic ascription can be seen in the prosecutorial processes of these same justice systems. Bargaining norms are determined by the going rates in particular courts for different categories of crime.[25] A stress toward universalistic ascription can be seen in the stress on due process standards set by the federal courts. All offenders anywhere are due the same protections, as citizens of a national organization. At the same time, universalistic ascription can lead to an emphasis on retribution for crime, while emphasis on particularistic achievement can stress that punishment should be decided on the basis of the individual offender's future behavior.

If indeed we should perceive organizational goals as sets of multiple constraints, or as the solutions to them, then perhaps the criminal justice organizations operating as they now do are achieving their goals as effectively as possible. To push the system toward maximization of a goal, such as retribution/deterrence, welfare, or fairness, to the exclusion of all other goals within the current goal set, might have dire results for the organizations. The level of environmental support might be reduced drastically, because the extent to which the organizations were perceived to address several values would be reduced dramatically. If the organizations were to pursue *only* their rational functions or *only* their symbolic functions, the endurance of the organizations might be considerably shortened. Perhaps it is the goal of criminal justice organizations to embody or manifest both the stresses toward achievement and the stresses toward ascription, to balance concerns for particularism and universalism, to be both rational and mythical.

RANCOROUS CONFLICT IN COMMUNITY DECISIONMAKING

In addition to the many studies that examine goal and value conflict in the social structure, a small number of investigations attempt to be more specific in categorizing the types of conflict that may take place in special circumstances. Among these studies are those that assume that conflict in American politics is a common, normal situation, but find that particular issues, and particular social and political structures, lend themselves to increased levels of conflict, in which the normal rules for governing disagreement are broken. Gamson identifies two means of carrying on conflict in local political decisionmaking. First there is the "conventional" means of debate, lobbying, voting, and the like, in which parties do not agree on what is to be done, but do agree upon the ways in which the disagreements should be weighted and balanced. Second, he identifies instances of "rancorous conflict," which is characterized by the belief that "norms about the waging of conflict in American communities have been violated."[26] In other words, there are occasions in which the predominant assumptions about the achievability of ultimate consensus break down, and the available compromises between parties are not satisfactory.

Rancorousness in political decisionmaking would seem a concept of special use in the examination of criminal justice policymaking, particularly at the local level. For one thing, rancorousness would seem especially prevalent in instances when the involved parties disagree about ends, rather than means to accomplish an end.[27] For another, rancorousness has a characteristic or a symptom that is also evident in criminal justice—the lack of motion, or inertia, over policy and program development. Those persons who have often lamented interia in the criminal justice sphere frequently blame it upon a lack of public interest. For example, Sykes suggests that prison walls hide offenders from the conforming public, so that the pains of imprisonment, or the fact of law breaking, need not visibly "prick the conscience" of the law-abiding.[28] Hamilton's historical review of police policymaking suggests that politicians isolated themselves from their police departments because active involvement in policymaking could not help their political careers.[29] Investigations of correctional executives suggest that these officials are primarily oriented toward the internal management of their organizations, and have not been trained in or interested in active involvement with the public. Jacobs, Geiss, and Cavanaugh, among others, discuss the low esteem given correctional employment by the public.[30] Bennington and Skelton recite instances in which public organizational officials blame low citizen participation in open meetings as a sign that the public is simply not interested in the operations of the agencies.[31]

The data used to support these assumptions about lack of public interest, upon closer scrutiny, may provide an alternative explanation of what happens. The claim that the public is not interested or is apathetic to criminal justice development is not actually consistent with the observations of goal conflict. If the public indeed did not care about what happened in criminal justice, there might be less inertia, since the executives might be able to do more as they pleased. Consistently low budgets for criminal justice operations and inordinate slowness in the implementation of reform, rather than demonstrate disinterest, does demonstrate immobility. But immobility can have other sources besides lack of concern. For example, Crain and Rosenthal relate immobility in community decisionmaking with high levels of citizen participation when various citizen groups have sufficient access to government to vent equally powerful competing viewpoints.[32] Gamson hypothesizes that such immobility is due to rancorous conflict and that rancorousness is common when the social structure exhibits high conduciveness to articulated opinion, high strain between competing interests, and low integration of interested parties.[33] These characteristics, says Gamson, are particularly prevalent in urbanized communities that are undergoing shifts in political control.[34]

Some of the previously reviewed public opinion survey data would support the existence of rancorousness in criminal justice policymaking, especially in urban centers where the issue of crime and its control is most acute. The Duffee and Ritti survey might suggest that the more educated suburban populations within metropolitan settings can articulately oppose deterrent-retributive strategies on grounds that they are not humanitarian, while being cool toward rehabilitative strategies on the grounds that they are not effective. Lower-class opinion, where it is organized, may object to rehabilitative strategies that are presented in such a way that the programs imply a reduction of retributive impact, while it opposes repressive strategies that ignore the high demand for concern about the futures of individual offenders.[35] Scull argues that community-based correctional and mental health programs are most frequently initiated in disorganized urban neighborhoods so that program executives can avoid such contradictory and immobilizing points of view, regardless of the fact that such locations are poor prospects for effective reintegration of offenders.[36]

In general, it would seem that community conflict resulting in low rates of criminal justice change can be a function *not of disinterest but of competing interest*, at least in some areas of the United States. Prime dimensions for analysis of criminal justice policymaking then would seem to be the interaction of centralized policy and programming forces against the decentralized or local expression of value. Within the last three decades there have been major shifts in policy decision locus. There has been an undeniable ascendancy of centralization of policy and program, particularly under the Kennedy and Johnson administrations. There is considerable evidence, however, that local decisionmakers have become skilled in blunting or diverting policy emphasis as it percolates down from Washington, with local communities taking federal resources and applying them to local priorities, despite evaluation and sanctioning measures built into federal programs.[37] Moreover, some political scientists raise the question that the apparent centralization is not the major shift in power that many have claimed it to be. Wood and Grozdins argue persuasively that while the centralization of government has increased on some dimensions, decisions as to how centralized resources are to be applied is still strongly influenced by the local level, both in the representation process and more so by the program implementation process in which local decision networks often effectively treat centralized professionals as advisors rather than as superior authorities.[38] Others argue that there are limits to growth of centralized power, and that locally relevant interests reassert themselves, whether in massive multi-site organizations or in federal-state-local relations.[39]

In any case, it would seem important to investigate the relationship between the potency of particular criminal justice strategies (both on the level of organizational structure and on the level of culturally espoused goals), and community power, or the relative power of local and centralized forms of politics. That is, are retribution and deterrence, or welfare, or some other goals of the criminal justice system, determined by the extent to which one group or another holds sway within particular situations or particular points in the historical development of the governing of communities? Some of the key concepts in addressing such questions will be introduced in the ultimate section of this chapter, and expanded into a general theoretical model in Chapter 8. Prior to that task, however, we wish to consider a third variation of community conflict, one that may be important to our ability to plot the course of rancorousness when it occurs.

THE COMMUNITY AS A FORUM FOR GAMES

This analysis has stressed that traditional treatments of criminal justice activity and reform are incomplete and often invalid because they utilize models of social behavior that are too simple. They usually stress general principles, values, and programs that are on the one hand supportive of only one American cultural and political tradition and are on the other hand related to hypothetical models of individuals, whose reactions to these programs are theoretically consistent with the program stimuli. These models ignore the facts that programs are organized to be implemented and that people are organized to respond in concrete social units that mediate not only policy but also personal perceptions of order and disorder. Hence, to be more exacting about criminal justice activity and the possibilities of reform, one must become critically concerned with both the operations of complex organizations and of communities.

If we are to understand why and how any specified criminal justice program or strategy will influence people, we must be willing to examine the community context of criminal justice. Many criminal justice organizations are still operating under auspices that are communal, or slightly larger. What these organizations do is certainly constrained by centralized sets of rules, laws, and resource distribution. But, police, prosecution, and judicial aspects of criminal justice are also heavily influenced by the communities that elect officials, argue over policy, and still to a large extent provide the financial resources for operations. Moreover, even organizations that have more centralized (state or federal) control centers are and will continue to be responsive to or accommodating of local determinations of program. Any centralized organization does not do its business from afar, but must provide local centers for information gathering, service delivery, and resource disbursement. It must also recruit and retain much personnel on bases influenced by local conditions, traditions, and power arrangements. There is no doubt that when policymaking and planning are remote from any particular local site, the organizational center can construct plans and programs that are not attentive to specific conditions and cannot be as accommodating to all local differences as organizations whose highest level of decisionmaking is itself local. Nevertheless, an organization that must engage people will remain to some extent a front line organization, in which policy is significantly reformulated by the information gathered at the local level and the actions taken by the local officials. What will then actually occur, flowing from centralized generation of objectives, will be partially a function of the varying priorities given local rather than central constraints.

Nor should we assume that the multiple constraints on organizational action are simply bifurcated between interests in central control, standardization, and policy implementation against local interest in amending central guidance to fit local conditions. Frequently liaisons will occur between some aspects of local interest and some aspect of central interest, against other local interests. For example, a centralized administration that demands standardization of program procedure may be more responsive to demand for due process regularity and fairness than a local administration concerned with individuating processes to meet temporal exigencies.[40] Hence, we can expect some local interests to appeal to some facet of central intervention and control as a means of gaining power over other local interests with competing or conflicting objectives. But we can also expect that two centrally initiated policies or program resource sets might simultaneously compete for local support and loyalty. Neither the central nor the local structures are necessarily cohesive. Under these conditions, the behavior of criminal justice, as a mix of local and central interests, and the behavior of many similar social service systems can meet on the local levels as if the community were a forum for games of power.

While it may be true that no effective analysis of criminal justice can evolve that ignores the concept of community in its statement of basic relations, one of the chief problems with utilizing the notion of community is the extremely arduous task of definition. Analysis, planning, and reform are all activities that seem to require the utilization of rather discrete entities that can be related, as black boxes, to other discrete entities. The key step in research and analysis is often the one of bounding the problem, and the key step in planning change is bounding the system. Without the existence of natural or arbitrary boundaries, we tend to have difficulties determining what is happening or making plans for future action.

Confronting the community, however, the analyst is almost required to find another means of describing the behavior that he observes. Unlike many social entities, communities do not have a formal organizational structure.[41] That is, one can describe many formal units, and informal ones, that seem to act within an area that we can allude to as a community, but the community itself is not a bounded system. There are, for example, school districts, municipal governments, local political parties, sanitation and transportation districts, local chambers of commerce, and many other organizations with local and overlapping boundaries. But no research has satisfactorily settled on any one set of such boundaries as those defining the community as an entity.

One means of handling this situation is simply to make an arbitrary selection of the existing boundaries. For example, researchers can first acknowledge that the community itself is not a legal entity, and that the legal jurisdictions that do occur across it or within it do not characterize the community itself, and then go on to select one set of political boundaries as a rough approximation of community. This procedure has its advantages. It is efficient and for some purposes may serve adequately. But if the questions we wish to deal with are the consequences of intersecting systems for any one of those systems, or for the people who are influenced by the patterns of intersection themselves, the selection of community as a discretely bounded unit must inherently bias the research.

The alternative approach to the analysis of community would treat it as not a bounded entity but as an ecological field upon which many more discrete systems engage each other. While some mathematical and psychological field models exist,[42] it has not been until recently that field theory has been applied to interorganizational engagements, in which the empirical field can be called a community. Two of the earliest works to do so are the seminal works of Emery and Trist, which attempt to type several kinds of environmental context, or field, in organizational theory,[43] and Terrebery, who attempted to build on this environmental typology to make some statements about different kinds of organizational planning.[44] More recently, Roland Warren and his associates sought to implement the concept of interorganizational field in the study of "community decision organizations."[45] While this Brandeis University team seems to have made significant strides in analyzing community power and community decision making, their operationalization of the community field concept is presently limited to the domain patterns that exist among six organizations in nine cities. Further work with the concept is necessary before we will be able to distinguish a community field rather than the subfield of interorganizational action that exists within the larger ecological system.

Nevertheless, we may have reached a point where some of the main characteristics of the community as a field may be used productively in reformulating criminal justice theory. If the community is a field upon which various social systems, differing in size, function, and degree of formalization intersect, we would wish to know how variations in the field may affect specific interactions, as well as how the interaction of the bounded systems can change the texture of that field.

The person who first termed the community field an ecology of games is Norton Long. In a rare journal article that utilized not a single footnote, Long argued that the community can be successfully analyzed neither as an organization nor as one of the more common types of system, because communities exhibit no central control, have no permanent boundaries, and evidence no consensus over social policies and program.[46] Long suggested that it might be effective to perceive of the community as a playing board, or field, upon which various groups and organizations were engaged in a host of different games. The community, he argued, is the overall pattern of these games, or an ecology of games.

Among the many pithy examples of games with which Long peppers his discussion one seems particularly useful to criminal justice analysis—the game played between power or social elites and the executives of service organizations. Long emphasized that many public and private organizations are supposedly overseen by social or political elites, who vie for roles as board members, council members, and agency trustees as a means of winning their own games of power, prestige, or social esteem. On the other hand, each separate organization operating under the guidance of these local dignitaries is staffed with professionals who are out to achieve their own objectives by mounting and implementing programs. Hence, the activity of an organization is partly a result of the tug of war between professional and salaried staffs against civic leaders. One objective of the staffs in this game may be to win sufficient status to enter the power or esteem game, or it may be to accomplish the program that will win them more professional esteem. In either case, the staffs of organizations often attempt to accomplish their goals by inverting the social and power structure above them, playing off one leadership group against another. At the same time the civic leaders will be vying to nurture organizational programs, the mobilization of which is a demonstration of their power.[47]

In this situation, the criteria of success are not those that we typically apply to criminal justice, such as reduction in crime or reduction in recidivism. Instead winners are those who enlarge their respective domains. Domain enlargement seems to be determined more by the power to initiate or mobilize action than by the power to accomplish the hypothesized consequences of the program. That is, within the criminal justice sphere of this ecology, success will not be measured in terms of actually deterring or rehabilitating, but instead in terms of convincing sufficient groups to back one sort of program rather than another. From this point of view, the real objective of the retribution/deterrence group is not to succeed at stated goals, but to overthrow the legitimating and implementing forces behind the welfare camp; vice versa, welfare succeeds to the extent that it can marshal sufficient resources to mount its programs.

That the American community is not an integrated entity, but a collection of conflicting groups, is nowhere better emphasized than in the community power and community development literature. Nieburg suggests that we are lulled into a false sense of unity in criminal justice because the high degree of ritual and formality in the process masks the high degree of disagreement about principal ends and functions.[48] But if this point of view holds sway in criminal justice circles, it is rapidly disappearing in discussions of other forms of community service and regulation. Blizek and Cederblom, discussing community development and social justice, elaborate on Long's notion of the community as a field in order to develop principles for professional interventionists on the community level. They argue persuasively that the community developer must choose sides and cannot stay morally neutral because the community cannot be considered a single entity in which dysfunctional or pathological parts can be sacrificed to the good of the entire system. Program developers, agency executives, and front line service providers must realize that they shall be choosing sides through the type of actions that they engage in. They are likely to be more effective for the group interest that they favor if they make an explicit choice.[49]

Bennington and Skelton's analysis of participation in government by the public also leads them to conclude that the community is not an organization, but a forum for the interaction of group interests. They liken organizational executives to professional gatekeepers, whose actions will ensure the responsiveness of their agencies to some interest groups and ensure its antagonism to other interests. While agency executives are not the source of power in community decisionmaking, they do have control of the organized resources for which different power groups compete.[50] They go on to suggest that the typical kinds of analyses that are utilized in program planning and evaluation (such as cost-benefit analysis) are inherently favorable to middle-class interests because the events to be minimized or maximized for this group are more readily quantifiable than the objectives of some other groups.[51] Their analysis would suggest that not only are some community groups in a better position to win a specified game than some other groups because of unequal distribution of pieces, but also that the type of game to be played or to consume most community energy is predetermined by the relative power of these various groups. This analysis would be supported by writers such as Bell, Beck, and Reich, who perceive that many current conflicts concerning agency programs concern the games to be allowed on the board, rather than arguments about how a specified game should be played.[52]

Finally, a complete conception of community, as the term will be useful to criminal justice analysis, must not only consider how conflicting and separate groups vie for power by engaging in program implementation. We also need to develop tools by which to study how various groups succeed or fail to enter the arena, or how they maintain the legitimacy to stay on the board, as eligible players in the ecology of games. In addition to the need to be attuned to goal and program formulation as a means of distributing power, and as a statement about which games will be selected for contest, we also need to know how the several potential organizational players come to be perceived as the appropriate contestants.

This question is of particular importance now, as criminal justice reform focuses on the auspices of intervention. For example, is a correctional organization a legitimate purveyor of helping services, or does the context of corrections imply that helping must be done by other organizations, external or neutral to the coercive aspect of intervention? Much discussion of this issue in the criminal justice literature focuses on the conflict of helping and controlling within the criminal justice agency, and the results of that conflict for staff-offender interaction and service delivery effectiveness. While this concern is of considerable importance to the future of criminal justice organizations as they now exist, this debate on intraorganizational conflict over functions tends to obscure some larger and equally important issues. A criminal justice planner may wish to know whether a police department or a correctional agency will have to engage in service delivery and, therefore, whether the agency needs to allocate resources to this function. From the perspective of the community field, however, the question may be quite different. From this perspective, we might reinterpret the debate over service and surveillance as an interorganizational conflict in which different players are seeking admission to the field, or to the game, at the expense of the traditional players.

To examine this question in this way, criminal justice analysis will have to employ the concept of organizational domain and develop means of measuring domain so that we can examine the extent to which changes in criminal justice goals are followed by shifts in range and scope of intervention, and so that we can examine the consequences of shift in domain upon the types and outcomes of services provided. The problem with the operationalization of the term organizational domain in the public sector is the difficulty with measurement. Domain of profit-making firms is usually measured in terms of percent of market controlled, or similar indicators. But many public organizational processes do not provide readily measurable indicators of organizational control of resources. Meyer suggests that organizational domain in the public sector must be perceived as "claimed domain." He suggests that public organizations, unlike firms, have no market for their goods, but do have assured monopolies on certain types of clients. However, the domain of the public organization is not assured by the size of the clientele so much as by the nature of the programs and activities that the organization can organize on alleged behalf of those clients. Hence, domain claim will center on the duration and scope of engagement with the client.[53] Arguments over scope and duration, says

Meyer, are political rather than market determinations, and an effective organization is one that effectively claims the largest domain.

Criminal justice analysis must include the concept of domain and be able to examine organizational domain as a means of assessing the ecology of games in the criminal justice sphere. If the games ecology application to criminal justice is useful, we should be able to reanalyze some common criminal justice events from this perspective. We will try here only to present some material that demonstrates the applicability of this analytical perspective. The utility of its use will be reserved for discussion in Chapter 8. In other words, the criminal justice system is open or vulnerable to the kind of gaming activity that we have described.[54] Presuming that some actors in the community field will have a vested interest in preserving the board for the types of games that they play best, we should see evidence in the criminal justice system of attempts to maintain in the arena the games that are best suited to the skills and resources of the parties in question.

In the area of policing, Robinson maintains that police-community relations is one such exercise among powerful community groups. That is, police-community group conflict is treated as a "police problem" and reduction of conflict is taken as a task to concern police, rather than alternative community groups. While police-community group conflict can be analyzed as a manifestation of broader structural conflict, and could conceivably involve city government administration as well as the business community, no steps have been taken to change the basic political structure of the community as a response to police-community conflict. Instead, strategies are designed and implemented for changing policing styles, increasing police knowledge of minority groups areas and minority problems, and instituting mechanisms by which to channel citizen complaint about the police. Maintaining this focus for resolution of police-community problems isolates the city administration, and the interest groups who prosper under this administration, from directly confronting insurgent groups. The police-community relations game is not played to be won, in effect, but as a means to reduce the likelihood that citizen dissatisfaction with their government will give rise to other kinds of games.[55]

Dession made the same basic case for the institution of helping professionals into the criminal justice system, although he saw within that introduction of noncoercive staff the seeds for the kinds of conflict that could result in the drastic redistribution of criminal justice resources. Writing in 1938, he suggested that there was at that time a significant imbalance in criminal justice among the degree of attention given the separable areas of substantive, procedural and administrative law. He argued that the introduction of new legislation in the substantive and procedural areas, to deal with new concepts of cause and responsibility, and therefore with new strategies for the punishment of crime, implied a change in criminal justice function and goals that was not embodied in the development of subsequent administrative regulation. Application of the concept of domain to his analysis would suggest that criminal justice organizations sought to expand in scope by introducing helping professionals into the system, but that the interests controlling the system did not intend to change essential operations and services so much as to utilize the professionals as legitimators of the new boundaries which the system claimed. Dession predicted, in 1938, that this strategy would be effective politically for the system until significant groups began to take seriously the promised accomplishment of the tasks that the introduction of the professionals implied. At that point, entire public confidence in the system of justice could break down, because the system was organized to accomplish goals symbolically (or satisfy evaluation by symbolic or token accomplishment of objectives), rather than to make the types of intervention that the newer substantive and procedural law purported to be concerned with.[56] Stated in another way, criminal justice in the 1930s began to speak as if the consequences of punishment should be utilized as a means of agency effectiveness. But the criminal justice system never organized to accomplish such ends; rather, it used the new rhetoric in order to mobilize programs. Effectiveness, defined as the ability to mobilize, was sufficient until some of the professionals entering the field decided to play a new game—to gain power by demonstrating the hollowness of the original system's claims to being a legitimate purveyor of help.

Recent analysis of changes in criminal procedure, particularly in the correctional process, would suggest that the concept of domain is relevant there as well. Sullivan and Tifft analyze the interaction of court and correctional agencies over such issues as due process at parole revocation as a process by which the two organizations try to establish a consensus on domain. Correctional organizations encroach on the sphere of the courts until that violation of basic rights is blatant. The courts must then insist that the correctional organizations adopt procedures or rituals that will demonstrate that the judicial domain has not been infringed. If the correctional organization will accommodate the courts to that extent, the court will not seek to alter operations and practices that the correctional organizations deem essential to its domain.[57]

Finally, one of the best examples of the utility of the game ecology applied to criminal justice is provided in Paul Lerman's analysis of the California Probation Subsidy and the Community Treatment Project.[58] Radical analysis of community treatment programs would suggest that the state finds decarceration cheaper and equally effective in controlling deviants. The liberal and conservative positions would revolve around whether the community options are more effective, and/or fairer, than incarcerative options. Were either the traditional or radical theories of criminal justice operations valid, the outcomes of the Probation Subsidy and the Community Treatment Project should have been quite different than they were. Lerman raises doubts about effectiveness and fairness while demonstrating that both projects were more expensive than the traditional options. Viable explanation of the expansion of community treatment in California, then, could not be based on the capitalist conspiracy or on the manifest goals of the programs to the organizations that sponsored them. Lerman demonstrates that the Department of Correction expanded despite a decline in prison population, and the clearest outcome of the two projects being the effective mobilization of state and local resources to the support of the correctional bureaucracies on both the state and local levels.

We have now examined three sets of literature and three alternatives to the assumption that the community is a coherent system and that planning for the control of its behavior can be done in such a way as to benefit all the groups in the long run. The goal conflict literature, the literature on rancorous conflict, and the literature on the community as a field all have in common some basic belief that conflict rather than consensus underlies the social structure and the dynamic interplay of social units. The question inevitably is raised whether this conflict approach is more valid than the consensus approach. Dahrendorf suggests that there can be no final determination of right and wrong, but rather the acceptance that the two approaches are useful for different purposes.[59] The consensus approach would appear more useful to those persons who wish, for whatever reason, to strengthen the criminal justice system. The conflict approach would appear more useful if we wish to study the functions performed by any particular organization in the social structure.

THE COMMUNITY AS THE CONTEXT OF CRIMINAL JUSTICE

The control models of criminal justice to be effective require the existence of an integrated society, or a social system that is accurately described within a consensus framework. Without that, the criminal justice system as a control system is useless, because there would be no notion of order against which the system could evaluate the observed variation of the behavior to be controlled. However, examination of recent literature on community power and organization raises severe doubt whether the consensus model of society is applicable to explanations of community decisionmaking, or to predictions of how and when what types of criminal justice programs will be implemented.

Given this evidence contrary to the accuracy of the control model as description and contrary to the feasibility of the control model as a guide to reform, what are some other ways to evaluate criminal justice operations, make predictions, and determine future revisions in criminal justice program and structure? This question provides the impetus for the analysis I shall undertake in the next chapter. In brief, the material reviewed here would seem to lead to a theoretical framework in which it is assumed that criminal justice operations are determined by community political and social structure. Making changes in any particular criminal justice agency must be done in light of information about the specific functions of that agency in that specific setting. Furthermore, if we are to make effective changes in some level or type of social order, we must begin outside the criminal justice system with redesign of basic living and working arrangements.

As we elaborate on these basic assumptions, the following themes or questions would seem to be the most important. First, what activities or institutionalized patterns of activity create a livable community? What social functions are relevant to the survival of a locality as a setting for civil, organized life? Second, if communities differ in the processes used to perform these functions, and differ perhaps in the extent to which one function is emphasized over another, how will criminal justice be altered by these variations? Third, to what extent are patterns of urbanization, industrialization, and bureaucratization limiting of effective means of community living? These three master change processes have seemed to alter considerably the loci of decisionmaking and power in American social structure. Articulation, or integration, across organizations and communities has decreased, leading to fragmentation in the specialization of labor. At the same time, policymaking and resource distribution decisions are increasingly made at higher levels of bureaucracy, or at levels of government and organization more detached from local levels of action. Are these trends inevitable, or will they level off or reverse themselves? What will happen to criminal justice if this trend continues? While the criminal justice system is relatively small, can increased attention to criminal justice as a social control mechanism reinforce or spur on these dynamics? Will the continued adherence to centralized controls, external to communities, weaken still further the sense of community from which our basic ideas of social order arise? Fourth, what is the relationship between the structure of community and the structure of complex organizations? Are communities to become more like complex organizations in the future? Or, stated another way, are communities to become more like bounded systems with central controls, with organizational membership replacing community membership for our sense of identity and our sense of order?

Chapter 8

Toward a Descriptive Theory of Criminal Justice—The Community as a Model of a Differentiated Social System

In the last chapter I presented a variety of evidence supporting the position that there is no single, widely accepted version of an American social order. Instead, the American social system appears to be a highly fragmented, differentiated, and complex mix of interest groups, value positions, and formal organizations. To be sure, there are several centralized pockets of power and influence that may exert a great deal of control over many dispersed groups of people. These modes of control may have several different sources of influence, ranging from intellectual and emotional appeal, through forms of resource bargaining and exchange, to coercion through law or force.

But liberal, conservative, and radical commentators alike tend to place too much weight on a single centralized power base, which they call the "state" or "society." They assume there is a hegemony of moral sentiment and political power that, for better or worse, provides unified, inexorable direction to individual members of society. In essense, both Moralist and Welfare groups assume there is a relatively simple and unidirectional causal link between this single coherent power base and individual human beings.

This conception of American society simply does not describe accurately the variety and conflict that are observable at all levels of social interaction. The "state," in the American system, is not a nationalized coherent entity but a hodgepodge collection of both formally and informally organized actors. These actors, whether persons, groups, bureaucracies, or complex agency networks, do not act in concerted fashion toward some predetermined American destiny. Instead they often act against each other, and very often they act for their own perceived immediate advantage rather than for the good of a larger collectivity.

In addition to the lack of integration of American society, or perhaps as one characteristic of that lack of integration, criminal justice systems do not display common structures and common purposes across various regions of the country, and they do not display a great deal of coherence and integration in any one area of the country. Nevertheless, I think that one can make some useful generalizations about criminal justice operations. I think one can, in fact, build a theory of criminal justice. But the theory must be descriptive. It must be sufficiently complex to accommodate observations of variety and conflict. In fact, it must attempt to predict which intraagency and interagency behaviors will predominate within specified subsets or differentiated subunits of the American social system.

In order to do these things, a theory of criminal justice cannot be based upon normative prescriptions for how a single criminal justice system should behave. Instead, a descriptive theory would be based upon an analytic scheme that captures the basic differentiations in American social system. Based on a framework that characterizes the various contexts of criminal justice operations, such a theory would help us understand how specific justice agencies will behave in specific circumstances.

In the last two chapters, I made a case for the proposition that criminal justice agencies operate at a relatively "low" level of social and political aggregation. In other words, variations in criminal justice operations are heavily determined by a relatively local set of constraints and a relatively local determination of public order. It is important to emphasize that the "local" nature of criminal justice does *not* suggest that more generic, national, or centralized concerns are insignificant. Nothing could be further from the truth. The federal government, particularly in the last two decades, has done much to standardize and unify criminal justice practices across the nation through the use of legal and economic influences such as block grant funding, standard setting, and a series of important Supreme Court decisions on criminal procedure and civil rights. State governments, also, have pushed for unification of local and regional practices and the upgrading of local agency personnel by subsidizing certain operations in return for compliance with standards. There are state inspectors of local jails, state funding and state technical services to county probation, increasingly centralized procedures and requirements for trial court administration, police training, and so on.

But there is a brand of modern social ecology that *includes* such centralized forms of control and influence. It includes them as relevant (at times overriding) variables that interact with more indigenous, localized variables that *in combination* provide the context for the style and quality of life that is observable in any particular area. One version of that study of social ecology is presented in this chapter. The principal proponent of this version of American social structure is Roland Warren. To designate those confluences of local and centralized forces that differentiate the social system into smaller subunits, Warren adopts the term "community." Since this term is unavoidable in a review of the social theory I want to use, I too will use the term.

It is important, particularly for criminal justice readers, to keep in mind that community, used in the following context, does not refer to neighborhoods, or to small, homogeneous towns, or to face-to-face collectivities whose well-being and group identity are juxtaposed against a "mass society" or urban sprawl or the national system. The term community, as used here, is a flexible, relatively unbounded ecological entity: an interaction field that may in some instances be as large and various as a metropolitan area and in some other instances as small and simple as a traditional village. For Warren and others of his tradition, some aspects of community can be understood only by tracing interorganizational networks that may stretch thousands of miles. Some other aspects of community may be as ephemeral and limited in space as a few neighbors relying upon each other for advice and mutual aid.

This use of the term community is definitely *not* common in criminal justice literature, where one may find discussions of police-community relations, neighborhood policing, community-based correction, and neighborhood justice centers. While there are some important exceptions, most criminal justice treatments of community tend to deal in cliché and oversimplification. There is usually a monolithic conception of "the community" just as there is a monolithic conception of "society" and "the state."

COMMUNITY DEFINED

Roland Warren defines community as "that combination of social units and systems which perform the major social functions having locality relevance."[1] He means that community exists when persons have local access to those activities necessary for daily living.[2] Hiller, defining community in terms of its elements, specified that it must have members, tests of admission, distinctive roles or functions, norms regulating conduct, and locality or area.[3] Hillery, examining ninety-four separate definitions of community, found that sixty-nine of them included the notions of specific activities or functions, area of locality, and common identity or common ties.[4] Warren comments that definitions of community are extremely problematic but unavoidable in examining American life. Summarizing the development of community as a theoretical construct, Warren observes that a principal problem with early definitions was the imposition of arbitrary constraints on the term, referring to some isolable entity or action independent of a broader society.[5] These approaches did not permit an adequate degree of mapping between the theories and the behavior of people. That is, while some notion of a limited geographical area seems essential to the idea of community, useful definitions must also accommodate interactions of social units both in the sense of categories equal to each other and of a category as a subunit of some larger entity. Hence, for the analysis of the performance of some relevant communal functions, one might need to proceed no further than the actions occurring across contiguous backyards. But to understand the performance (and the possible inadequacies) of some community functions, it will be necessary to examine the interaction of many local governments vying against each other for priority of state or federal funds.

Warren suggests three possible approaches to the study of community, or to the process of making statements about community activity. One approach is the development of ideal types, confining statements to a level that will apply only to particular categories of community. A second approach seeks specification of relationships on such a general level that these statements might apply in any setting. The third approach is more integrative. One can consider "some of the important dimensions on which communities differ from each other, relate these dimensions to general statements applicable to all communities, and then 'locate' any particular community or type of community under discussion at a particular point along such a dimension."[6]

Because we are concerned here with criminal justice as much or more than community per se, the extent to which we can elaborate a theory of community itself is limited. Statements made here about community may seem too general and superficial to a student of community organization. On the other hand, because we are concerned with criminal justice as an aspect of community, persons who have concentrated their lives on the examination of operating criminal justice agencies are likely to complain that the conception of criminal justice here is too broad. As a clarification of this second problem, the reader might recall Van den Haag's justification for limiting his examination to the effective distribution of criminal penalties, independent of alleged merits or weaknesses in the system of social justice. Accepting such a legalistic distinction, one is relegated to the existing frames of reference and to the search for efficiencies in a system whose effectiveness can only be ignored, or by fiat defined in accordance with temporal political power or persuasiveness. Rather than apologize for the inadequacies of the present approach, as judged by the standards of these broader or lesser limits of vision, we can do only two things. One, while attempting to be as specific and empirically sound about community as possible, we admit that the notion of community here still plays the role of metatheory to a specific inquiry (as systems theory does to operations research). Second, we answer to those who would claim the discussion of criminal justice is too broad that the explanation presented in terms of community is simply more accurate than the competing explanations.

It is to this last point that the implications of modern community theory for criminal justice are most useful. Criminal justice analysis based upon control assumptions depends heavily upon the "institutional" approach to social systems. That is, the analyst concentrates upon the activities of groups and organizations that are taken to be empirical examples of major social institutions, such as economic, political, religious, and so on. In contradistinction, community theory that focuses on functions for localized living assumes that any institution or patterned structure of people can perform several functions at the same time, and different functions at various times. For example, an institution such as the family, which used to perform primary production and socialization functions, as well as offer care and nurturance, is now arguably less involved in production functions than the business and banking institutions and less involved in socialization than the public educational system.

While often identified as representative of the same institution in every community, I have shown that criminal justice agencies may have varied functions for the communities in which they operate. I have also shown that while one locality-relevant function can be performed under varied auspices (or varied institutions), the alteration of auspice can have significant impact on the extent to which the people's daily needs are thereby met. For example, the social functions of an early constable system may not be the same as those of a modern police force, and the consequences of an urban probation agency may not be the same as those produced by the informal volunteerism of John Augustus.

The following analysis is based upon these assumptions: first, communities are varied in type and in the quality of life they provide. There may be no ideal community in the abstract sense, and the problems of community will have both different sources and solutions.[7] Communities themselves, as subunits of a larger social system, may differ on the functions they perform for this larger system.[8] In terms of organizational functions for a social system such as a community, "types of organizations . . . will vary as much within each type as between types."[9] While organizations survive as they are functional for community, we can assume no direct relationship between the endurance of an organization, or its development and expansion, and the community functions to which it claims contributions.[10] While criminal agencies may have an interest in community order, we may have to make a choice between preservation of organizations and performance of social order functions.

Three important themes are recurrent in literature of community:

1. Community as a functional spatial unit meeting subsistence needs of people in the area
2. Community as a unit of patterned social interaction
3. Community as a cultural-symbolic unit of collective identity[11]

All three of these dimensions would seem important to the operation of criminal justice. (1) Communities that meet subsistence needs with varying degrees of effectiveness and by varying methods are likely to give varying amounts of attention to either law enforcement or maintenance of order. One would also assume that communities that meet the subsistence needs of the greatest proportion of their members will have lowest crime rates. Moreover, communities that rely upon illegal means to meet a significant proportion of subsistence needs are likely to view criminal justice quite differently than communities in which the majority of the members want protection of their legally obtained goods and resources from those who are less fortunate. (2) Communities as units of patterned social interaction are likely to be quite significant to the extent that the police are mediators of social disturbance rather than enforcers of the state law. In this context, the events that the police recognize as worthy of mediation will depend heavily upon community notions of what is normal.[12] (3) Finally, community as a cultural-symbolic unit of collective identity should be particularly significant in the determination of community tolerance-intolerance for particular behaviors and groups of people. For example, some communities contain strong values against the acceptance of public welfare. They may also have a strong sense that deviance in the community should be handled there ("we take care of our own"). Other communities may be much more open to state or federal level assistance and intervention, and to the use of remote state facilities for the handling of deviants and criminals.

INDUSTRIALIZATION, URBANIZATION, AND BUREAUCRATIZATION

Most definitions of community have some common elements, suggesting that some generic characteristics underlie the many changes that have taken place. Yet it is also clear the community structure has undergone remarkable change, and with it have occurred changes in criminal justice operations, as aspects of community. An examination of the evolution of the British police will highlight how the changes in English policing over time seemed heavily influenced by changes in the economic base of communities. The social structure changed significantly as capital and labor concentrated in cities. People interacted more in their performance of economically structured roles than in their membership as persons in small villages and towns. The role of elected, amateur policeman did not fit well with roles of merchant, laborer, manufacturer, and the like, and the role of police officer finally became a remunerated position as well. Following the trends of industrialization and urbanization, the organization of public offices had to change. The Police Act of 1829 not only established the role of paid police officer, it necessarily authorized a new management system as well. The creation of a large number of salaried officers required the ordering of authority in hierarchical positions and rules for the interaction of incumbents of different offices within this hierarchy. While the constable managed himself, industrialized cities brought about the need to bureaucratize in order to discharge the responsibilities of public services.

Roland Warren calls these triplets of modern social structure the "master change processes" that have reshaped the nature of American community.[13] The result, says Warren, has been the general weakening of community autonomy and the increasing dependence of community upon extra-local units and forces for the performance of local functions. Silver suggests that these changes in community have included alterations in the moral or normative dimension:

> The nationalization of civil rights, federal involvement in municipal programs like housing, the erosion of the power of localities to control the content of mass media, pressure from judiciaries on informal and quasilegal police practices—all mean that smaller formations come to see themselves as less able to control or influence their moral destiny.[14]

Indeed, the dependence of communities on extra-local units has increased to the point, says one economist, that communities themselves may be the victims of crime. Large corporations that do not depend upon any one community site for their conduct of business place low priority on community opinion and communities' problems when determining business policy.[15]

The increasing size and complexity of bureaucracy, together with the increased technology of industrialization, has had its impact on the relationship of community members to the agencies of criminal justice. In the 1890s the police station house functioned as a community action center. Meals and lodging were frequently provided for poor or traveling persons, and neighbors congregated there seeking solutions to a wide variety of problems. Furthermore, the individual police officer was alone on his beat, immersed in the social situation of the persons he policed and relatively cut off from other police and his station house superiors. Consequently, he learned to handle problems informally, on the spot, and by himself. Isolation of the police from the people became significant in the 1930s with the introduction of radios and patrol cars.[16] By 1968, the National Advisory Commission on Civil Disorders noted the motorization and mobilization of the police had sacrificed the possibility of informal contact with the citizenry to the demands for internal, bureaucratic efficiencies.[17]

Separation of community interest from agency determination of operations is also visible in corrections. Large urban probation departments and jail facilities are relatively inaccessible to the bulk of the community even though they may be local units of government. The distance from private citizens and even organized citizen groups to the top levels of a city correctional bureaucracy is almost as large as if the organizations were run by a distant state government

Moreover, many of the bureaucracies that do implement community correctional programs such as probation, parole, or halfway houses are responsive to influences beyond the local community. Policymakers in state governments may be almost as independent of any particular community they affect as are large corporations.

But the impact of bureaucratization on criminal justice interface with the community is not limited to matters of technology and size. The common meanings of police professionalism also signal a growing commitment of the officials to organizational rules, procedures and technology: "Professionalization may operate to cement conservative bureaucratic philosophies to law enforcement on level of rationality never before achieved."[18] Professionalization of police as it is generally practiced increases rather than retards the organizational tendencies toward isolation and remoteness from the public. The result has been exacerbation of already strained relations, particularly in ghetto areas.[19]

While the bureaucratization of criminal justice has had extreme impacts upon the ability of community groups to communicate with and control criminal justice operations, it would be a mistake to suggest that the impetus for the changing interaction has come from the public agencies. Bureaucratization seems to be a concommitant of the other two "master change processes," not something that agency heads will do because of their political or ideological inclinations.

In many ways, the characteristics usually associated with bureaucracy alone appear to be outcomes of urbanization itself. While the major conceptual framework in this study is drawn from the larger literature on community, it may be helpful to examine briefly some of the characteristics of urban community, in particular. Louis Wirth suggests that: "The central problem of the sociologist of the city is to discover the forms of social action and organization that typically emerge in relatively permanent, compact settlements of large numbers of heterogeneous individuals."[20] The key variables, in Wirth's opinion, are (1) large size, (2) density of population, and (3) heterogeneity of population. Spatial density seems particularly important because the more compact the space in which a wide variety of interactions must take place, the more the nature and types of interactions themselves seem to change. Density leads to the segregation of different interactions (functions) into relatively distinguishable roles, and these functions tend to be concentrated into relatively specialized sections within the dense area.[21] When this functional segregation is coupled with large populations, one result is the segmentalization of human relationships and reduction of the possibility that individuals will make contact as "full personalities."[22]

Because individuals have a variety of roles to play in urban communities, and because a large variety of behavior has to be tolerated, "in large cities there are much stronger norms about 'deliberately not noticing' the behavior of other people. This means that in cities, much more behavior is *only* inquired into by the police."[23]

While small, sparsely settled, homogeneous communities may be held together by the simultaneous conducting of a large variety of social functions in an integrated fashion, urban communities have to elaborate new forms of control to deal with functional specialization. According to Wirth, two forms of control that frequently emerge are competition and formal control.[24] "Competition" as described by Wirth seems reminiscent of the "winner-take-all" motif that Chambliss and Seidman associated with the emergence of states.[25] I interpret "formal control" as a reliance on bureaucratic order that is similar to the formal norms or laws that form the basis of state social control.

Why then all the fuss about bureaucracy and community, if the end result for criminal justice is the reliance on the coercive behavior associated with the state? The answer is not easy, but important. The mere fact that certain behaviors appear similar to those known to be produced by a certain antecedent does not demonstrate that a causal relationship exists. It is a common phenomenon in a variety of disciplines to find that quite similar events can be explained in very different ways. Doctors are quite familiar with the causal ambiguity of certain symptoms. Psychologists may find that fear produces flight in some circumstances or organisms and aggressions in others. General systems theorists speak of the principle of equifinality, referring to the ability of complex systems to arrive at similar end states through a variety of different processes. To the extent that the behaviors of the criminal justice system are explainable in terms of community and complex organization, applying a theory of the state will not have much utility for prediction or control. If a theory of the state were sufficient, then all states should have similar criminal justice systems, which is not true.

The organization of criminal justice contains more variety than its attachment to the state would appear to generate. Even if all states tend to industrialize, bureaucratize, and urbanize, it seems quite doubtful that overthrowing or abolishing states as forms of government would stop or reverse these trends. Indeed, it would seem the more heterogeneous, dense, and large that communities become, the less that their subsumption under states (capitalist, communist, or other) would appear capable of explaining them. And if we are to deal with the negative effects of external, coercive control upon groups of people, then we clearly need to generate alternative forms of social and community organization in addition to or instead of alternative forms of state government.

WARREN'S MODEL OF COMMUNITY

The impacts of industrializtion, urbanization, and bureaucratization may be equally or more important than the impact of the state upon the behavior of people in twentieth century America. Indeed, arguing that the capitalist state in the United States is the prime mover of criminal justice, even radicals accept the existence of the state itself as a kind of centralized control brought about by the changes in the economic basis of life. Thus, even from a radical perspective, one could argue that the type of criminal justice we have is determined by the organization of people for the performance of primary social functions. While we could agree to some extent with the foundations of a radical analysis of criminal justice, the radical emphasis on capitalism and upon the hegemony of the industrial-political complex is somewhat misplaced. Bell, for example, amply rebuts the current Marxian position regarding social control. He suggests that the technological axis of post-industrial society, whether socialist or capitalist, leads to many similar characteristics in social structure, and to many similar social problems.[26] Dahrendorf, concentrating upon power distribution rather than technological change, reaches conclusions similar to Bell's. He stresses that distribution of power through formal hierarchies, and the control of organization by managers rather than owners, shifts the predominating influences in twentieth century politics from the location of wealth to the location of authority.[27]

Urbanization, while arguably a consequence of industrialization, brings with it problems not predicated on industrialization alone. Large numbers of heterogeneous people living in a dense or relatively small area create problems of interdependence and control that can hamper industrialization and provide problems for bureaucratic authority.

An adequate theory of criminal justice in the United States must deal accurately with all three of these trends, rather than with the simpler notions of the individual and the state. Hence the most adequate framework for criminal justice theory is a model of community, providing that model can incorporate all the above trends. Many models of community will not do so, because they are limited to the "ideal type approach." That is, the generalized statements of relationship that they allow are limited to certain points along the urbanization continuum. Roland Warren and his associates,[28] taking an integrative approach to community, provide a model sufficiently wide and broad to encompass most, if not all, of the relevant questions concerning the conceptualization and operation of criminal justice.

As stated above, Warren defines community as the arrangement of groups, organizations, and larger systems that provide locality-relevant functions.[29] The functions that Warren suggests must be performed with some degree of effectiveness in order for community to exist are:

1. Production-distribution-consumption
2. Socialization
3. Social control
4. Social participation
5. Mutual support

The production function is primarily the economic one of local participation in the processes by which goods and services are made and delivered, and the structure of work that these processes entail.[30] While this function is generally considered the province of industry, business, and finance, Warren, Bell, and others stress that the auspices under which the function occurs are rapidly changing.[31] Thus all organizations, formal and informal, must be considered as they contribute to this function.

Socialization is the process by which members of society take on the knowledge, values, and norms of their own society. Socialization in the earlier part of the life cycle is perhaps the most significant type, and consequently, the contributions of families and schools to socialization have been most frequently stressed. But it is true of at least American society that socialization is becoming increasingly problematic as knowledge, values, and behavior patterns that are most useful at one stage of the life cycle are often no longer appropriate for another stage. Hence resocialization processes are increasingly observed as important, whether we are speaking of an unemployed executive learning new skills in mid-career, the aged learning how to cope with retirement and separation from family, or the delinquent learning to cope with the demand of incarceration or release on parole. Hence, socialization is now a function that is diffused through many organizations and across the life cycle.

Social control, according to Warren, "involves the process through which a group influences the behavior of its members toward conformity with its norms."[32] He suggests that social control has traditionally been considered the province of formal government, since government has ultimate coercive power over its citizens.[33] This may imply that criminal justice agencies are to some extent involved in control activities. Warren makes no assumption, however, that criminal justice agencies, or any other organizations of formal government, are the only or the most effective auspice of social control. Quite different than the Welfare or Moralist conceptions of social control is Warren's emphasis on the extent to which the auspice of control activity provides *local access* to norm enforcement. Again, Warren's concern is with outcomes or functions of social arrangements on the local level. In other words, in some communities criminal justice operations may contribute to social control, but in other types of communities the same operations may not.

The fourth locality-relevant function is social participation. Perhaps the weakest part of Warren's model is the absence of definition of this function, despite its apparent importance. In neither his original presentation of the model nor in his later elaboration on social participation does Warren do more than provide definition by example.[34] He suggests that social participation is typically seen as an activity provided by churches and other voluntary associations. He then mentions that the informal activities within many formal organizations provide for some types of face-to-face, primary group interaction during the performance of other roles and duties by organizational members. Forced to read between the lines, we can conclude that social participation is that function by which members of a locality obtain a sense of membership or identity with other persons in their area, irrespective of their roles in secondary, or formal, organizations. That is, social participation is probably most important to developing a sense of belonging to an area, and the strength of this function then should be highly significant to the ability of people in one area to cut across their ethnic, occupational, or class differences, and act as a community.

Warren points out that it is perhaps the social participation function that has been most weakened by urbanization, bureaucratization, and industrialization. Increased mobility results in persons identifying more with their organizations of employment than with one of the many areas that they will live in for short periods of time. Specialization of labor also frequently results in a fragmented approach to community planning, so that no group or organization feels responsibility for the overall quality of life in an area. People specialize instead in matters of health, education, land use, and so on, so that even concerted efforts at improvement are focused on a narrow band of problems, and isolated from the development of area-wide rather than sectoral allegiances.

The church, or religious activities, is frequently mentioned as a good example of social participation in that such activity allegedly gives people an opportunity to meet as members of a primary group and develop a "we-feeling" that is lacking in other modes of daily interchange. However, churches themselves are relatively fragmented, with many denominations hierarchically related to some central policymaking body and only weakly linked to other religious organizations in the same locality.

Many students of community organizations cite the move toward the suburbs in the 1950s as evidence of people trying to regain a lost sense of community.[35] Wood would argue that the unwillingness of suburban governments to join in regional governmental arrangements with the central city of an area is at least partially founded on an unwillingness to lose control over decisions about community.[36]

The function of social participation would appear to be potentially very powerful for an analysis of criminal justice, since it contributes to identity, belonging, group definition and group membership. To the extent that the function can be defined usefully, it may provide a new path by which to investigate the symbolic functions of criminal justice, such as whether a community can be made to believe that retribution has been given or whether the due process rights of a community member have been violated.

The last community function is that of mutual support. By this term Warren means simply "the type of help which is proffered in those instances where individual and family crises present needs which are not otherwise satisfied in the usual pattern or organized social behavior."[37] Warren is careful to distinguish what he means by mutual support from Durkheim's notion of organic solidarity or Kropotkins's notion of mutual aid,[38] and suggests that Kropotkin and Durkheim were both referring to a more fundamental interdependence or symbiosis by which the welfare of one group was linked to the welfare of all others. This idea of mutual interdependence is quite important to Warren's analysis, but he does not consider it under the heading of mutual support. Mutual support is to be understood as aid-giving in times of trouble. Warren suggests health and welfare services as examples. He also points out that health and welfare, and other forms of crisis care, can and frequently are organized in our society so that organic solidarity or mutual aid is lacking in the performance of mutual support. For example, indigent pregnant women seeking medical care may presently have to go to several agencies and meet several sometimes conflicting eligibility criteria in order to receive complete prenatal care. Or, the proferring of health services may not be coordinated with other kinds of welfare functions, so that while health care in and of itself might be adequate, housing and sanitation may not be. Advances made in one area of care may be negated by neglect in another area.

Equally important to identifying community functions is the examination of the particular structural arrangements for performing those functions. Just as complex bureaucratic organizations may have different decision and control networks and different production technologies, communities differ markedly in the way that production, socialization, social control, social participation, and mutual support activities are carried out.

Warren suggests four separate dimensions upon which communities may differ: (1) local autonomy, or the independence of the local area from outside sources, may range from independent to dependent. (2) Local services areas or functional delivery areas may coincide or differ. (3) Psychological identification with the local area may be strong or weak. (4) Horizontal articulation across functional units may be strong or weak.[39]

While these four dimensions may all be important and logically separate, this presentation will concentrate upon only two of these dimensions, the issues of autonomy and of horizontal articulation. It would seem that lack of autonomy in functional performance may lead to lack of coincidence in functional areas. For many reasons, school districts, health catchment areas, judicial districts, and so on may overlap rather than be coterminous. But overlap would seem very likely when such activities are organized in separate, hierarchically arranged service systems where the interdependence between need areas is not recognized. Second, identification with a locality would seem partially dependent both on area autonomy and on its horizontal articulation. While some persons might argue that psychological identification must precede structural interdependence, most research would suggest the reverse.[40] Also, it is not clear that the dimension of psychological identification with an area is not already covered by the function of social participation. Thus, the two dimensions most essential to an analysis of how locality-relevant functions are organized would appear to be the vertical dimension (autonomy) and the horizontal dimension.

The vertical dimension of community structure refers to the degree to which a local social unit is tied to or dependent on a non–local system for the performance of its locality-relevant functions. The horizontal dimension of community refers to the degree to which various groups, organizations, and systems within a community are interrelated for the performance of one function or the performance across functions.[41]

The vertical dimensions might be weak, for example, to the extent that most locally consumed goods and services are produced and distributed by local private organizations. The vertical dimension would be strong to the extent that members of a community are dependent on large corporations and state or federal government for the provision of goods and services. Similarly, the community has relative autonomy on the vertical dimension of the socialization function to the extent that local schools are independent of state or federal revenue and non–local policy and curriculum decisions. The vertical dimensions of social control might be considered weaker in a city with a strong, centralized political mechanism and its own police and regulatory agencies than in a city that contracts for state police services. Communities that depend upon broader (or higher) governmental structures for the performance of social control functions (such as the town that contracts for police services) are influenced by a relatively strong vertical dimension.

The horizontal dimension of the various functions is strong to the extent that different community units interface and cooperate with each other. For example, a "company town" in which many if not all members depend upon one organization for production activities and many participatory and support services can be considered to have a strong horizontal dimension. Likewise, small, rich, and predominately white suburban communities such as Winnetka, Illinois, and Brighton, New York, have a strong horizontal dimension because the population is relatively homogeneous, most persons in the community have the same values, and behavioral anticipations are generally consensual. There is usually little diversification in the community influence network: people influential in police policy, school board elections, and important church functions are either the same, or know and cooperate with each other.[42]

All community social functions are influenced in some degree by both horizontal and vertical structures. City and town governments, no matter how powerful in their own right, are chartered and constrained by state government. Local school boards depend to some degree upon state departments of education. County prosecutors and local police enforce state laws and are constrained by federal constitutional standards. On the horizontal dimensions, even communities with fairly fragmented and dispersed participatory and support organizations may be integrated to some extent by local political mechanisms, chambers of commerce, community clients, and other coordinating agencies.

The major conclusion from observing contemporary American communities is that the horizontal dimension has tended to weaken and the vertical dimension has tended to strengthen dramatically in the last fifty years. Industrialization, urbanization, and bureaucratization are predominant forces that have tended to make communities dependent on various vertical linkages for the performance of social functions. Corporations of national and international scope, with diversified interests, have tended to take on to a great extent the production-distribution-consumption functions that were once the province of individual and local entrepreneurs. State and federal governments have been increasingly responsible for support and operation of local schools and have simultaneously been more demanding that state and national standards be met or implemented at the local level. Social control functions are increasingly state and federal concerns, as are many social participation and mutual support activities. This trend has tended to mean that various local units charged with the delivery stages of different functional activities have less in common with each other and less loyalty to each other, or to local citizenry, than to the superstructures at the state and national levels to which they belong.[43] Health, welfare, and justice activities that may once have been performed locally, and policy decisions about each, are now made at central headquarters far removed from local incidents and local problems, as well as in a manner that reduces interaction among these units.[44]

THE VERTICAL AND HORIZONTAL AXES AND CRIMINAL JUSTICE

The elaboration of community functions might enable us to understand better why the outputs of criminal justice agencies might differ according to the community in which they are bedded. Hence, this aspect of the model might be useful in discussions of criminal justice goal selection. Only in communities with the same functional needs would we expect criminal justice to function in the same way, everything else being equal.

But of course, everything else is not equal. Not only may criminal justice agencies and systems vary in the extent to which they contribute to one community function rather than another, but also different structural arrangements might be required in order to achieve the same function in different communities. For example, it is a long-standing problem, as yet unanalyzed, that programmatic structures accepted in one community simply cannot be grafted onto another. Recent LEAA mystification as to why replications of community corrections projects have remarkably different planning processes and results serves as only one example.[45]

In relationship to this problem, it is the community axes, rather than functions alone, that would seem to help the most. As an example of this, let us isolate just one function for the purposes of explication, and attempt to trace how different criminal justice program structures might be related to community structure in general.

In Figure 8.1, the two axes, vertical relations and horizontal articulation, are treated as orthogonal dimensions. Thus we can consider localities that differ on the values of these two dimensions, or differ on the kinds of structure by which a locality-relevant function is achieved. Theoretically, there would seem to be four ideal types of locality on this structural basis. We can imagine on the one hand localities with strong horizontal patterns and low vertical dependence, localities with strong vertical relations and

	Low Horizontal articulation	High
High Vertical relations	Fragmented community, norms unclear, responsibilities for functions parcelled to various organizations that quibble over turf. Welfare law management, with legitimacy of organization over individual.	Interdependent community, organizational jurisdictions blurred, with formal mechanisms used to coordinate activities. Legitimacy dependent on interactive capacity.
Low	Disorganized area, or mass society. Norm observance low, offender and victims treated individually; formal law keeping, with little legitimacy granted to officials of state.	Solidary community, norms unified and concrete with few local organizations responsible for many functions, informal norm enforcement based on membership and peer pressure.

Figure 8–1. Community structural axes and the social control function.

low horizontal interface, localities with simultaneously high vertical and horizontal relations, and localities that are weak on both dimensions. In relation to the last type, we might geographically designate such areas as "communities," and yet one would expect that functional delivery is ineffective and that we are dealing here with a loss or lack of community. In the other areas, it would appear that all functions are performed to some degree, although perhaps with quite different results. That is, in the localities that are relatively high on at least one dimension, one might argue that peoples' needs are met. Yet because these different structures imply very different auspices for the delivery of functions, different constraints will be operating, and therefore the strategies selected by these different auspices can be expected to vary.

Elaborating this typology on the function of social control alone, we can specify in rudimentary fashion what we would expect both in terms of functional auspice as well as in terms of social control outcomes. Where both the vertical and horizontal patterns of community are weak, we would hypothesize that the community itself is weak. We would expect in such instances that norms are not clearly defined and that many behaviors that would bring about some sort of reaction in other areas will not receive any organized sanction. If there is no local group commitment either to socialization or to building and maintaining a sense of group identity, social control activity will not be organized or effective. On the one hand, there will be no group boundaries against which to define deviant action, and on the other hand there will be no processes by which groups inculcate mutual standards in individuals. To the extent that criminal justice activity occurs in such places, it is likely to involve response to major crimes or major group crises. Since these localities will exist within states, some observance of law enforcement will continue in these areas, but the officials of state agencies are likely to be seen as outsiders who must rely on the formal authority of the law and upon coercive sanctions in order to rationalize their intervention. That is, criminal justice is likely to be seen as distant and have little legitimacy. Criminal justice officials may conceive of themselves in this situation as ministerial agents, but without a local group concern for outcomes or processes, criminal justice agents are likely to contain, rather than prevent or intervene, and in those instances where they feel they must act, their boundary-spanning repertoire is likely to be corrupt or brutal.

In localities where there is high interdependence, or strong horizontal articulation of the organization of various functions, we would be dealing with what might be called a solidary community. In such instances, there will be a strong, predominating "we-feeling", a clear sense of group boundaries, and responsibilities for community functions will be the province of a relatively small number of both informal and formal organizations, all of which are closely interlocked and all of which are relatively independent of external financial support or policy influence. Social control in such situations will rely primarily on informal mechanisms, such as peer pressure and public approval, and the fact that everybody knows everyone else's business. There is little opportunity for norm-violating behavior. In such places even formal criminal justice agencies will operate in ways commensurate with local definitions of propriety. Agency processes are likely to be informal, and invocation of the criminal sanction is likely to be infrequent. When used, sanctioning decisions are likely to center on whether the offender is perceived as an outsider or an insider. If the offender is a local citizen, a decision to keep the punishment local is really a signal that the community considers itself to be confronting a local problem. If such a community transfers its punishment to a state agency, it is in effect ostracizing, defining that offender as no longer belonging to the group.

Such communities are not likely to resort to harsh penalties, such as lengthy prison sentences, in most instances. Social control is more likely to be of the remedial, negotiative, restitutive kind. However, retribution in the form of ostracism to prison may become an issue in one of two ways. One would expect that transient offenders are more likely to be treated harshly, since they do not have claim on community membership. One would also expect that these communities can become retributively oriented when they feel the present sense of order is threatened. This may occur particularly when such communities are waning, as when a predominate life style and set of norms is being displaced by the entrance of significant groups of others, or by the ascension to power of previously dispossessed minorities. In this instance, one may see "political law enforcement" rather than negotiation, with the austerity of the formal criminal justice system called upon to defend old norms from new incursions.

In some communities, locality-relevant functions are heavily dependent upon vertically organized specialty organizations, and there is little interdependence among these organizations. Such communities are likely to be highly diversified with multiple and conflicting power bases, with different organizations initiated and operated as a means to meet the disparate functional needs of the area. This situation we might call the fragmented or pluralistic community, where norms are multiple and perhaps conflicting, and responsibilities for functions are parcelled out to separate organizations. These organizations may battle over turf, or have significant domain disputes. Or, as Warren, Rose, and Bergunder have suggested, these organizations may come to a relatively well understood agreement on organizational missions and therefore have very little interaction with each other.[46] Because such communities rely on hierarchically organized units with relatively narrow specialities, there is often a press for professional management and client-centered programming within the various organizations, whether we are dealing with mental health, municipal planning, or police and correctional services. We would see in this type of locality something we might call "welfare law management" in which organizations are concerned with the organizational posture toward specified individual clients, without great regard for the community or group identity of the individuals involved. The aim is likely to be the reduction of future crime when the criminal justice system is involved, rather than a concern for maintaining an existing normative pattern. Such systems might become concerned with specific deterrence, incapacitation, or rehabilitation, but it is less likely that they will be judged effective against criteria of retribution or prevention of anomie for any of the many conflicting and diverse groups that form their constituency.

Finally, we can conceive of communities that present both frequent exchange and interaction with units external to the community, but at the same time the various units providing community functions are relatively well integrated. It is doubtful that there are many such communities in the United States today, and examples of the nature of social control in such areas are difficult to give. This type of community may be unstable and revert relatively quickly to one of the other forms previously described. Hypothetically, however, such an interdependent community would seem to be one in which auspices for community functions are blurred by informal and personal or formal, interorganizational mechanisms by which to coordinate services toward the meeting of community needs and by which to coordinate external resources or policy decisions with local determinations of need. Legitimacy of agencies in such communities would seem to depend upon their integrative capacities. Administration of formal organizations involved in social control would seem to be a difficult activity here. Such communities are likely to seek or to need complex organizations funded by outside forces in order to deliver satisfactory services, but such communities are not likely to be satisfied with public bureaucracies that operate independently of each other and concentrate on independent subparts of the total community.

It is possible that criminal justice structures such as team policing[47] or federally funded but locally determined correctional programs[48] represent attempts to create such a balance.

SUMMARY

This chapter has elaborated a model of community function and structure that incorporates a greater variety of behavior and a larger number of social units than is true of most other social models that have formed the basis of criminal justice analysis. Unlike other beginning points, this model would portend the development of a theory of criminal justice. It would do so because it allows for statements of relationship about, individuals, groups, and organizations, and the arrangement of these into complex social systems. It would allow us to predict variations in criminal justice operation based upon measures of specified dimensions. It would also provide a broader base for policy analysis and planning that would allow us to link proposed changes in processes and operational structures to identified needs in an area, rather than have us depend upon planned changes that are narrowly justified upon some *a priori* plan for criminal justice as it should be.

The utility of the model is of course an open question. It should be evaluated in terms of its accuracy as a description of relationships and in terms of its prediction power relative to proposed implementations of change. This assessment is naturally a long and complex process that should be attempted gradually.

The next chapter merely begins this process by (1) analyzing some criminal justice operations in relation to community functions, and (2) specifying where possible how location upon the vertical/horizontal matrix may alter functions to which any particular auspice might contribute.

Chapter 9

Criminal Justice Functions in Various Settings—Production, Socialization, and Social Control

I intend to demonstrate in Chapters 9 and 10 that criminal justice analysis has often been faulty and generalizations from it either scanty or inaccurate because an inappropriate framework for analysis has often been used. Attempts at criminal justice theory have usually sought to stipulate effects of the "system" upon outcomes such as crime rate, sense of safety or order, or recidivism. In contrast, this chapter presents reports of criminal justice behavior within a model of community. Hence, rather than seek generalizations about effective police behavior, of effective correctional programs, and so on, I hope to be able to specify types of criminal justice behaviors from some generalizations about community.

The procedure will be perhaps too simple, but it may serve as a starting point. I shall review the locality-relevant functions serially, specifying when and to what extent criminal justice agencies may be involved, depending upon their location along the vertical and horizontal dimensions of community.

THE PRODUCTION FUNCTION

The question of how criminal justice may contribute to the community function of production, distribution, and consumption should be understood as an inquiry into how criminal justice *itself* contributes directly to the economic structure of a community or to the processes of labor specialization, economic exchange, distribution of products and services, and so on. The inquiry here is directed toward the elaboration of criminal justice as an enterprise in its own right, rather than as a control or sanctioning system that maintains or strengthens a separate set of economic relationships. To the extent that a Marxian analysis emphasizes the utilization of the criminal law and the administration of justice as a means of protecting an existing economic structure, that analysis is more relevant to social control than to productivity. In contrast, the key questions here involve what function, if any, criminal justice serves in producing jobs, distributing goods and services, structuring the labor force, and so on.

Warren's analysis of the production function of community is limited. In elaborating his model, he is satisfied with (1) demonstrating certain examples of production organization, and (2) describing basic changes in production as community axes have shifted. By way of example, the unit he selects is a general private business organization. He begins with the point that American economic structure is based primarily on private ownership and management of specialized organizations for the manufacture and delivery of various goods and services. Since labor is specialized, there must be local access to a system of exchange of goods and services. The supposed benefits of such a system are increased production through greater efficiency and the availability of a greater range of goods and services for consumption than would be available under less specialized systems.

Another claimed outcome of a specialized labor and exchange system is that it requires, or results in, greater "interdependence" of various economic units. "Interdependence," used in this context, however, requires some qualification. Durkheim's theory of division of labor leads to the hypothesis that as labor becomes more specialized, there "must" be greater articulation among the specialized units, or various needs will go unmet.[1] Warren would agree, to some extent, but would also emphasize the probabilistic quality of the connection. Warren suggests that the increased vertical structure of community functions has significantly reduced articulation across units within many communities. Hence, Warren is using "interdependence" as a neutral term. As units of labor become more specialized, each person, or each group of people, are *factually* more dependent on other units in order to obtain all the goods and services they may need in order to survive or in order to embellish life. Thus, while specialization may lead to interdependence, it is an *empirical* question whether the problems presented by this interdependency are actually solved. As Chambliss and Seidman have stated, while specialization of labor is allegedly both more efficient as well as conducive to greater consumptive choice, a money economy limits that greater freedom to those who can afford it.² In other words, the greater interdependence produced by specialization uniformly provides to all people the need for exchange or services and goods but limits to only some groups the means by which such exchange can take place.

Hence, the kind of interdependence produced by specialization of labor should not be confused with the activities of mutual aid that Kropotkin observed in village communities or with the organized solidarity that Durkheim theoretically predicted for a modern economic system. Indeed, Kropotkin theorized that as labor becomes specialized and as distribution of land and technology becomes concentrated in small groups rather than communally, solidarity of the community breaks down.³ For example, he observed that emancipated serfs in many areas of Russia decided to pool the lands they had been awarded at emancipation so that all the members of the village would have their survival needs met.⁴

On another level, however, it is possible to say that articulation among economic units has increased in the United States. Integration has increased on the production and distribution rather than the individual consumption end of the continuum. As private business organizations have become the model auspice of production and distribution, they have increasingly sought to expand markets outside the context of the local plant. Hence, there has been a greater articulation of production and distribution across various communities so that business companies are more dependent upon their vertical articulation and coordination and less dependent on the extent to which the company in any one site serves and is served by a local community.⁵ Firms may also depend more on each other for procurement of raw materials or disbursement of products. But these companies are often less concerned or affected by the extent to which their internal organization or interorganizational arrangements provides local community access to either the profitability of the firm or to the goods and services that the company produces. Thus it is not unusual to find successful enterprises in economically depressed areas. The insurance companies centered in Hartford, Connecticut, are not immediately or greatly affected by the deterioration of Hartford as a community, nor is General Electric greatly affected by the deterioration of Schenectady, New York.

Many experts have hypothesized that economic specialization has proceeded to such a point that entire communities can be characterized by the type of economic activity that takes place within them. For example, Hawley classified communities in the United States into nine types, depending upon the kinds of production that takes place within them. These types range from communities specializing in manufacturing through communities that specialize in resorts and retirement.⁶

Albert J. Reiss used this observation as a starting point for an inquiry into community social and demographic structure. He hypothesized that the structural characteristics of a community would be intimately related to the economic functions that its population performed.[7] Reiss suggested that communities may be seen as having two major forms of economic activity: (1) They can act to satisfy local demand. This activity he called the maintenance function of a community. (2) Communities can function to export their economic output, meaning that communities could be involved in satisfying non–local demands for goods, services, or capital.[8] Reiss denoted communities that had greater than average export activity as "specialized" communities. He discovered that specialized communities had markedly different social stratification patterns compared to communities with other types of specialization and communities that were not specialized. For example, communities that specialized in manufacturing had truncated class patterns, with significantly fewer people in either the highest or the lowest income brackets. In contrast, communities specializing in financial services displayed a higher pyramidal structure, with greater contrasts between the richest and the poorest members of the community.[9]

Meyer has argued that economic specialization of communities is a major determinant of community vulnerability to immoral and illegal corporate practices. Communities that specialize economically tend to lose control over the behaviors of their economic sectors, or in Warren's terms lose access to the locality-relevant function of production.[10]

PRODUCTION FUNCTIONS OF CRIMINAL JUSTICE

While there may be many other ways in which community economic function may relate to criminal justice, I wish to mention just two here as suggestive of the kinds of analysis that must proceed if we are to understand the economic role of criminal justice. In either example, the criminal justice system may be said to provide a functional activity for the local community, but the results for both the community and the justice system are markedly different.

Let us take the negative example first. This involves the symbiotic relationship between organized and professional crime and the criminal justice system in some communities.

Crime as a Specialty

Chambliss and Seidman insist that organized and professional crime exists in many communities side by side with law enforcement and criminal justice agencies that vigorously prosecute other types of crime. They suggest that certain types of crime are not prosecuted because it is rewarding to the system to allow it to continue.[11] The services provided by crime to criminal justice take at least four different forms. Professional and organized criminals can provide information to law enforcement agencies, they can help to "solve crime" by clearing crimes upon arrest for another offense in return for leniency, they can provide direct payment to agents of law enforcement, and they can help to control crime and disruption in communities because organized and professional crime, like any other business, works best in a stable atmosphere.[12]

Criminal organizations can and do provide such services to law enforcement agencies and agents in areas where the criminal justice system can provide the situation that makes such crime profitable: criminalization of certain demanded services and activities provides the tariff that reduces the supply in relation to the demand.[13]

Thomas Schelling's analysis is limited to organized rather than professional crime, and yet it lends credibility to Chambliss and Seidman's general conclusions. Schelling suggests that organized crime is not essentially in the business of providing illicit services or goods but rather in the business of controlling the people who do.[14] That is, organized crime is the business of controlling or governing opportunity and jurisdiction. Schelling suggests that only certain kinds of crime can lend themselves to organization in the sense of governed jurisdiction. One requirement is that the technology of the crime must lend itself to organization. Schelling points out that prostitution, gambling, and drugs require a stable place of business as well as protection from the law. Hence these types of crime are open to extortion from organized criminals, who can locate the places of illicit business as easily as can the customers. Second, illicit business must lend itself to suppression of supply. That is, the crime must be such that not anyone can deal, as would be the case with selling cigarettes or liquor to minors. Schelling concludes, "So if an organization seeks governing authority in the underworld, we should expect it to seek exclusive authority, or at least to seek stable jurisdictional sharing with other authorities so that, all together they constitute a hierarchy without competition."[15] Schelling suggests that if this is the true aspect of organized crime, then it can have a symbiotic association with law enforcement in some areas, since in those areas organized crime acts as a control on deviance, suppressing the supply and increasing the cost to the consumer.[16]

This sort of control does as much or more, in some cases, than law enforcement can do to control crime, particularly where the legitimacy of the law and legal intervention may be questioned. Chambliss and Seidman suggest that the kinds of communities in which this kind of relationship can and does exist is limited. Organized crime and criminal justice goals are congruent in areas where (1) there is a fragmented normative and value situation, and (2) there are actual or arbitrary barriers to consumption of goods or services desired by some but not all segments of the population. In such places, the criminal justice-oriented crime network acts to redistribute goods and services that are available legally (or at least without detection) to some segments of the population but not to others.[17] The localities where this relationship can occur is the fragmented community, in which there is a high vertical arrangement for the production function, and low integration across the various units of the community. In these cases, institutionalized deviance provides access on the local level that might otherwise be lacking in the production function. Chambliss and Seidman suggest that it is also in such communities that the criminal justice apparatus can "atone" for laxity or corruption in one area by acting more harshly in other areas. Hence, they suggest that in the fragmented community, retribution will be demanded from ordinary criminals to balance the immunity provided to organized criminals in the economic function of institutionalized deviance.[18]

Criminal Justice as a Specialty

If the structure of the highly fragmented, vertically organized city can lead to the illicit forms of specialization described above, it can have other consequences as well. Another form of economic specialization that might be considered in relation to criminal justice is provided by James Jacobs in his description of the relationship between the Vienna, Illinois, correctional facility and the town.[19]

Jacobs points out that community correctional reform, such as has been spurred on by the dissatisfaction with institutional corrections in the last decade, has often run up against severe community resistance. In order to avoid such resistance, correctional planners have often resorted to locating community facilities in disorganized communities where strong opposition to programs cannot occur. This kind of avoidance of conflict, suggests Jacobs, really defeats the whole point of community programs, since the disorganized communities do not contain the kinds of social resources that correctional experts assume are necessary in the reintegration process. Analyzing this problem, Jacobs concludes that in large urban communities, the correctional program is often insufficiently important to the community that resistance on some grounds, such as danger, cannot be overcome by community support in other areas, such as economic importance.

In this context, Jacobs discusses some remarkable cooperation between the town of Vienna, Illinois, and a new open prison built in the community. He reports a high degree of exchange between the prison and the townspeople, with inmates frequently utilizing the town itself and the townspeople freely utilizing the prison facility as well. Noting that the community originally objected to the location of the prison, Jacobs suggests that the prison was able to locate in Vienna because the prison was sufficiently economically important to the small town that Vienna eventually acquiesced to placement of the facility and ultimately cooperated with apparent satisfaction in the facility's correctional programs. Jacobs concludes that a workable alternative to settling community correctional programs in disorganized areas is to settle them in areas where the correctional organization itself can become the production specialization of the community. This relationship between community and justice agency is quite similar to the relationship that Meyer describes between small towns and large corporations that seek tax rebates or other accommodations from the town in return for the increased jobs that the company location will bring.[20] Yet this relationship is apparently successful as a correctional reform, whereas other instances of company dominance of the community economic function may lead to severe economic dislocation, squandering of natural resources, or other problems.

Variations on the Horizontal Dimension

Perhaps one distinction between the apparently positive results of the economic specialization in the correctional example and the apparently negative results in the organized crime example is the extent to which the economically dominant organization is tied into other community functions. Jacobs provides many examples of ways in which the Vienna correctional organization is integrated with other community functions beyond the economic one. Chambliss and Seidman and Schelling, however, provide few if any examples of how the criminal organization-law enforcement connection provides other functions for the communities involved. (Although some might argue that organized crime has an entertainment value, perhaps a social participation function, Schelling adequately refutes this suggestion.) Warren points out that most production function units, such as business organizations, have only superficial horizontal ties on the local level to either each other or to the other kinds of community functions.[21] Since the Vienna agency has many other social functions beyond production, its domination of that function leads to the meeting of other needs of the community.[22]

But this leads us to another major difference between the negative and the positive examples of criminal justice contribution to the production function. In the prison example, the community involved was relatively small, with a population that was culturally homogeneous. There were few conflicting points of view or conflicting power centers in this community; thus what was "good" for one part of the community was in most cases good for other parts of the community. In the case of corruption, the communities involved were quite different. There were many different power and value groups involved, and it would be difficult or impossible in that situation to suggest that what was functional for one group would also be functional for all others. Chambliss and Seidman suggest that the case of the small, homogeneous community is the one case where a corrupt criminal justice system is least likely to prosper.[23]

In summary, the contribution of criminal justice agencies to the economic or production function of communities has been relatively ignored. Whether this is the case because the contribution is not significant or frequent is possible, but not likely. It seems more likely that the production function of criminal justice has been downplayed in comparison to the function criminal justice supposedly serves for guaranteeing the economic exchange relationship among *other* actors and organizations. This role, too, is certainly important, but more appropriately discussed under the topic of social control.

THE SOCIALIZATION FUNCTION

Socialization, according to Warren, is "the process through which individuals . . . acquire the knowledge, values, and behavior patterns of their society and learn behavior appropriate to the various social roles which their society provides for."[24] It is within the context of community that the individual goes through this learning process. Most observers agree that the structure in which these processes takes place has changed significantly within this century. The learning processes that historically had been the province of family, neighborhood, and informal peer groups are now heavily influenced, if not replaced, by socialization through complex organizations, notably schools.

It is frequently argued that if the socialization processes in the United States were more effective, there would be considerably less social control required, or that there would be fewer deviant events to govern. Criminal justice executives are quick to point out that their ability to socialize people is quite limited, and by the time that the criminal justice system has jurisdiction over an individual, it is frequently "too late."[25]

This kind of criticism of the socialization processes in the United States is relatively inappropriate. It is frequently if not always based upon standards of socialization that if actually applied today might create more chaos and alienation than we currently observe. For example, it is essential in our current society that people can play many roles at the same time, and that they learn fairly well both how to segment these separate roles as well as how to respond to the same person who at different times is "wearing different hats." Socialization is now more complex, or perhaps more accurately, there must be several socialization processes for the different aspects of a person's life. Socialization today may not be effective in instilling familial traditions, such as building and maintaining loyalty and respect for parents and grandparents. Yet a socialization process that continued to do this could be very ineffective for providing individuals with the skills that they need in order to live in a technologically advanced situation where life in complex organizations requires the ability to live in bureaucratic rather than familial settings, or to pack up and move to a new community and a new school system every five years. This is not to say that socialization processes today are effective in all respects—far from it. Nevertheless, the American school system, for example, does produce a large number of engineers, business executives, public administrators, and so on, who have both the technical and social skills to operate in the situations in which they are placed.

In general, a major change in socialization processes over the last fifty years has involved the gradual switch in auspice of socialization from the province of familial and communal settings to that of formal organizations and government. It is not unusual today for children from the age of three to spend as much as a third of each day in formal organizations rather than with parents. Nursery schools and day care centers have emerged as necessary for the care and upbringing of children, as it has become increasingly common for both parents (or the only one) to be working. By the time children enter adolescence, it is likely that school organizations see more of an individual per day than do parents. But it is not merely the reduction of parental responsibility for socialization that is important. Equally, if not more significant, is the shift in responsibility from informal community-wide socialization to socialization by distinct units of community.

Kropotkin's classic anthropological work suggests that communal socialization may have been equally or more important than socialization through distinct familial units in many areas through the latter parts of the nineteenth century.[26] Indeed, he provides a strong argument for the proposition that socialization in communal settings antedates the clustering of persons into smaller family units. In either case, the contribution of the community to socialization processes has significantly changed in structure as well as in content so that today segments of community, rather than the community as a unit, are responsible for various socialization processes. As this dynamic has progressed, socialization has become increasingly specific to particular settings and groups, and the socialization patterns established in these more specialized groups are less well coordinated with each other. One hundred years ago, it was not unusual in many communities for almost all socialization agents to know each other as well as the individuals being socialized. Today, in contrast, it is unusual if the policeman, the parent, the school teacher, and the friends all know each other.

MORALIST AND WELFARE MISCONCEPTIONS

The contribution of criminal justice to the socialization processes of communities is not well studied. The two dominant criminal justice ideologies contain two competing assumptions about criminal justice socialization. The Moralist group tends to rely upon the symbolic functions of criminal justice in socialization. For example, the suggestion is made that the criminal justice system, including the criminal code itself, bolsters or reinforces the socialization processes that are supposed to take place within the primary auspice of socialization. Thus it is proposed that the existence of punishment for "doing bad things" is incorporated in the process of family discipline or school discipline, or that the existence of criminal deterrents provides an external sanction that functions as an alternative to the socialization processes of loyalty, shame, guilt, and positive moral education. The Welfare group, in contrast, tends to describe the socialization function of criminal justice and related systems as a replacement for primary socialization units when those units fail. The primary example of this set of assumptions is the establishment of the juvenile court as a substitute for the family.[27]

Both of these schools of thought regarding socialization are relatively silly. The problems with the Welfare approach have perhaps been adequately dealt with elsewhere.[28] Briefly put, the Welfare approach ignores significant distinctions between the foundations of judicial and parental intervention, and fails to deal with the ethnocentric model of the family that the organizations of justice are supposed to replace. The Moralist conception of the criminal justice socialization contribution is even less adequate. The Welfare group argues with some plausibility that we have faultily implemented a family model of criminal justice but that the conception of socialization is basically sound.[29]

In contrast, the Moralist group seems almost willfully to ignore all empirically based studies of socialization and the relationship between that process and criminal punishment. The basic weakness is that threat of punishment and/or its implementation tend to weaken rather than to reinforce the normal learning processes. Sociological investigations have demonstrated that external punishments for wrongdoing are relied upon in family or school situations where socialization is ineffective.[30] A number of anthropological studies have demonstrated that external and notably criminal punishment systems replace rather than reinforce family and communal socialization.[31] Psychological studies forcefully distinguish between the different processes of punishment and discipline as well as between the distinctive outcomes of the two processes when applied to children.[32]

The Moralist conception of socialization fails to recognize that socialization is a broad term referring not only to the inculcation of moral principles but to the assimilation of knowledge and technological skills as well. There is a good deal of evidence that moral responsibilities and recognition or reciprocity between individuals is closely related to the extent that these knowledge and skills are also shared, and distributed effectively among the group.[33] Psychologists and anthropologists alike agree that persons place a priority on not harming each other only after or only as the socialization processes also accounts for the basic survival and security needs of all group members.[34]

CRIMINAL JUSTICE SOCIALIZATION

In contrast to the ways in which the socialization contribution of criminal justice has been explained in the past, an approach based upon the model of community would point us toward investigations of ways in which criminal justice agencies structure the process of socialization at the community level and to the examination of the content of the learning processes that groups accommodate because of the kinds of contact with the justice system that they experience.

Perhaps the clearest example of socialization through criminal justice is that of "state-raised youth," in which most if not all of the interaction skills and interpersonal expectations of groups occur in the context of criminal justice or related agencies. One would expect in these instances that to the extent that socialization is effective, the groups so engaged with the criminal justice agencies learn how to survive and prosper within the organizational setting, but that what they learn may be inappropriate to other settings. Such is certainly the case with the socialization of groups that Irwin and Cressey identify as formulating a "convict culture" in their adult lives.[35] While it is not known how many persons are significantly affected in this way, political and sociological analysis of this occurrence suggests that state (or agency) responsibility for socialization is structured so that this agency responsibility for care, nurturance, and learning of some youths reinforces the auspices under which that process operates. In other words, as socialization in families was conducted so that one result was maintenance of families, socialization in agencies is conducted so that the agencies are maintained.[36] Systems of foster home placements, and new Youth Service Bureaus, while not part of the criminal justice system, probably demonstrate similar consequences. Groups who depend upon these institutions for their survival and their education will learn behaviors that are more appropriate to life within these agencies rather than behaviors that are transportable to different settings.

Socialization contribution of the police may be less significant than the socialization contribution of closed institutions to their inmates. Yet many observers have commented on the institutionalization of reciprocal behaviors between police and gangs of juveniles, particularly in urban ghettoes. Wolfgang and Ferracuti point out that the police and gang members formulate highly reliable expectations of each other, and that the police agents in such settings adopt value and behavior patterns that are consistent with that situation. The socialization process that occurs in this interaction is quite different than might take place in a family setting. The young learn that the appropriateness of behavior is judged in terms of its surveillance, that what is correct is not ethical behavior but behavior that wins that game.[37]

The Horizontal Dimension and Socialization by Agencies

Inquiries will be necessary around the issue of criminal justice interface with other organizations and informal units of the community that perform socialization functions. The evidence seems persuasive that criminal justice or juvenile justice apparatus for socialization have dramatically different results than socialization by family and informal groups, but we know little of the kind of interorganizational arrangements that may exist between agencies of justice and the more traditional auspices of socialization.

For example, it may be important to know about the interface between the police, juvenile probation, or juvenile residential centers and the families, peer groups, and schools in particular communities. Wilson's examination of police behavior is only suggestive in this regard. His examination of service style police agencies would suggest that the linkages between these police departments and families and schools in the community are quite different than the linkages present in agencies using legalistic or watchman styles.[38] Much of the difference Wilson attributes to the vertical and horizontal structures of the communities, although he does not use those terms. Service style policing tends to appear in communities with strong horizontal articulation, strong "we-feeling," and coincidence in authority structures. Civic leaders in these communities, who are also the politicians, expect the police to quell trouble by providing aid through informal channels. Hence, police engage actively the cooperation of school and family members in order to keep local juveniles in line. Toch, Grant, and Galvin suggest that similar linkages between police and families or social service units may emerge in larger, more heterogenous communities, but only with considerably more difficulty.[39] In instances where trouble and disruption is handled by referral and by working things through, the linkages established between criminal justice and non–justice community units in effect "simplify" the system, to use Mills's terminology.[40] A variety of informal pressures from various directions are all applied to the process of socialization. Consequently, social control and socialization are more difficult to distinguish, and the contradictory results that are often found in complex systems do not occur.[41]

Correctional linkages to the same units in the community may be equally important to the kind of socialization that takes place. Sullivan suggests that school officials may not place as much stigma on students with juvenile records, or be as quick to ask that they leave school, if the probation department is willing to work with school officials on problems of school discipline rather than acquiece to requests that troublesome students be kept out of school.[42] Similarly, Street, Vinter, and Perrow report significantly different attitudes by school officials toward youth in half-way house settings, depending on the relationship between the correctional agency and the schools.[43]

IMPACT OF CRIMINAL JUSTICE ON OTHER SOCIALIZATION AUSPICES

Besides those interorganizational arrangements that might directly involve a limited number of students as members of both community schools and criminal justice organizations, other relationships between school systems and criminal justice may be quite important. Some schools attempt to replicate the criminal justice apparatus within the school itself, perhaps only as a means of keeping order, but often under the assumption that students should learn the processes and issues involved in justice settings. My own high school, for example, had at one point a "dress court," in which elected student representatives were responsible for monitoring the dress code, holding hearings, and deciding on punishment. Inevitably, this procedure pitted the dominant middle-class youth in the enforcement and judicial positions against that small number of working-class youth who were the frequent offenders. While the system perhaps did not instruct either group of students in the value of fair procedure and deliberation, it did tend to instruct both groups about class differences. Jules Henry's classic work on the public school system, while not so specific as this, demonstrates quite well how the school system reflects or duplicates class and value conflicts that are also found in the criminal justice system.[44]

On another level, the intervention of criminal justice in the school systems had quite another set of outcomes. The increasing attention to due process in the criminal procedure has changed certain long-standing school procedures. School officials can no longer search student lockers at will and punish students for any contraband found therein. This is not to suggest that socialization would be aided by having the courts ignore the arbitrary and unilateral disciplinary procedures frequently found within the school. But it does serve to point out some fundamental conflicts between procedures appropriate to social control and procedures or relationships appropriate to informal socialization.

Finally, the criminal justice contribution to socialization requires examination of the symbolic, vicarious messages that the criminal justice system in a community may provide and how those messages may affect the quality of socialization in the community. We have already rejected the Moralist suggestion that the image of punishment institutionalized in the criminal justice system aids indirectly in the socialization process. That is, it is not necessary to utilize the existence of criminal justice, the stigma for criminal punishment, and related symbols as means of reinforcing informal socialization. In fact, reliance upon external punishment as a means of gaining compliance seems to be the result of ineffective socialization. Nevertheless, we do not know enough about the impact of criminal justice as portrayed on television, or the impact of a clearly corrupt police department, or the impact of a clearly discriminatory justice system upon a group's acceptance of norms, or upon a group's image of the community it lives in. It might also be important to investigate the effects of the conflicting images frequently cast by the criminal justice system: for example, the ideal of the adversary system cast against the now well-known practices of plea bargaining. In any event, it is likely that the criminal justice system will have different socialization functions in different communities. To the extent that these functions might be important, it would be foolhardy to alter criminal justice operations in accordance with a specific model of justice organization as opposed to judging performance in specified settings.

THE SOCIAL CONTROL FUNCTION

Warren's definition of social control is the processes taken by a group to ensure conformity with its norms. Yet he means by this something far more general than would be implied by the definitions of social control given by Welfare or Moralist forces in criminal justice circles. By norm, Warren apparently includes any form of standardized or patterned behavior. And he correctly assumes that maintaining order, or the capacity to structure behavior, is necessary if not synonymous with community living.[45] By and large, his conception of social control is *not* based upon an image of the criminal law or the agencies of criminal justice, although he argues that the location of these formal organizations within government justify treating units of government as the principal purveyors of social control, because their processes for social control include the use of ultimate coercion. But his example of a social control agency is not the police or the courts, or the criminal justice systems, but municipal government. In short, the essence of social control, for Warren, is not the application of criminal sanctions to individuals, but the managing of relationships among groups in a local area.

He is quick to point out that governmental units have many other functions beyond those of social control. A local government can finance and operate a swimming pool as an alternative to having this aspect of the entertainment economy conducted by a private organization. Local government is concerned with schools, welfare to families, licensing and vending, and so on. Governments are organizations, and, as such, they are usually multifunctional, as is the criminal justice system.

Socialization and Social Control Distinguished

An important aspect of social control within the community model is its distinction from the function of socialization. The need to make the distinction is clearly a concern to Warren, as he spends several pages on it and still probably fails to delineate the functions adequately. Part of the problem arises from the fact that socialization is in part the learning of norms, and that this learning process includes many techniques of norm enforcement. That is, some behaviors are rewarded and others are not until the individual is not only cognizant of what the norms are, but learns as well how to learn, so that he can adapt to new situations.

Some people attempt to distinguish, then, between socialization and social control by contrasting the internalization of norms (socialization) and the reaction to externally imposed limits (social control). This distinction is clearly inadequate, as it is virtually impossible to locate one set of controls as entirely outside the individual and another set that is or becomes totally internal.[46] Moreover, whether motivations are internal or external depends partially upon situation and partially upon culture and changes in it. What one set of people may do because it is consistent with their own conceptions of self, another set may do in order to gain esteem or prestige from others.[47]

Another part of the difficulty may be that social control, as distinct from socialization, is not always clearly evident in social groups. Anthropological investigations of primitive cultures and social investigations of small groups, and even of some communities, demonstrate that there are no social control processes or structures separate from the informal face-to-face ones that also are the main instrumentalities of socialization.[48] These studies, particularly those of Homans, but including Mills and Banton, would suggest that the term social control in these undifferentiated, simple, systems is perhaps synonymous with the idea of socialization. In any case, the processes are so similar in structure (informal and ad hoc) that they are difficult, if not impossible, to distinguish.

I have argued in Chapter 5 that one of the difficulties with current criminal justice theories is their application of the notion of social control as it might apply to simple societies and small groups to the complex situation of modern communities. Warren's model of community supports this contention. That is, Warren suggests that social control as a community function emerges when the elaboration of the social system (the community) includes a separation of informal group processes from formal group processes. In examining the consequences of this separation, Warren relies on a definition of social control propounded by Hollingshead when that scholar attempted to resuscitate the term in the 1940s. Hollingshead defined social control as the organization of a social group, as opposed to its means of handling crises situations such as crime.[49] Warren then argues that if social control can be conceived of as the order or organization of the social group, *it becomes a separate function only when that order is increasingly problematic, or when the tasks of survival are so completely differentiated that their various components must be coordinated.*[50] In effect, then, Warren is defining social control as the management of all other community-relevant functions. Hence, social control as "norm enforcement" more accurately describes activities and organizations in community that marshal the processes of production, socialization, social participation, and mutual support into a coherent pattern.

This point of view is entirely consistent with more recent studies of human organization as systems. For example, both Kuhn and Katz and Kahn suggest that the management function in formal organizations, as a distinct activity, emerges only as specialization of labor and socialization of persons into particular roles is sufficiently fractionated that integration of various subdivisions is necessary.[51] Within this framework, it is to be expected that our current knowledge about, technology for, and management of social order are not yet capable of providing the effective integration of other community-functional units. We are just beginning to examine in sophisticated fashion the processes required for the management of single formal organizations. Social control for communities is even less developed. Since social control is the last of the community functions to develop, we should expect that the capacity of our social systems to elaborate and divide far outstrips our capacity to control and coordinate this activity.

The images of totalitarian social control, perhaps epitomized in Orwell's *1984*, are, beyond being dystopias, inaccurate and inapplicable to the kinds of social control problems presented by a complex society. "States," in the sense of extremely centralized, omnipotent, and omniscient mechanisms of control, are unlikely to be effective as means of governing the kinds and amounts of variety that a complex social system can produce. Modern communities are, and probably should be, more concerned with the specter of total chaos, or entropy, than with the specter of overly rigid, bureaucratic, centralized governments.[52] The state, envisioned as radicals might, is a relatively primitive management form. It will break down before it is achieved. In this sense, a Marxian insistence on the inherent contradictions in the capitalist (or any other) state may have a certain allegorical accuracy, but probably none other. A more correct prediction of the evolution of the governing process of communities is probably provided in Kropotkin's description of the reemergence of village communities in Russia despite state attempts to efface them. Effective order was simply not possible from a centralized locus.[53] But neither should this suggestion evoke the strong fears usually associated with the mention of "anarchy." It is unlikely that we will enter, and probably inaccurate history to suspect that we have come from, a situation of "every man for himself." The evolution of social control, instead, most likely speaks of new forms of order, in which centralized and decentralized managements have joint and mutually supportive functions.

Social Control and The Community Axes

Within the community model, inquiries about the contribution of criminal justice should begin with an examination of the extent to which criminal justice agencies and their interaction assist in the maintenance of order, or organization, as Hollingshead used the term. That is, to what extent does the operation of criminal justice contribute to the integration of other locality-relevant functions?

Within this inquiry, we must remember that functional performance is somewhat dependent upon the structure, the vertical and horizontal dimensions, of particular community systems. Warren's model demonstrates succinctly that the same community functions are performed under different auspices as the axes of community change. We should also expect, then, that the functions performed by the *same* agencies may be quite different in communities with different horizontal and vertical dimensions.

The extent to which the criminal justice system has been studied within a broadly defined framework of the managerial function is quite deficient. The typical focus is on the system as it handles the offender, or specified groups of offenders, or potential criminals. There are no theoretical or empirically established linkages between this kind of activity and the management of community functions. About as close as most policy and research gets to the question is the current recognition that we know little about the general deterrent functions of the system. But as we have seen in

Chapters 2 and 4, the dominance of the Moralist group in the raising of this question means that we are always asking the wrong questions. Conceptualizations of deterrence and retribution simply end up refocusing the attention of research upon individual response to law and rule enforcement. This approach is totally inadequate to the definitions of individual, groups, communities, and community organization or management.[54]

On the theoretical level, the discussion of functional integration and criminal justice is sparse. The typical source is Parsons, or Katz and Kahn (following Parsons), both of whom suggest that these organizations take troublemakers out of the group so that the remaining group can continue to perform.[55] As we have said before, this notion of integration is inadequate to the kind of system a community is.[56] The most telling weakness in this approach is that the removal (as of a presumed pathology) fails to make the parts remaining "better integrated." The problems of inadequate management persist.[57]

The more promising approach begins with the assumption that the community is complex, differentiated, and conflicting. Beginnings in this direction have occurred in the police area. Reiss and Bordua, for example, discuss the police as a boundary-spanning mechanism, an organization whose task is the coordination of conflicting elements: "Unlike many organizations, however, the police have as their fundamental task the creation and maintenance of, and their participation in, external relationships. Indeed, the central meaning of police authority itself is its significance as a mechanism for managing relationships."[58] Some of the work of Wilson and Bittner is similar, to the extent that they emphasize containment, control, and the structuring of a behavioral ecology, rather than the police activity of apprehension, arrest, and sanctioning of individuals.[59]

Perhaps the greatest deficiency in the examination of the criminal justice system within the framework of social control as management is the absence of definitive material linking the coordinating or management function to the processes that occur because the agencies of justice (like other parts of government) are adaptive social structures in their own right, as well as being economies for the conduct of integration.[60] The study of this dual existence is important because communities are not single, complex organizations with a unified management. Thus the key question of the serious study of social control is: *What structural arrangements, if any, allow the managerial units of communities to retain the primacy of managerial or coordinating functions and spend the least amount of resources in the maintenance of their own system boundaries, or in the seeking of survival?*

Work on this question is just beginning. Elling and Halebsky suggest that we must focus on the influences exerted on public organizations by the nature of community stratification (or their values on the horizontal and vertical dimensions). They found that the community stratification system operated as an external constraint to which the organization had to adapt. Certain organizations become associated with certain levels in the hierarchy of statuses in the community. These differential associations with different community groups will associate the formal organization with one set of values rather than another, regardless of the overt goals of that organization.[61] For example, organizations obtain sponsorship from different loci on the vertical axis of community: "Sponsorship differentiates between organizations so as to associate them with elements of the community which have varying ability to channel support to the organization."[62] Hence, these associations with different levels of community power and authority will heavily determine both the extent to which the organization can obtain support from the environment, and the kinds of support it can seek. Elling and Halebsky found, for example, that various hospitals are associated with different types of patients, and this association significantly limits the kinds of services they can provide, the kinds of technology they can afford, as well as the kinds of evaluations they receive.[63]

In a study related to his recent work on urban reform, Warren extended this kind of analysis by dividing organizational community associations into two sets. He suggested that we must identify both input and output constituencies of organizations. The former will provide funding and influence goals, the latter will be the target for programs.[64] The disparity between these two constituencies varies considerably. In some kinds of business enterprise, and in some community governments, the two sets may be close to identical. But in many public organizations, the input constituency is found high on the vertical dimension and the output constituency is relatively low.

CRIMINAL JUSTICE AGENCIES AND SOCIAL CONTROL

Chambliss and Seidman attempt to apply this kind of analysis to criminal justice. Their book may be the only existing work that seeks to explore the social control function of criminal justice agencies from a perspective consonant with the community model. They propose that "rule creation and rule enforcement will take place when such creation or enforcement increase the rewards for the agencies and their officials, and they will not take place when they are conducive to organizational strain."[65] They then suggest that the criminal law and its implementation will differentially reflect the perspectives, values, and definitions of reality of upper classes and not be responsive to the values and end of the lower classes because of the distribution of these classes into the input and output constituencies.[66] Studies by Geis and Cavanaugh, Piliavin, Rokeach, and many others confirm this thesis.[67]

The problems with analyzing criminal justice as contributing to the social control function is that even most analysis that take the managerial perspective of social control stops at this point, as Chambliss and Seidman do. It is not sufficient to demonstrate discriminations in the system nor even to reinterpret discrimination as externally imposed constraint. We must go on to ask why these things happen and what can be done, if anything, to change them.

Of particular importance in this context is the examination of the processes that occur as reactions to the differential constituencies, both on the issue of what happens to the technologies of management and what happens to the organizations that are supposed to manage because they are also adaptive social systems. For example, the recognition of differential makeup and power among input and output constituencies is not, in itself, problematic. Problems are observed when this differentiation is seen as improper, ineffective, or both. Wilson suggests that it is change in the perceived effectiveness and propriety of the constraints of police operations that has led to current police problems: "The fact that the police can no longer take for granted that non-criminal citizens are also non-hostile citizens may be the most important problem which even the technologically proficient department must face."[68] Wilson argues that it is this problem, not the original limitations on police practice themselves, that leads the police to devalue public opinion and to rely instead on internal sources of morale and internal criteria of effectiveness.[69] Banton's analysis of police reaction to outside challenge is similar.[70]

Left unanswered, however, are questions concerning the limitations on the criminal justice management repertoire that results from this internal focus. Are concerns for the deterrent, retributive, and rehabilitative actions in criminal justice primarily internally selected technologies, or is this limitation to concentration on both negative sanctions and individuals a constraint imposed from some remaining, external source?

While many commentators, such as Lerman, suggest that this concentration is primarily an internal one,[71] other writers leave room for doubt. For example, McIntyre writes: "When administrators and officials of public and quasi-public organizations were asked about the most effective remedies for crime, they suggested the amelioration of social conditions far more frequently than did members of the general public."[72] Hence an unanswered question is whether the ineffective and minor role played by criminal justice in management, or coordination, of community functions is a result of the limited technologies that these organizations select as they close off from conflicting external constituencies, or whether it is a result of limitations in repertoire imposed by some external groups regardless of the potential of these agencies for more creative managerial action.

Chapter 10

Criminal Justice Functions in Various Settings— Social Participation and Mutual Support

SOCIAL PARTICIPATION FUNCTION

The fourth locality-relevant function is that of social participation. Warren sees this function as crucial to the continuation of the concept of community to sociological analysis, because it is participation, and particularly voluntary participation, that maintains for groups the importance of their geographical closeness as a determinant of when and how they interact.[1] Yet Warren finds that even this function of providing individuals with access to joint and voluntary activities and providing a sense of mutual belonging has been influenced heavily by bureaucratization, urbanization, and industrialization. Even voluntary associations for civic improvement, entertainment, and friendship have become formalized in this century, so that just as one joins an organization in order to earn a living, one now joins an association such as a country club, church, or a health campaign in order to retain a sense of primary group interaction and belonging.

A variety of studies have demonstrated that associations of all types in American communities have become more stratified in membership and narrower in purpose. Persons with higher education and higher economic status more frequently are joiners than people with lesser economic means and less education. As American society has become stratified economically, and the division of labor has become more specialized, people have begun to travel farther in order to participate in groups that are relevant to them. And frequently, these groups are attached to causes that have specialized national or regional significance. It is rare these days for everyone in a community to associate informally in the same marketplace, send their children to the same school, and to attend the same church.

Warren argues that the lowering of social participation or its restriction to only some social strata is related to a lowered general sense of personal effectiveness in regard to public issues. Spitzer relates a reduction in social participation to the centralization of civic action. Growth of the state, he argues, led to subordination of the local community, or to reduction of the belief that individual well-being is related to the mutual well-being of all others in a particular area. Centralized government tends to become the only bond of union among loose aggregations of individuals.[2] Warren suggests that increased stratification has meant a divergence between mutual interest and propinquity. There is no longer a common culture and a common set of problems facing people who live fairly close to each other.[3]

Warren's example of a social unit providing one of the greatest amounts of social participation in modern communities is the church, defined broadly as any type of religious association. He points out that most church groups today are fairly autonomous in relation to each other but fairly dependent upon sectarian or denominational relationships that extend across communities. Thus even if church membership provides a greater sense of participation in a primary group than other secondary associations, this participation is far narrower and specialized than elementary communal religions, which, according to Durkheim, were almost synonomous with the sense of community itself.[4]

While the lessened sense of community participation is extremely important to analysis of modern community, the trend toward splintering and specialization can be overemphasized. Some types of trend analysis would suggest that all expansions reach their own limits, at which point they are either reversed, or a new dynamic shows predominance in structuring relationships.[5]

Grozdins would argue that the centralization of government and its impact on participation of a public nature have always been overemphasized. His incisive analysis of the local orientation of both state and federal governments provides a strong counterpoint to those who suggest that government is increasingly distant from local determination.[6] Wood's analysis of suburban communities also dampens the emphasis on the inexorable nature of the externalization of both community governance and community participation. But Wood's analysis adds a new dimension that Grozdins, taken alone, tends to miss. Wood suggests that the city of 1950, with its suburbs, has fewer characteristics of centralization and mass society than the Victorian city of 1850. Suburbia demonstrates massive urban sweep, perhaps, but also shows considerably more decentralization and segmentation than community organizations of the past.[7] "The essential qualities for the grass roots faith—propinquity, homogeneity, a special kind of interdependence, a disposition to democratic participation in the Western tradition—shows signs of flowering again."[8] But this new flowering, Wood staunchly insists, is not a reversion to some earlier time, but a synthesis of small town independence and large-scale organization and positive, professional government.[9]

On a very different plane, Geoffrey Vickers cogently writes that the prime difficulty with modern institutions, particularly economic ones, is that they are incapable of handling a cultural shift from emphasis on achievement to emphasis on belonging and membership.[10] He suggests that current strain in industrialized societies such as England and the United States is not simply a product of the fact that satisfactory welfare of all can no longer be achieved in proportion to the contribution of each individual. It is more accurate to state that the definitions of social worth and contribution are changing, as it is recognized that the well-being of the best-off depends upon improvement in the social conditions of the worst-off. Thus Vickers concludes that a sense of membership in community, rather than contribution of achievement in a narrow segment of life, is becoming increasingly important in determining both the right of association and participation and in the quality of the outcomes of associations.

CRIMINAL JUSTICE AND SOCIAL PARTICIPATION

These trends are visible in the operation of criminal justice systems in several respects. Even one of the most centralized aspects of criminal justice policy and administration, the Law Enforcement Assistance Administration, has changed in the ten years of its existence from attempting to remake all criminal justice operations of all communities along one version of "correct" procedures and practices to rather explicitly accommodating local differences and local needs. Perhaps one of the best examples of this sort of change is visible in the alteration of the perception of the President's Commission on Law Enforcement and the Administration of Justice as providing a blueprint for action to the status of the National Advisory Commission on Criminal Justice Standards and Goals as providing guidelines that were to be modified at every level of government before locally enforceable standards could be enunciated. This change from federal prescription of change to federal facilitation of locally determined change is of course only partial. Some observers may feel that the change, particularly as relevant to the process of standards and goals, is more adequately described as local resistance to needed change. But in any event, it is demonstration that policy, at least in that instance, was not to be dictated in concert with ideology and program models that were incongruent with existing differences in political orientation and practice.

Even so, this change from federal enunciation of policy to some interdependent action between centralized and decentralized units of decision-making is probably more limited to a change in interorganizational relations among existing criminal justice agencies than it is a change in the auspice under which criminal justice activity takes place. Even criminal justice standards and goal activity at the "local level" was to a large degree dominated by the perceptions and authority of the established agencies rather than by new coalitions of local power.

The extent to which criminal justice provides access on the local level for the function of social participation is quite limited. But analysis of this function lags behind the analysis of other criminal justice activities. The most immediate impacts can probably be grouped into three areas: definitions of membership, including enunciation of civil rights, dramaturgical effects of public ritual, and avenues of voluntary association within criminal justice programs.

Definitions of Membership

The function, in relation to membership, is visible in several regards. Probably most important is appellate court leadership in the elaboration of citizenship rights that adhere regardless of status as a defendant or an offender. The "due process revolution" is more accurately analyzed as a revolution in the understanding of what characteristics of individuals are relevant to their inclusion in political groups than as a revolution in criminal justice procedure. In fact, it is probably only as decisions about rights affect the understanding of legitimacy and political association that they can be called revolutionary. Actual operating procedures of agencies have changed only a little in respect to any particular decision. Thus, these are not operating policy decisions so much as they are statements explicating cultural values and norms.

As such, due process decisions have often mistakenly been analyzed in relation to their impact on social control, on which their impact is actually either neutral or contradictory. If social control is the organization of a people that leads to obedience of norms, due process changes may be seen to have increased, rather than to have reduced, social control. But they are relevant to protecting norms of belonging, membership, and personal worth (that is the positive side of freedom) rather than norms proscribing particular crimes. Were this not so, the interest in protection afforded by rights would be irrelevant after conviction, unless one was concerned with prosecution of a convict for a new crime. That is, if the due process rationale rested on the accuracy of decisions produced by an adversarial process, they would be salient no longer, once a decision of guilt had been reached, or if an unfair procedure was demonstrably accurate (as many illegal searches may show themselves to be). This is perhaps the greatest fault in Packer's analysis of due process: while he begins by stressing the relationship between membership and the recognition of rights, he finally likens the due process safeguards in the criminal process to those of quality control mechanisms in a factory assembly line process. This quality control aspect of appellate review might of course be important, but it remains irrelevant to definitions of membership, belonging, and association of individuals as persons in a common community. An effective crime control process, irrespective of its concern for an individual's worth as a member of community, could conceivably have a high interest in quality control merely for the sake of ascertaining that the real culprits were caught. And certainly, many procedures could provide such accuracy without recourse to exclusionary rules or like mechanisms of enforcing norms about individual worth.[11]

To the extent that accuracy rather than membership was the crucial concern to due process, we would find that the correctional system, which contains only offenders who have been judged to have violated some community norms, would be relatively autonomous from the applications of due process. Correctional agencies have been, of course, the last area of judicial intervention, probably because in this area the concerns over accuracy of procedure and fairness of procedure can be most dramatically separated: "The traditional self-definition of powers and function in correction is that, once an offender has been convicted and sentenced . . . (he) may make *requests* not *demands*; he may be accorded *privileges* but he has no *rights*. . . ."[12] Yet this hands-off doctrine regarding the rights of convicted offenders has been modified if not repealed. Interestingly, the offenders' rights first protected in practice were those that were not clearly associated with the administration of corrections, but went directly to the notion of the offender as a citizen. Thus correctional practice that interfered with the practice of religion and practices of correctional discipline that failed rudimentary standards of health and hygiene were some of the first to be challenged.[13] As the consideration of rights narrowed to questions of liberty, the courts were slower to intervene, and the correctional administrations more recalcitrant. And as could be expected, delineation of which rights of offenders, regarding their concern for liberty, remained after a legal conviction had been achieved, appeared first in the area of delayed sentencing, then in probation and parole, and only recently as it might relate to good time loses or solitary confinement for offenders who are imprisoned already.[14]

John Griffiths's major article challenging the validity of Packer's analysis of due process in criminal justice focuses directly on these issues. Griffiths challenges Packer's inattention to correctional process, pointing out that certain rights are not lost after the presumption of innocence no longer protects the guilty party. Instead, a totally separate rationale for treating offenders (or anyone else) with fairness and propriety, and for minimizing the scope of state intervention, is based upon the idea that individuals have ongoing claims on membership in the social system and must be treated in a manner commensurate with that continuing membership.[15]

Dramaturgical Effects

A second area where the criminal justice system can be seen as contributing to the function of social participation is the dramatic one. The trial and related formal proceedings of the criminal process can provide a symbolic, vicarious form of participation for citizens in a community undertaking. The value of this dramatic contribution is probably minimal under current circumstances. Most criminal cases do not proceed by way of trial, and the frequency of vicarious participation in determinations of guilt and innocence has been relegated to the occasional infamous offender or celebrated cause. The criminal troubles of Spiro Agnew, Patty Hearst, and the Chicago Seven probably provide some evidence that community opinion and sense of participation can still be marshaled by the system in extreme circumstances. (Although none of these particular cases provided any sense that justice was done.)

Nieburg argues that the criminal justice system can help to unify the community through its portrayal of community norms challenged and upheld: "The legal process may be viewed as a set of unifying myths which serve a wide range of uses, including those of a theater in the round, a circumambient divertimento that dramatizes and gives meaning to our lives, even if it lies a little."[16] Packer presents a similar case for the criminal justice process as a means of dramatizing community:

> The ritual of the criminal trial becomes for all of us a kind of psychodrama in which we participate vicariously, a morality play in which innocence is protected, injury requited, and the wrongdoer punished. . . . These public rituals . . . strengthen the identification of the majority with a value system that places a premium on law-abiding behavior.[17]

The problem with this contribution of criminal justice is that, if it once did what Packer suggests, it now seems often to do the opposite. Even if we could locate a "majority," it is doubtful that the current dramatization of the criminal justice operation's highlights a premium on law-abiding behavior. The other question is what the same ritual dramatization does for the minority (or minorities) who might be watching. The problem, which Packer misses, Nieburg understands: simply the messages dramatized in the formal criminal procedure have these reinforcing effects only to a point and only when the two or more components, given the same information, act in the same ways about it.[18] Or to paraphrase Nieburg, perhaps the drama visibly lies too often.

Association with Agencies

There are, of course, ways in which the criminal justice system can open avenues for face-to-face rather than vicarious participation. Witnessing an important trial, for example, may once have been an important community event. Participating as a jury member may also have been seen as a civic duty. It is rare these days if ordinary citizens take time off from other pursuits to watch a trial, and it is unlikely that there is space in the courtroom for the few that do. As for citizens' participation in the trial process, the system simply has not found a way to treat witnesses or prospective jurors with efficiency or consideration. And the requirement to participate is now often seen as a personal nuisance rather than a public duty.

On the other hand, other forms of participation are expanding. Within the last ten years, a variety of opportunities for voluntary assistance in both the police and correctional areas have opened up.[19] The influx of volunteers into police and correctional work have brought with it the expected conflicts over professional autonomy, volunteer inexperience, overzealousness, and lack of commitment. But in some instances, voluntary participation in criminal justice might raise in new forms the question of whether social control functions need to be performed under the auspice of formal state agencies. Another question that it might raise is the extent to which the actions of participation change the perceptions of volunteers about membership, rights, and group boundaries. Does volunteering in criminal justice self-select only those persons who are most tolerant or liberal, or does the act of participating alter the volunteer's conception of the offender in relation to community? A particularly important avenue of investigation in this regard would be those programs that seek a voluntary commitment from victims to work out a program of restitution with the offender.

THE MUTUAL SUPPORT FUNCTION

It is over its contribution to the mutual support function that much of the current controversy in criminal justice comes to a head. That is, can agencies who must provide some forms of social control also provide services in times of trouble? Yet the controversy and the apparent dilemmas of service and control under one source have rarely been framed within the community function model. Hence, the punishment/treatment argument is sometimes couched in language that would suggest that services and retribution are alternative means to the same end, that of social control.[20] At other times, critics have raised the question in terms of whether the correctional system can serve political and educational functions simultaneously. For example, Katz and Kahn analyze prisons as contributing either to socialization through reeducation or to social control by isolating offenders and hence integrating the remaining members of a community.[21]

It is not clear, however, that conflicts in the criminal justice system arise only out of disagreement about means of controlling deviant actors or only out of placing priority on resocialization rather than incapacitation. Indeed, as the discussion on socialization and social control has demonstrated, socialization and social control are closely associated anyway. Application of the community model suggests that there is another perspective that may shed some light on the controversy in criminal justice. Examination of criminal justice activity in terms of locality-relevant functions suggests that much time and a great many resources are expended in providing mutual support. Much of this activity can be justified on grounds independent of whether or not effective socialization or social control is also thus provided.

Warren presents the local, voluntary health association as a unit typical of mutual support on the local level. He suggests that such units of community are horizontally articulated with other health and non–health activities on the local level through community councils, and they are usually organized vertically in association with a national health organization. His analysis demonstrates that provision of help in crisis or unusual situations has become an increasingly bureaucratized activity in both the public and the private sectors and that, in addition, these units of mutual support have become increasingly specialized in one type of problem.[22] Kropotkin would add to these generalizations that aid-giving has become stratified, the rich aiding the rich and the poor taking care of their own. He would stress that in the modern community there is too little of mutual interest among classes to facilitate sharing across class boundaries.[23]

Many writers have stressed the dysfunctional aspects of bureaucratization and specialization in the area of service provision. It is not always clear whether they are complaining about social service activity that is guided or provided by agents who are accountable to some extra-community authority, or whether they are simply ranting against the size and complexity of some social service undertakings, even if they are run by local agencies. At any rate, many complaints are heard about the inefficiencies and the sense of powerlessness and anonymity introduced into social service provision when the delivery provider is some form of government. Perhaps the following statement is typical:

> Government is best when it is mostly in the community. In handling relief, health, sanitation, police and safety, local management calls for the participation of community members or their local representatives . . . . To whatever extent is feasible, the functions of government should remain in the hands of those immediately affected—in the community.[24]

What such comments fail to address is that there can be no easy answer to what "in the community" means. There are certainly many examples, racial prejudice in the South being just one, in which state or federal representatives might be more characteristic of all the constituencies on the local level than some of the local governments. We cannot dismiss all state and federal government programs as being non-local in character any more than we can generalize that all municipal or county governments are responsive to or capable of handling the needs of all the people within their jurisdictions.

Nor should we dismiss out of hand, as is often done in the criminal justice area, the potential of public rather than private voluntary services. Private philanthropy is often as bureaucratized as public social services and often geared to a more specific clientele. In some instances, public, governmental provision of mutual support may be the most feasible plan of action.

MUTUAL SUPPORT BY CRIMINAL JUSTICE

Questions will and should arise whether criminal justice agencies should be engaged in service provision in addition to their other functions. That is, perhaps another public auspice is more effective, or cheaper, or has a better handle on what the needs of particular groups happen to be. However, many instances of mutual support by the criminal justice system go unchallenged by even the most rigorous critics of the system. In these areas, the question may not be whether the criminal justice system should be providing services, but how it can organize to provide such services more quickly and more effectively. Some instances are reported in research that appear to suggest that criminal justice agencies not only *should* provide a particular service, but that they actually provide more effective and more comprehensive service than the known or planned alternatives can promise.

Probably the area of service provision in which there is the least question of criminal justice domain legitimacy is that of general crisis service provision by the police. Wilson and others have found that a large majority of police-civilian contact is categorizable as service provision.[25] This service activity remains large and important even when simple requests for information and regulatory duties such as traffic patrol are excluded. It is a simple fact that the police are often the first outside party on the scene, and frequently the only service-providing agency operating on a twenty-four-hour basis. Social agency officials riding experimentally with police in Oakland, California, observed that the police not only handled personal problems when these were at their most difficult stage, but that the police actually dealt with types of problems and classes of people with problems that the nine-to-five service agencies rarely saw.[26]

Most recommendations concerning police activity in this area involve not divesting the police of responsibility but training the police, or special police units, so they can deal with service calls more effectively and more quickly.[27] Much of this training involves imparting to police officers the skills they need to diagnose crisis behavior, intervene effectively, and provide appropriate follow-up. But a new form of program in this area is somewhat different. For example, the San Diego Community Profile Project, funded by the Police Foundation, had as its objectives the expansion of the police officer role, establishing new ways that the police could offer service to the community, and systematizing their ability to provide referrals as well as direct service.[28] Toch, Grant, and Galvin offer similar examples from a program in Oakland in which not only were police skills enhanced, but interorganizational linkages among community groups, service agencies, and the police were changed, with the goal that the police would have a broader social service role.[29] In other words, mutual support in the police area is not merely progressing on the level of enabling the police officer to conduct individual interventions more effectively; it is also progressing in that the organizational domain of the police organization in the mutual support area is expanding.[30] This development offers stark contrast to current trends in the correctional area, where the challenges to correctional service provision are serious.

Beyond discussions of mutual support to an undifferentiated public, criminal justice provides services to some rather special clienteles. Before we discuss two of these in some detail, it is important to point out that the classification of any person in need of service is difficult and always somewhat arbitrary. While both victims and offenders as client groups may present some special problems, we should always be aware that denotation of persons as victims or offenders does not always tell us very much about their problems or their needs for services.

Police activity in the area of service delivery is quite likely to engage persons who at some other time (or with a narrower repertoire of problem-solving skills by the police at the instant time of intervention) would be treated as offenders rather than as persons in need of service. The Oakland study relates many instances in which the police might have responded through the invocation of the criminal sanction rather than through talking a crisis through, or by providing referral to a service agency. A variety of new police programs, such as training in the handling of family disputes and transportation or referral of alcoholics to detoxification and treatment programs suggest the ambiguity of many events calling for some response to trouble. Utilization of the criminal sanction is often only one possibility.

The perception of the police as service providers does not seem to diminish the police sphere of action. It only changes outcomes in particular cases. That the police need not and often should not resort to the negative sanctions of the criminal process is quite apparent. "The image of the police officers must be radically changed to consider that as a part of the broad category of occupations which deal with people who are sometimes difficult to handle."[31] Yet the implications of this trend for the image of criminal justice, particularly for planning purposes, is not known. We know, for example, that a police officer's response in ambiguous situations is often determined by the criteria of evaluation that he perceives to be most relevant, whether those be formal sanctions by the department or informal approval or castigation by fellow officers. Police utilization of service response therefore goes up when the police department rewards and the locker room culture does not punish helpful rather than law-invoking behavior. But we do not know how many persons who are served rather than arrested therefore do not become offenders at some other time. In any event, it is difficult to integrate the recent trends in police work to emphasize service with the trends in the correctional area to emphasize punishment, particularly since the people propounding the second trend often treat the police as the frontpiece of the criminal justice system. It is difficult to make sense out of the notion that crimes should be treated equally and the condition of the offender should be separated from consideration of punishment when at the same time the police are apparently demonstrating the accuracy of the statement that crimes are not simply events but also official decisions on how to handle events.

Support for Victims

One type of person in need who is of particular concern to the criminal justice system is the victim of crime. It has long been complained that the system provides too little concern, let alone service, to the victim. And we have seen in the last few years considerable increase in interest in victimization as well as in ways that the system can allow the victim to participate in the criminal process. Of course, there are many other service providers who may be concerned with victims, including insurance companies, family, church, counseling services, lawyers, and medical agencies. It has often been argued that since the crime is committed against the state, the criminal justice system is not concerned with the welfare or the attitudes of the victim. But as the study of victimization increases, we are learning that the effectiveness of crime prevention may often be greater if it concentrates on victims and potential victims rather than on offenders. An interesting study in Washington, D.C., also discovered that persons once involved with the system as defendants often reappear as witnesses and victims. In other words, the populations that may play these different roles are not distinct.[32]

One kind of service that the criminal justice system can provide to victims is restitution for crime. This practice is not new. Many probationary dispositions have included orders for restitution. And many offenders and some probation officers complain that the chief aspect of the probation officer's role is that of collection agent. But of the newer restitution programs, perhaps the most innovative aspect is the greater participation provided for the victim in both the amount of and means of making restitution. In some programs, the victim sits down with the offender in a session to deliberate how restitution will be made.[33] Such programs bring out in a new context the ancient tradition that the offender was responsible for correcting the trouble he had caused. In some societies, victims of murder were replaced by the offenders, who were adopted by the families of the victims and had to carry out the victims' obligations and roles.[34]

The new concern with victims, and the police impetus in the service area, should again caution us not to limit the conception of the criminal justice system to the narrow one of how effectively and quickly it can apply negative sanctions to offenders. Of course, we are more or less relegated to that narrow conception the more we become convinced that the criminal justice system can base its authority of intervention simply or only on the adjudication of guilt. If this is so, then we are constrained to planning for and evaluating punishments to offenders. But this point of view makes it difficult to predict or explain why the various components of the system seem to engage in many other sorts of action that are totally unrelated to the application of negative sanctions.

Services to Offenders

This brings us to the second type of special client: offenders as receivers of mutual support. Regardless of whether the provision of service is in any way related to reducing recidivism to the commission of the crime for which the offender has been incarcerated, it is undeniable that a majority of offenders come from that portion of the population that has a wide variety of frequent and chronic problems, ranging from poor physical condition to many sorts of social disabilities such as poor education and lack of vocational skills, to emotional and psychological problems. In the past, many correctional service programs have been justified, at least in public statements of correctional objectives, on the grounds that provision of service to offenders will enhance the prospects for reducing future crime by these offenders. That is, provision of mutual support has been justified on its social control potential.

There is, however, little data to suggest that provision of service to offenders is successful, or that provision of successful services leads in turn to reduction in recidivism. Based on these findings, we reach conclusions such as: "With few and isolated exceptions, the rehabilitative efforts that have been reported so far have had no appreciable effect on recidivism."[35] While Martinson's evaluation of correctional programs is replete with methodological and logical fallacies,[36] the entire controversy concerning whether or not correctional treatment programs are effective misses the main issue: that many offenders, regardless of how they are to be punished (unless they are executed) also need many problem solution strategies in order to survive in accordance with even relatively meager expectations about the quality of life. Data showing that offenders are also often victims, or, given another approach by the police department, perhaps not involved in the criminal process anyway, suggest that service provision to persons in need has both a set of technologies and an ethical justification completely separate from the impact of service provision on the quality of social control. We do not include in a hospital admission interview questions pertaining to whether the fixing of a broken leg or the suturing of a wound will reduce the chances that the patient will or will not commit crime in the future. We do not generally consider whether provision of food and clothing to the poor will be instrumental in quelling revolt. One asks instead if it is needed.

The attachment of promises about crime control or recidivism reduction to the issue of service provision to offenders has perhaps had several detrimental effects on the criminal justice system. The common complaint currently, of course, is that it makes treatment or service provision a sham by requiring offenders to accept help in order to reduce their punishment. But perhaps the more crucial problem is that it has raised societal expectations that the mutual support function and the social control function are positively related, in the short run, and that all offers of help to those in need should be repaid by them, in the short run. In other words, social ethics has been replaced by manipulation for utilitarian gain.

The difficulty, of course, is that the second problem is related to the first. It is doubtful that offenders would be coerced into service acceptance without this broader cultural belief that problem solution should have payoff for the providers, in terms more tangible than gratification for having helped. And this raises the chicken-egg problem. Has corrections sold a bill of goods to the political constituencies that fund correctional agencies, or have these constituencies demanded this type of alleged payoff in order to fund any helping programs at all? There are probably no ultimate answers to this question, although some data suggest that (1) a variety of publics exist with different attitudes toward this question, but (2) in general, public respondents seem able to separate issue of service from issues of punishment.[37] One problem is that publics are often not given a choice: they are asked to opt for punishment *or* service provision, or to place priorities on the social control and the mutual support functions. This situation places community groups in a forced choice situation relative to correctional policy that does not accurately map the community structure in which they generally participate. In communities, *both* social control and mutual support are necessary.

On another level, the question of whether service provision and social control effectiveness are or must be inextricably linked disappears. That is, how can correctional agencies, or other public organizations as well, perform social control and mutual support functions at the same time? To the extent that policy and programmatic changes can make both functions more accomplishable, the apparent dilemma is explained as an aspect of unsophisticated managerial practice.

Managing Services and Control

Research on the effectiveness of mutual support in correctional agencies is lacking, and a great deal of ground will have to be covered before we can ascertain which linkages between mutual support and social control are most effective for the performance of either function. At this point, correctional policy is in a stage of significant revision, with the decoupling of mutual support and punishment as a key ingredient in the deliberations. New program formulations, however, are slow to emerge, and discussion tends to hover about two issues which may not be the crucial ones. On the one hand there is now a concern that separating punishment, or length of sentence, from participation in services is more ethical, or more honest. On the other, there seems to be an assumption that service provision will be more effective if it is delivered by persons who are not also engaged in punishment. There is some suggestion also that punishment will be more effective if it is not confounded with treatment issues and technologies. But some of the persons arguing for separation of functions tend to speak as if punishment is immune to criteria of effectiveness. That is, punishment is to be evaluated only in the sense that punishment is correctly imposed on those who do wrong. If retribution is all that the correctional system is asked to deliver, whether punished criminals commit new crimes is irrelevant.

At any rate, the first two concerns, (1) that separating punishment and service provision will be more honest, and (2) that service provision will be more effective if provided under separate auspices, are notions that warrant discussion and research. Whether or not punishment independent of service provision is an ethical advance probably depends upon the other side of the question. Is there an implicit statement in this argument that service provision can be ignored? It might certainly be said that service provision is more honest if its acceptance is not forced by making it an alternative to punishment. Yet many of the new programs that are based on the manifest purpose of separating the two functions do not in fact make the separation. For example, many diversion programs, such as probation without conviction, simply twist the service and punishment relationship around, pushing the offender to accept treatment services as an alternative to conviction rather than as a means of reducing length of incarceration. Thus one is merely raising the specter of punishment in prison as the club by which to enforce service reception rather than raising as the club the discretion of the parole board.[38] Hence some programs do not remove the dishonesty from the correctional system, they merely move its consequences from inside the prison to field services, or from intraorganizational locus to interorganizational locus.

The second problem is that many correctional reforms that include separation of services from punishment determination assume that other organizations are more competent to provide services and that therefore the services provided to offenders by these organizations will be more effective. This assumption thus ignores many instances of research that show social service programs in general have at least doubtful effectiveness. Moreover, the suggestions for separation often ignore the problems of making services to offenders accessible, once separation takes place. Not dealt with, for example, is the fact that service provision under correctional auspices provides offenders with a monopoly on services so provided. Alternative forms of accessibility are not usually discussed.

One set of research activities involving halfway houses for adult male felons in Pennsylvania shed some light on the issue of alternative service provision mechanisms, as well as upon types of offender problems. Duffee, Meyer, and Warner reported that problems of offenders reentering the community from prison could be categorized into three broad classes: hard problems such as transportation, clothing, location of a job, and finding sufficient financial resources to finance the first few weeks on the street; soft problems such as adjustments with family, or the expressed desire to talk things through with somebody; and problems related to correctional supervision status, such as associating with other offenders or dealing with the conflicts between job schedules and the curfew rules of the halfway house.[39] Each set of problems appeared to have relatively distinct problem solution mechanisms. Most of the hard problems that reached resolution were attacked through dependence on another agency. In contrast, most soft problems that reached resolution were approached informally rather than through dependence on any agency. Finally, most center-related problems, if resolved prior to release from supervision, were solved through some deliberation between the offender and the correctional agency staff.[40] The study concluded, in part, that correctional agencies were more competent to handle some problems than others, that greater discrimination had to be used in assessing both problems and needs themselves and in assessing the solutions available, and that the service role of correctional agents might be more effective if it concentrated on building interorganizational linkages rather than in direct service delivery.[41]

This study and a few others like it[42] also point out, however, that many offender problems are not fixed, once and for all, regardless of the problem solution mechanism used. Many offenders fall into that class in which, under present conditions, situations such as unemployment and lack of money are recurrent experiences regardless of instant service delivery quality. We will probably not shed much light upon the relationship between mutual support activity and social control until systematic researches are conducted on the social problem profile of the offender over a long period of time rather than at one point in time, in which the comparison group is nonoffenders rather than other offenders.

Public Service Delivery

A final point I wish to raise relative to the mutual support function of criminal justice agencies is relatively independent of the social control function that also might be performed. That is, what are the characteristics of service provision within the context of public organizations? Are some dynamics operating in the organizational context that reduce or impede service delivery that are independent of the extent to which the agency happens to be also an organization of punishment? Why is it that many service problems in health, welfare, and mental health appear to be quite similar to those in correction, regardless of the fact that these other agencies are not constrained by the fact that they also administer the criminal sanction? Some observers would respond that these similarities simply demonstrate that all such organizations are involved to a large degree in social control, and that in almost all cases the provision of service is a means to accomplish control rather than a means to reduce suffering, inadequacy, or inadequate opportunity. This is, of course, a strong possibility, particularly since the evidence is convincing that most organizations have multiple functions for community. Nevertheless, this point of view should not be adopted unless other explanations of service ineffectiveness can be explained away.

The alternative explanation would focus on the processes of organizations as they expand to achieve certain tasks or objectives of a problem-solving variety, that is, to contribute to some community function, while at the same time maintaining themselves as stable entities. Selznick's classic formulation of the problems is provided in four propositions:

1. Bureaucracies delegate functions in a cooperative effort to accomplish an overall objective;
2. The act of delegation leads to bifurcation of interest between the delegator and his agents;
3. This bifurcation leads both to issues of control of the internal organization as well as to the informal structure of the organization,
4. Which results in the problem that the basic operational problems for the organization increasingly become those of internal stability and their solutions, so that organizational elaboration is better explained in terms of the internal relevance of these actions than in terms of the professed goals of the system.[43]

In brief, if it is true that within the nature of complex organizations community functions and organizational maintenance become bifurcated, then part of the problem with service delivery in correction (and other parts of the criminal justice system) is related not to functional conflict but to organizational structure, and that problem might remain even if the supposed conflict between custody or punishment and treatment or service delivery were removed.

But the alternative answer on this level is of course incomplete. It is not sufficient to elaborate on the processes of complex organizations, or bureaucracies as a special case, in order to explain the ineffectiveness of service delivery. Another angle must be introduced that concerns the technology of the services, and the nature of the problems to be solved, within the organizational context.

The theorist who has probably done the most in this regard is Charles Perrow. He attempts to explain organizational structural differentiation in terms of the service tasks to be performed. He suggests that action in organizations engaged in human problems must account for the variations with which the organization involves the client. Whether the organizational action on behalf of the client will be routine or nonroutine depends upon whether the organization treats the client as highly variable or relatively uniform and stable, and whether the problems presented by clients are well understood or not well understood.[44] Coupled with Selznick's principles regarding delegation of tasks and resulting maintenance problems, Perrow's analysis would suggest that organizational approaches to clients (and therefore the kinds of problems the organization is both responsive to and competent to handle) depend on whether the technology of the helping process is at all compatible with the informal organizational structure that results from delegation of authority and resulting split interest on the part of workers and supervisors. Some couplings of managerial control strategies vis-à-vis subordinates may not be commensurate with the roles that staff should play with clients, if client problems are to be solved.[45]

Examples of the resulting inefficiencies for service delivery because of conflicts between organizational maintenance needs and service delivery technology are frequent. Lerman's analysis of the California Community Treatment Program led him to conclude that the organizational actions were dominated by the need to control staff toward demonstrating program success rather than helping clients.[46] McCleary reviews the problems that parole officer discretion presents for the political survival of the organizations, and concludes that helping activities are sacrificed to reputation building.[47] Similarly, Fogel finds that prison treatment programs are structured in order to maintain an organizational climate rather than to alter behavior of offenders.[48]

Chapter 11

Criminal Justice Reform in the Context of Social Change

The model of community that I have used examines the functional requisites for groups' survival and the changes in the level or quality of these functions that occur as community structure changes. The examination of criminal justice operations in various settings would suggest that this "system" of agencies may contribute in various ways to several community functions, and that the contributions made tend to vary, depending on (1) the level of authority at which decisions are made and resources distributed, and (2) the extent to which the agencies are integrated with other types of community activity. These conclusions have been drawn, as much as possible, from empirical accounts of various criminal justice agencies. These many empirical enquiries have been ordered here in a rather new fashion—the community model suggests an order and relevancy of what would be diverse observations if those observations were catalogued within more traditional frameworks. But even to the extent that I have succeeded in providing some coherence to these data within this framework, the accomplishment has been no more than to suggest a potential of a new angle of vision.

But should this potential prove fruitful, one result would be the insistence that criminal justice planning and program reform (as that in any other area) must proceed from an examination of the functional output of a variety of intersecting groups and systems within particular localities.

To the extent that people are concerned with the quality of life, rather than with the maintenance of particular agencies, one must begin with questions about which arrangements of people produce what results for those people.

Cast against such conclusions, a major problem with much current criminal justice analysis is that many of its forms proceed from nonviable assumptions about social order. There is, however, little doubt about the assertion that needs of many American citizens go unmet; and there is little doubt about the assertion that basic conceptions of human need are changing. It would also seem supportable to say that social institutions designed to meet human needs frequently lag behind both the problems confronted by people and the conceptions of what their problems are. Many problem-handling agencies seem unable to develop structures rationally linked to the reduction of the initiating problems.

Through the 1960s the typical approach to this recognition of the problems within (or of) our social, economic, and political institutions had been the one of program development within specialized areas of recognized need, and/or the divestment of one auspice for delivery and the creation of replacement systems. Thus we have experienced welfare reform, health reform, educational reform, and criminal justice reform.

But often the evaluations regarding the implementation of new programs and new agencies have been negative. Or there have been claims made that the typical evaluation designs are not conducive to valid conclusions, that we are pumping money down a variety of conduits that may turn out to be drains.

The decade of the seventies has seen the development of some new themes that claim, superficially at least, to be "new" approaches. Of these newer approaches to social ills, two seem most prominent, although they may be combined. We see, for example, recent policy formulations born of the discovery that many human problems confound each other—that the technology capable of improving health cannot be delivered because of clients' low education, or that persons with improved employment skills suffer entrance into a retrenched labor market. In other words, some persons have remarked that program delivery designed to address certain problems is contaminated by other problems, or possibly by the forms of delivery themselves. Stemming from these findings, programs have emerged that concern "multi-problem clients" and "multi-service centers." The other significant approach stemming from negative evaluations has followed something of the benign neglect mode—that is, many groups now call for "holding the line" or containing persons who are judged recalcitrant to well-intended problem solution efforts.

These newest approaches often fail to behave differently than the solutions they have replaced. Multi-service centers often resemble supermarket collections of the same old services rather than new approaches to human problem resolution. And the new restrained, hold-the-line approach is in fact often no more than another set of specialized services—doses of sour rather than sweet medicine.

Observations of continuing disorganization, or increasing problem rates, seem to keep pace with the types of problem-solving programs that are put together. Some persons have begun to associate the two, causally, suggesting that many of our social ills may be germinated by the way in which we attempt to deal with them. Hence, we hear prophecies that "community is disappearing," that bureaucracy is taking over, that centralized government is administering to a mass society.

No more evidence exists to support these contentions than to support the contentions of the policymakers and program delivery specialists who claim to have found new and effective solutions. For every empirical investigation that may support claims of one doom, we can find another that demonstrates the counter-doom. Many community studies, for example, seem to suggest that we are not headed for mass society and centralized control, but instead toward increasing polarization of groups and to breakdown in the capacity for central control.

Careful examination of criminal justice highlights the existence of such competing claims. There is some evidence that criminal justice is nationalizing, that agencies of justice are professionalizing, and that group commitments to common values and standards for behavior are being replaced with the ethic that any action is good if one can get away with it. But on the other side, there is evidence that criminal justice is decentralizing, that federal level policymakers have reduced if not abandoned their commitment to prescribing local agency operations, and that the biggest bang may not come from the biggest buck.

Intrigued by such conflicting information, I have tried to accomplish three basic things in this book: (1) to trace the intellectual development of the concept of social control; (2) to compare actual criminal justice operations, constraints, and capacities to the models of the system that are usually employed; and (3) to provide a new framework for the analysis of the social function and value of criminal justice operations. These activities have led me to the following conclusions:

1. The decoupling of the concept of social control from that of the integration of social functions has led to the expansion of agencies but not to the clarification of, or the creation of, order.

2. Formal, external means for controlling human behavior are not functional equivalents to informal means of resolving interpersonal group conflicts.

3. The steps that would apparently be necessary in order to create a system of criminal justice that operated toward planned objectives would

be resisted by the agencies involved, by the communities that still legitimate the existence of some of those agencies, and by the absence of resources, to say nothing of inherent contradictions in the assumptions underlying the attempt.

But while I find these conclusions supportable upon existing evidence, it is also clear to me that social processes are not reversible. We do not deindustrialize, deurbanize, and debureaucratize—at least we cannot do so in the sense that is often portrayed by either conservative or radical critics of the "system." We will not all return to the soil, nor to the natural workings of a free market, self-determination system.

Social structure and culture will, of course, continue to change. These changes will be seen alternatively as motions backward, forward, or sideways depending upon the costs and benefits adhering to different groups who are positioned differently to the course of change. Among the changes that we are likely to see, however, some have lower probability than others. The chances seem small that all individual behavior will suddenly uncouple from group moorings, and that a Weberian/Taylorian organization of an entire people will ensue. It also seems unlikely that various social groups will polarize to such an extent that only continual, violent conflict will link the ghetto and Wall Street, or Africa and Europe.

It is likely, however, that social organization will elaborate more quickly than the processes by which to integrate such elaboration. It is likely that increased change in many social spheres—technological, cultural, and political—will lead to more frequent and drastic oscillations in both conceptions and measurements of social order. We apparently do not know how to remove highly negative from highly positive innovation, neither in nuclear research nor in human governance.

Nevertheless, some guidance may be obtained through a more thorough investigation of the relationships among hierarchies of power, with the noticeable increase in specialization and technical expertise that these may bring, and the coordination of human endeavor across these specialized divisions of power and expertise. These vertical and horizontal dimensions of action are observable in many levels of social structure, from those of small groups, to complex organizations, to local congregations of people, to vast systems of business and government. But we do not know as yet how the consequences of these dimensions relate to each other across the various levels of social grouping. In other words, we do not know which elements or kinds of human resources can be effectively organized at a central level and which kinds of human resources must remain open to distribution in accordance with face-to-face sharing and negotiation at the level of personal interaction.

With this level of uncertainty in what we are doing to ourselves, social policy formulated and implemented in the guise that it is informed by past mistakes may be one way in which an American society can travel down the path of low probability but high cost outcome, which even the proposers of such actions seek manifestly to avoid.

It will alter little to say that we have not learned because we cannot even identify our past mistakes. It may be true, as Wilkins has said so many times, that degree of knowledge and indecision or inaction are directly associated. But even if this is true, for the knowledgeable man then to drop out of decisionmaking is to leave power to true believers.

Thus, in the field of criminal justice, as in other fields, uncertainty must lead to action. The course of this exploration has led me to many questions, and to many hunches about what should or should not be tried in both criminal justice and in community politics. The core of these rough guides to action can be stated simply:

1. Federal level criminal justice activity is better to the extent that it generates variety rather than similarity.
2. Variety is more safely done in the form of research than specified action.
3. Research can be constrained negatively by narrowing the selection of the persons to conduct it and those to host it to the "experts" who have done it in the past.
4. We should be less concerned with the immediate policy relevance of research than with the quality of its conduct, and less concerned with evaluation than basic research.
5. We need to be more concerned with the negative side effects of the things we consider good than with unraveling the mystical nature of these negative effects taken alone.
6. What we now know as "criminal justice" we know as such only because we ignore its interconnections with the rest of the world.

But the expansion and ordering of these guides into a new paradigm for action is a difficult, unattended task. In this final chapter I feel competent only to take two initial steps. First, stretching as it does from jurisprudential and treatment ideology through systems approaches to community structure, the analysis certainly requires review and summary. This review should include, if possible, the attempt to relate the Moralist and Welfare conceptions of criminal justice to the alternative that I propose. Second, using as my base this comparison between the traditional and the new approaches, I shall attempt to suggest some directions in which the community-theoretical approach might take us, both on the level of empirical research and on the level of social policy reformulation.

A COMPARISON OF FRAMEWORKS

I have contrasted three approaches to the analysis of criminal justice. I believe that two of these, which I have called the Moralist and Welfare approaches, represent the two predominating frameworks within which crime and criminal justice operations are analyzed and from which emanate the largest number of recommendations for reform of the criminal justice system.

Some readers may feel that I made one of two critical errors in my presentation of the Welfare and Moralist positions. Some might suggest that these two positions are so blatantly deficient that I devoted too much time to their review and critique. If this perception were correct, then this work could have been considerably shorter. But this criticism would not detract from the validity of the alternative that I subsequently presented. My judgment in this matter may have bored some readers, but I think that these two positions are sufficiently viable political, if not intellectual, positions that a systematic presentation was justified. Other readers may feel, on the contrary, that my presentation of these positions was unfair—that in effect I established these positions as straw horses by which to establish my own stalking. If I anticipate this criticism correctly, the key point is that I imputed to Moralist and Welfare positions objectives to which they in fact did not aim. In some sense, this criticism is also correct. That is, Van den Haag, Packer, Clark, Menninger, Wilson, von Hirsch, Dershowitz, and other such writers may actually be arguing only among themselves. One can compare and contrast these various works on the normative reformation of criminal justice in order to select the existing option that is "best" within their shared framework of assumptions. Indeed, if we are to maintain the kind of criminal justice system we have, there is some obvious utility in this activity. If there are to be police chiefs, judges, wardens, and what not, I, too, would like to be able to pick the sets of guidelines these executives might follow.

However, I disagree that it is therefore unfair to compare what the Moralist and Welfare positions, in general, have to offer relative to alternative frames of reference for the analysis of social harmony, social order, and the quality of life. In other words, I do think that voters, legislatures, agency executives, and other people respond to Moralist and Welfare prescriptions as procedures by which to solve human problems and increase some sense of community good. In many quarters, they are not taken as merely alternative calculations of agency efficiency.

If my analysis of the Moralist and Welfare positions is accurate, these positions are sufficiently similar that on some levels of abstraction they may be combined. Both Welfare and Moralist theorists take a simplistic approach that seeks to explain and control crime in the following way.

These simple approaches begin by contrasting a "generalized deviant" to a "generalized, encompassing social unit." One invents a relatively simple mechanism—a "generalized agency"—that performs as if it were a tool of the "encompassing unit" to "fix" the deviant so that he will then perform much like a miniature version of the "encompassing unit." These approaches might be called "anthropomorphic" because they treat the "fixing agency" and the "umbrella social unit" as if they were larger versions of the "fixed deviant." That is, the "fixing agency" and the "umbrella unit" are described as if they followed the same basic principles of motivation and organization that characterize the "fixed person." It is probably more accurate, however, to describe this approach as humanistic, because the dynamics ascribed to all three units in the analysis are not actually the projected characteristics of an anthropoid. Instead, the "umbrella unit," the "fixing unit," and the "deviant unit" are all characterizable as images of some (usually one) humanitarian theme. There can be several versions of this approach, because one can select one of several possible themes. I have examined here two such versions. The Moralist approach seems to be a ramification of the Rational theme, while the Welfare approach is a ramification of the Healthy theme. These two themes seem to be replacements for the Religious theme, but all three have in common the understanding of society as a projection of an abstract model of a virtue that is to be attained through the use of instruments, whether they be altars, rules, or scalpels. Such approaches seek to maximize a particular, singular value. Such maximization is considered desirable because all other values are believed to be subordinate to or variations of that basic value.

In contrast, the community theory approach begins with a greater variety of analytical units. The larger of these units, such as the national economic system, the federal government system, the community field, and complex, formal organizations, cannot be reduced to or explained as the aggregate results of the smaller units, such as small, informal groups or individuals. Or in reverse, it is assumed that the behavior of the larger units is not a mere projection of principles that accurately predict the behavior of the smaller units.

But in addition to the inclusion of more analytical units, the community theory approach also assumes multiple and at times conflicting processes and dynamics may be at work within any of the analytical units at any particular level of complexity and size. Probably the most important of these assumed multiple activities are those that are referred to as the "horizontal" and "vertical" dimensions, which seem to capture significant aspects of social structure in almost all units beyond that of the individual human being.

More work must be done both concerning the conceptualization and measurement of these dimensions and concerning their effects on social functions. Nevertheless, already completed research that examines these dimensions suggests what is perhaps the greatest difference between the humanistic and the community theory approaches to the criminal justice system. That difference is: the simpler approaches seek to describe and to plan for change in the system as if complex organizations (the fixing agency) were merely instruments for the maximization of a value, while the community theory approach stresses that such units of social action are in fact viable entities in their own right rather than merely instruments of social utility. This particular difference leads to the conclusion that these units are not constructed in order to maximize one value but rather to satisfice (as Simon puts it) or to provide multiple, perhaps conflicting, functions under conditions of high uncertainty. In fact, attempts to maximize one value may threaten the survival of these units in one or both of two ways. Emphasis on a single set of instrumentalities can disturb the internal polity of the organization so that coordination and support across subunits may be hampered. Or, succeeding in the achievement of an internal consensus about value selection, the activity of the unit can become so directed toward a rationalized pursuit that support of multiple external polities is damaged beyond repair and the unit is no longer seen as a legitimate contender for environmental support.

RELATIONSHIP BETWEEN FRAMEWORKS

Since the Welfare and Moralist framework is apparently the predominant one for criminal justice analysis, I find it compelling to inquire why this predominance exists. Were the community framework in fact more accurate, one would think it might replace the other as a means of analysis. But so far it has not. Does the community model of criminal justice suggest any reasons for the imbalance between the alleged accuracy of the models and their frequency of use? An answer to this question may or may not lead to a tip in the balance, but at least it might serve to locate the blinkers on our current angle of vision.

In this regard, I would suggest, a bit tentatively, that the humanistic approach is narrower and less accurate, but for some purposes it is more useful than the community approach. Because the humanistic approach attempts to maximize a value through concerted action, it leads to a number of short-term advantages. First, it appears politically assertive. Second, it promises certainty, if only because of its ability to reduce the world to a small set of instrumentally linked and operationally similar units of action. Third, it enables the mobilization of resources toward one end, and therefore implies for the mobilized group considerable aggrandizement of high status, financial gain, and power. Fourth, by ignoring many structural similarities beneath the many specific differences in the several humanitarian themes, it provides a sense of "improvement" to whatever specific theme is next adopted. Fifth, and again by stressing superficial differences, each particular program mobilization delays accounts of failure until "final evaluations are in." Sixth, by delaying recognition of failure as long as possible, it allows prolongation of enjoyed power, esteem, and financial reward. Seventh, by ignoring many of the potential inputs to program mobilization, this approach facilitates the interpretation of dissent as "noise" and then uses the existence of noisemakers as justification for the continuation of the program. Lastly, this series of seven short-run efficiencies enables the mobilized program to rationalize its aggrandized power as benefitting all people—or at least all people who fit into the truncated version of the social system.

Such a framework for action is in fact powerful and relatively resilient. It often fails only in the limited sense that the specific groups and organizations fade in and out of power while the basic structure of the system remains the same. For example, a particular police chief, correctional commissioner, or political party may "fail," and leadership of program mobilization may change hands. But even these kinds of failures are often minimal: the police chief or the commissioner often finds another system in which his theme is just coming to power, and the political party may win the next election.

Such limited failures occur, despite the power of the system, because these intendedly rational programs do subscribe at least halfheartedly to the collection and analysis of information. Since, at least in this country, information systems are generally broader than the specific power structure can control, then information may eventually jar loose the existing dominant coalition. We will then see new programs mobilized around new themes. Welfare gives way to Morals, at least temporarily.

However, these limited failures, in which the underlying structure remains relatively stable, may give way to greater instability over time. This happens for two related reasons. On the one hand, the vulnerability of humanistic approaches to long-range rather than short-range failure makes this approach increasingly vulnerable as social time speeds up—that is, as increased information complexity and variety continually reduces the length of the feedback loop between initial mobilization and receipt of information disconfirming program assumptions. On the other hand, increased rate of turnover in program leadership and operating assumptions tend to disturb the underlying structure of the system. There will be increasingly loud and frequent noise about *any* potential program for mobilization. In our financial system, it becomes increasingly difficult to ignore the consequences of structurally similar program themes on the depletion of natural resources. Long-range failure catches up with short-range success too soon. In the criminal justice system, the rapidity with which one theme divests another seems somewhat slower. Many groups seem willing to "bank" on deterrence/retribution as a program structuring distinct from welfare. But it seems likely that long range failure will catch up with this system, too.

To what extent can this process be explained by the community model? Can this kind of process be located within the community model, and if so, what kinds of actions might the model imply as a corrective for this kind of process?

If it is correct that the traditional approaches to criminal justice reform seek to maximize particular values at the expense of others, then these sequentially mobilized program themes may be themselves regarded as facets of specialization of labor. Each position argues for the particular capacities and competencies of one set of agency functions at the expense of others. For example, it is argued that the criminal justice apparatus cannot be both punitive and rehabilitative. We hear that it cannot be utilized as a means to better the conditions or the personal capacities of offenders and simultaneously as a means of reinforcing community standards of conduct. Both Welfare and Moralist arguments stress the instrumental potential of one set of system technologies over another. But, as we have seen in Chapter 4, the relevant questions in the Welfare/Moralist controversy are not fundamental. Both sides argue that their set of technologies is the better way of strengthening American "society"—an entity about which both sides present some vague but common images.

As I have suggested, it is quite possible that this presumably mortal combat is not very mortal after all. To the extent that the Moralist group succeeds in reducing the welfare functions of criminal justice, Welfare-oriented programs in other agency systems may be increased. While there is in fact a sometimes vicious struggle over which social technology is the best means to the same end, the end result of this struggle may be relatively insignificant in terms of casualties. The resolution is apparently achievable through a careful domain partitioning in which welfare provides "Health" or helping services outside the criminal process.

Indeed, there are recent indications that the power struggle may result in a closer partnership than one would expect, given the vociferousness with which the two sides attack each other. It appears, for example, that the deterrent forces will allow treatment to take place (and will not even complain about its coerciveness), if the welfare programs are sequenced before or after the punitive process. Thus offenders are now being "allowed" to "choose" rehabilitative probation without conviction as an alternative to prosecution, and some detainees are now allowed to choose supervised release if they are not rich enough to post bond or socially stable enough to score well on release on recognizance (ROR) criteria. In other words, there are some signs now that welfare programs will be permitted relatively close proximity to the punitive process, so long as participation in treatment programs is not used as a means of managing the stability or the reward structure in the prison itself. The offender will be coerced into avoiding punishment by accepting treatment rather than coerced into reducing punishment by accepting treatment.

One could conclude that what we are witnessing now in sentencing reform, in penal code revision, in separation of the surveillance and assistance aspects of parole, and in other program divisions is a domain struggle between factions of opposing professional elites, and perhaps between entire organizations. Each is seeking a legitimate sphere of activity in which there is relative autonomy from the decision criteria, resource claims, and operating principles of the competing group. It is much less a war over what American society should look like or how it should treat its citizens than it is a war over who should preside. Since neither group has sufficient power to stamp the other out, and since both sides pay at least some lip service to the legitimacy of the other, these machinations of reform do not generally result in supplanting one technology with the other. Instead jurisdiction is arranged so that the costs of competition are minimized, much as Thomas Schelling suggests organized crime factions may split up territory.

In Chapter 7 this kind of struggle, on a more general level, was analyzed as an ecology of games. Warren, Rose, and Burgunder have done an admirable job of describing similar interactions among six "Community Decision Organizations" in nine cities. They stress that while these organizations may argue with each other over the virtues of particular technologies or services to be applied to a particular individual or problem, they engage in such conflict in very limited circumstances. When the legitimacy of the organization is not threatened and when domains are sufficiently clear, the organizations are generally cooperative and exhibit, as Warren and his colleagues call it, an "institutional thought structure." This thought structure is quite similar, if not identical, to that which I have described here as the humanistic approach, which mediates an umbrella society and problem individuals through a fixing agency.

Within the community model, the final definition of social control was those activities that integrate social functions at the local level. If this definition is workable, then the behaviors of Moralist or Welfare reform are not in fact social control efforts but are themselves characteristic of the lack of social control. Rule enforcement and provision of welfare are advanced as specialized technologies. Professional loyalties and organizational competition for domain result in ideological arguments to maximize one set of activities rather than another. But the result most frequently is the institutionalization of separate, respected domains. Thus Welfare and

Moralist forces can each establish parallel, vertical systems for mobilization of their separate activities.

I presented this kind of activity in Chapter 8 as an example of community structure with high vertical and weak horizontal dimensions. It is the kind of structure in which the injustices or ineffectiveness of one system of activities are balanced by the constraining or counteractions of other systems. It may provide a certain type of order and solve a certain number of problems. But the order provided is essentially the unplanned pattern that results from the separate actions of autonomous technological systems. The kinds of problems solved are relatively specific. The welfare system may provide emergency assistance in crisis situations, indigent pregnant women may obtain prenatal care in a clinic, some well-known gang leaders may be taken off the streets. But such an arrangement of services is not likely to be able to deal with the chronic nature of such problems. And the recognition of such areas as "communities" seems primarily a result of the plurality of power in the several vertical arrangements of technology. If any single theme ever succeeded in reducing the power of competing themes, the result could well be the emergence of "mass society" in which individuals would be reduced to the roles they play within or for one large, technical system.

The community model would suggest that there are alternative forms of social structure. One extreme case would be the increased autonomy of localities from vertically related organizations, the dismantling of economic and political superstructures, and the reemergence of small, self-contained living groups. One option, in other words, is to devise means of reducing centralization and bureaucratization while increasing the horizontal dimension. This option seems to me extremely far-fetched. It seems likely, for example, that "self-contained" subsistence economies, new extended families, and communes, all of which clearly indicate a group choice for this kind of structure, all depend upon the existence of the very technological systems that these groups deplore. They are able to create their new insularity only because they can rely on external, formal systems for assistance and support.

But the other alternative is implied in these observations. It may be possible to decentralize and debureaucratize certain segments of social organization while retaining other centralized elements and in fact increasing their effectiveness. One can, for example, centralize computer services without centralizing decisions on what to compute. It may be possible to centralize health services, as in health maintenance organizations, without reducing quality of care. Distinct religious denominations might save a great deal of money by sharing one facility and staggering time of use. Professional football teams seem able to pool information on prospective talent without reducing their ability to obtain skillful players or to compete on the field.

These examples are relatively trivial, but they might suggest some avenues for future research as well as some areas in which social policy might shift, if the aim is to reduce social problems rather than expand the organizational networks for meeting these problems. In the next section, I will outline some possibilities. There is neither space nor time to attempt to predict which of these possibilities is most valuable, most feasible, or least threatening.

SOME KEY RESEARCH AREAS

If the community model has potential for explaining why criminal justice behaves as it does, a variety of research areas would open up for (1) investigating the validity of the basic constructs and theoretical relationships, (2) investigating means by which theoretic specialty can be reduced and activities of coordination and integration increased, and (3) investigating outcome of such activities.

Specific research questions are so numerous that an attempt to be specific would amount only to a distillation of the research questions addressed in Chapters 6 through 11. It is probably more valuable to identify some general research emphases that can serve to distinguish the community approach from the research of the more traditional variety.

One exceedingly difficult task within the community approach is the attempt to specify some indicators of social order that are independent of both the present problem-solving repertoire and of vested organizational interest. If our current means of defining social order and dealing with social problems lock us into themes attached to specific technologies, we are not going to progress very far. For example, the notion that "crime" or "mental illness" are significant social problems seems to press people toward reliance upon existing bureaucracies. One of our social problems may be, for example, that we rely upon police as a means of obtaining feelings of safety or protection when the police as an organization are dependent on some sense of danger.

The extent to which we pose the problems of people in terms that stifle their options is surprising. For example, when conceptualizing what an offender may "need" when released from prison, some persons respond that offenders "need counseling." Counseling, however, is neither a need nor an accurate way to codify the troubles that may give rise to a counseling response. We have implied in the way we describe the problem that offenders require a particular set of problem responses and professional assistance, regardless of what the problem might be.

On another level, it may also be stifling to certain agencies to categorize them as dealing with the "crime problem," or to identify them as belonging to a "criminal justice system." Organizations may have many capacities that are wasted when we ignore some of their functions by stressing others.

Before criminal justice can become a rational enterprise, we must find ways of specifying social relationships that do not depend on already codified and institutionalized responses. Relative to criminal justice, we need to find ways of deciding when an area is safe to live in, or satisfying to live in, or orderly, or peaceful, that do not depend on definitions of events as crimes or on classifications of official responses to such events.

Most present criminal justice research, for all its alleged ultimate concern for order and social harmony, seems virtually ignorant of any positive concept of social order. It relies instead on measurements of crime and delinquency. Such research may be of interest to some criminal justice agencies. But even if actions taken by these agencies demonstrate reduction of crime, we have no way of knowing whether the candle is worth the game. We might simply be redefining crime as illness and committing people to hospitals rather than to prisons. Or we may simply become so tolerant that acts now defined as crimes are simply ignored. Or it may be that our actions have left most people so weak from starvation that they lack the physical strength to bother their neighbors.

In short, we need a tremendous amount of research on the notions of the quality of life and of social harmony. Our aim must be good societies, not crimeless ones. Thus the development of social indicators, which are also outcome criteria or objectives, is extremely important.

Second, we need to step up research on the nature of organizational and interorganizational behavior. These phenomena have already been studied with some sophistication. But so far the nature of the focus has been somewhat narrow, if this research is to be relevant to the production of social order. Despite great reams of data and theory on organizational structure, internal dynamics, management, and so on, there is little usable material on the output of organizations and organizational networks for social systems. Hence, the first area of research, on social indicators, and the second are related. We often speak of complex organizations as instruments of societal goals, but there is little effort to measure how and whether organizational activities in fact can contribute to such goals. A related question concerns organizations as systems. If the internal politics of organizations do seem to lead them away from initiating societal goals and toward maintenance of organizational stability, how can this gradual process of organizational insularity be retarded or reversed? Should we find ways of making organizations self-destruct or reorganize periodically? Or can they be effectively governed and coordinated so that stable, complex systems learn to retain or increase their yield to the social order?

A third broad area of inquiry concerns the notion of community. From Warren's point of view, community is a term by which to order statements about patterns of group life and about the variety of ways to provide the physical and social supports for group life to exist. As long as people tend to congregate, cluster, and interact, community will remain fundamental to our conceptions of social order. But we now lack the means to specify the differences in community among various localities. Methods of specifying the extent to which locality-relevant functions are performed may conceivably be handled by designations of social indicators. But methods of specifying community structure—of measuring the relative strength of autonomy and integration—will need a great deal of work. If this task can be accomplished, we may be able to investigate how social indicators vary over different structures as well as determine whether processes for accomplishing social functions become transformed as more basic structural change takes place. For example, are the police engaged in the same social outputs when the source of funds changes? Are universities altered in social function as their independence of the local area increases? Are private and public welfare essentially concerned with the same functions? Or is one more concerned with mutual support and another with social participation or socialization? Is work release designed and supported on the local level supportive of retaining offenders or supplying local business with cheap labor? What happens when the same program obtains federal support?

In summary, our last twenty years of criminological and criminal justice research has not really left us woefully ignorant of crime. But much of it has left us ignorant of the significance of crime for anything that we may wish to achieve under the label of "social improvement." We behave much like medical men whose treatment of troubles was unattached to any standards of health. We apply medicine, set bones, cut out tumors, but without knowledge of whether the patient is better off when we have exhausted the tricks in our kit. Often, we cannot even define who the patient is. The analogy is particularly apt, since we have reached a point where we are willing to doubt that the patient was sick in the first place, but our response to this doubt is to hit the patient with a cudgel. We are likely to be striking out at ourselves.

I do not think that the situation is hopeless. As Warren concludes, the reported death of the community is greatly exaggerated. It is likely that we possess a great deal of data about community structure and about the changes in locality-relevant function that occur as we change that structure. Because our search for data has been myopic, it is quite likely that our reconstructions of what our programs have done to community order will be sketchy. But research on completed program endeavors may uncover a great deal of valid information relevant to outlining new research activity and new thrusts for social action.

The research findings reported in the second half of this book suggest only a few ways in which old findings might be useful in establishing a new paradigm. But it will take considerable imagination to use our piecemeal data in this way. We will have to redefine chaff and wheat and restructure our sifting process. For example, Lerman's reanalysis of the data on the California Community Treatment Project and the Probation Subsidy is exciting, but for findings that Lerman himself almost throws away. He seems most concerned with debunking some lofty program claims for high accomplishment of program objectives. His success at this debunking is partially dependent upon his definitions of program success, which are as challengeable as the originals. But in the midst of this process, Lerman produces a rare case study of interaction among various levels of government and various levels of public service bureaucracy. This story is rich with information relevant to the mobilization process. But these data escape many commentators. For example, all that Martinson does with this history is catch the few statements that lend credence to his belief that treatment does not work. Certainly we need to go further than such secondary analysis will permit. But I think there is a vein of information, now considered waste, that we could readily appropriate to valuable use.

POTENTIAL SHIFTS IN SOCIAL POLICY AND ACTION

New research activity is not enough. We must engage in some new kinds of social action, including policy formation. One type of action, of course, would be the consideration of social research as action. This statement might seem only a clever play on words, but it represents considerably more than that. I mean that the basic learning process, as explicated in the scientific method, should become a means of structuring action. This, of course, is not in itself a new suggestion and is likely to be cast away with the offhand comment that "here is simply another scientist wishing to be on top rather than on tap."

I would disagree with that answer and with the idea that social policy has ever been structured by a research process. We have little research as yet on the processes and structures of policy formation and implementation. In a very loose way, we might say that criminal justice action is guided by research, in the senses that action is often partially legitimized by research, particularly of an evaluative sort, and that specific programs are sometimes changed or dismantled when there is sufficient evidence about inefficiency. But at least in the criminal justice area, research activity is characterized by monopsony—the activity and the products of the supplier are controlled by the investments and needs of the buyer. Criminal justice researchers will investigate restitution or victimization because such endeavors are politically supported. We will find ways of creating parity in qualifications and procedures among rural and urban or lower and higher court systems if at some level policymakers wish it done. The research buyer controls the research process so long as the buyer controls the questions. Under these conditions the buyer can even seek negative information about particular achievements.

Under these conditions, researchers generally operate to legitimize the structure of social action as it is. Researchers often struggle feverishly to guard their autonomy under these conditions. They prefer grants to contracts and they feel more comfortable dealing with research institutes than practitioners or policymakers. But their autonomy is often displayed only by their ability to predict a "hot" research area prior to their receipt of requests for proposals. They often settle for investigating problems that are already in the "pipeline," as it is called. But to the extent that the research buyers determine the salient research issues, criminal justice research will legitimize organizational technologies that are implied in how the questions are posed.

Analysis of the relationship between research and action can open up a number of areas to policy reformulation. How can we generate more variety in the way we pose questions about social problems? Can we find ways to include dissent as information rather than noise? Or how can we increase the legitimacy of diverse groups to pose questions? How can we increase our awareness of the range of social problems to which any one organized response is considered an answer? Can we find ways to solve one set of problems without engendering or maintaining another set? Or can we solve a problem for one population without creating a problem for another population? (For example, a recent *New Yorker* cartoon displayed a sensitivity for interlocking problems that social investigation too often ignores. In this cartoon, a long line of people were queued up in front of the "unemployment desk." In the second picture, there were two desks with half the applicants in front of each. In the last picture of the series, all persons were employed at desks, and the applicant lines had disappeared. The implication, of course, is that welfare work is itself a form of welfare. But the cartoonist forgot to add that we discriminate in terms of which group will perform as applicants and which as applicators.)

At the bottom line, I think, social policy should be altered in such a way that implementation alters the structure of policy formation. This attempt is likely to be extremely threatening, so much so that even people who see some wisdom in it will claim it is utopian. But this possibility does not really change my beliefs about what should be done. What would happen, for example, if we perceived social action agencies as the consumers of social problems generated by a controlling public? What university courses would be offered if curriculum were determined by a board of students?

What would happen to welfare services if agencies were staffed and organized by "clients"?

These are perhaps trivial examples because they imply a kind of organization similar to what we have, changing only some decisionmaking power. Yet such questions might be applied creatively to the research process in several ways. For example, what might happen to the kinds of research questions asked if we had a monopoly—that is, if suppliers rather than buyers controlled the question market? Or more intriguing, what if we changed the locus of the monopoly? Perhaps offenders and victims should raise the research questions. Perhaps unions of front line staff rather than management could become concerned with research. What would happen to our answers then? Or, in a slightly different mode, what would a protection of human subjects protocol look like if it were constructed by human subjects rather than an elite panel of users and producers?

While I regard as a high priority the need to shake up the current relationship between policy, research, and action, I am also aware that some kinds of disruption have more enduring benefits than others. Two results of disruption that any serious disorganizer may wish to avoid are (1) the propensity of the established system for backlash, and (2) the propensity of a new set of actors to reinvent the old structure rather than a new system. To avoid the first problem, one needs to protect innovative activities until they are well established. If an old system is able to co-opt a new activity, the old system will often defuse the specific innovation, and learn how to head off innovation in the future. To avoid the second problem, one should probably seek those kinds of reorganization that do not require new personnel. We are more likely to get truly innovative behavior out of an experienced policeman committed to a new set of activities than we are from a new policeman operating under the same old constraints.

But avoiding backlash and avoiding the reestablishment of old systems under new names are not easy tasks. Why is it that, like Sisyphus, we often exert so much energy climbing our mountainous social problems only to find the objects of our exertion almost crush us as they come rolling back down the mountain? Why is it that we expend so much time and energy inventing new means of locomotion only to discover upon completion a shiny new wheel? Maybe the boulder should be pushed around the mountain, or perhaps we should outlaw locomotion and see what we can accomplish where we are. Or to be more specific, perhaps we should try to be novel with what we now see as mundane things, rather than seek new ways of accomplishing our old tasks.

To summarize, in the social action area, it is likely that disruption of our current action paradigms and invention of new ones is more likely to be enduring to the extent that we can find ways for our current actors to relate to each other *slightly* differently, rather than to have them reverse roles completely, and rather than to pretend that we can conceive and implement a totally new system. If it is not feasible, for example, to change directly who poses research questions in criminal justice, perhaps we can at least alter the relative importance given the different actors in the research process.

One step, for example, might be to feed back findings to everyone who generated information. If we were researching the relationship between fear of crime and objective probability of victimization in an area, the researchers might go back to each interviewee with an oral report equal in length to the original interview. Interviewees might then get out of research what they put into it. The conductors of research would also have to calculate the cost of interviewee time in their budget because they would have to pay it back in dissemination time. Moreover, presuming the ultimate user in this type of research is the respondent as potential victim, the respondent's opinion about the research report might be utilized in formulating any policy about fear of crime before action was undertaken.

But some other, more novel, steps might be taken. Research projects might include direct payment to any subjects engaged in the research. So that subjects did not receive double payment, the time that they spent engaged in the research might be subtracted from any other means of income. This procedure might force researchers to coordinate their diverse activities so that all potential research questions to the same subject were asked at the same time, for the same payment. This inclusion of the respondent in the research project budget is also likely to increase the willingness of subjects to participate in research. It is no more likely to produce invalid information than the approaches we use now, when respondents "volunteer."

This approach is likely to be quite useful when the research population is also perceived as the problem population and when the research in question is used as a basis for intervention into their lives. For example, we might pay all welfare clients who are willing to sit through the eligibility interview and orientation. On the grounds that the welfare recipient is necessary to the maintenance of the system, this payment can be justified. But it might also be justified on the grounds that those clients engaged the longest with welfare workers would be those clients who were most greatly rewarded. The same process might be applied in corrections. Offenders might be paid a certain amount upon incarceration and then taxed or charged for any service they wished to have. Offenders wishing to avoid high taxes might buy only general dormitory accommodations and mediocre food. Offenders wishing more protection, better food, psychological services, and whatever, would pay considerably more. However, we might also pay offenders according to the degree to which they contribute to our knowledge of crime. Therefore, an offender who pays a considerable amount for psychological services, but whose treatment process contributes to new knowledge about intervention techniques, might receive a rebate.

But if this approach is useful, it is more likely to be effective when the units of action are larger than the individual research subject or the individual offender. Altering relationships among informal groups, organizations, and interorganizational systems would seem most likely to have successful results for criminal justice.

Right now reducing crime is not very profitable, or at least its reduction benefits only certain groups and not others. For example, most retail companies pass on the cost of stolen goods to the buyer. Buyers pay for both losses due to employee crime and losses due to consumer theft. Even if some company succeeds in reducing such theft, it probably increases its profit margin rather than reduce the price of its goods. Hence the company may benefit from effective surveillance, but the consumer does not. Perhaps we could have companies report to consumers how much of the item cost was due to loss from crime and/or to expense of private police and surveillance equipment. Customers might then choose to shop in the store with the least crime.

Some states are now experimenting with "community corrections" acts, or other means of rewarding local jurisdictions for keeping offenders "in the community." This kind of incentive program does seem to be a weak stab at altering some systemic relationships. But more novel incentive programs might be possible. Could we find ways to reward communities for maintaining low crime rates? Or better yet, can we find ways to reward areas for lowering social problem rates? If our aim, in the long run, is to increase social control rather than reduce crime, we should find ways to increase the *net* gain of social "goods" to a local area rather than ways to increase the effectiveness of special programs.

Net gains in the quality of life are unlikely to be achieved by feeding organizational and professional activities that are dependent upon the existence of particular kinds of social problems. Thus, while specific steps in research and action may take many years, some general action strategies might be designed fairly soon. These strategies would be "procedurally rigorous" rather than "content-rigorous." They would be conducive to gains in knowledge rather than gains in political and organizational power.

On the research side, we could seek ways of centralizing the conduct of and the facilities for research while simultaneously decentralizing the sources of questions and the uses to which answers might be put. It would seem ineffective, for example, to maintain separate centers for educational, welfare, health, and criminal justice research. We might do better research in these areas if the research were *not* conducted by persons committed to such problems as areas for inquiry. We might also do better if various researchers using similar techniques were combined. It seems wasteful to have one survey research endeavor mounted around questions of delinquency while another is mounted on questions of school achievement. The variables are probably related to each other anyway, as is research that uses agency documents or census data, or requires participant observers in designated settings. Finally, research should be given back to all the people who produce it, not just the few who paid for it directly or are immediately concerned with its use. Researchers are supposedly interested in the validity of their findings, but they rarely test findings against the reactions of information producers.

In the realm of social action, the dilemmas of specialization and coordination or integration may be less resolvable than in social science. At least in the research realm, a relatively diverse set of investigators subscribes to a generic statement of processes. This appears to be less the case in social practice, although the present appearance may be more the product of professional domain claims than to real differences in practice. To put it another way, a key question about social practice might be whether or not we can invent a new language to describe how certain actors respond to other actors, or to situations. Is there a generic set of skills that might apply to calming down angry people, to increasing the participation of alienated people, or to protecting the rights of service recipients? Is there a generic set of skills that might apply to managing organizations or reducing waste? Is there a generic set of social outcomes that most groups seek to achieve, or are rewarding situations fundamentally different for different classes of people?

I doubt we now have answers to such questions, but we probably never will, unless we are willing to disengage social research from current social action. I am not sufficiently prescient to know what options will be taken. I would assume, however, that opting for criminal justice is opting for crime.

Notes

CHAPTER 1

1. Ernest Van den Haag, *Punishing Criminals* (New York: Basic Books, 1975): Herbert Packer, *The Limits of the Criminal Sanction* (Stanford, Calif.: Stanford University Press, 1968): Richard Quinney, *Class, State and Crime* (New York: David McKay, 1977).
2. For example, compare the Marxist examination of community corrections and community mental health in Andrew T. Scull, *Decarceration* (Englewood Cliffs, N.J.: Prentice-Hall, 1977) to the evaluations of community corrections in Paul Lerman, *Community Treatment and Social Control* (Chicago: University of Chicago Press, 1974). Scull assumes that decarceration efforts are pursued because of their economic benefit to the system, independent of any effects on recidivism. Lerman, who tends to be radical himself, demonstrates that the California Community Treatment Program and the Probation Subsidy were both *more expensive* than the institutional strategies, as well as less effective.
3. The most telling analyses, in terms of the breakdown between national policy formulation and intervention programs on the local level, are outside the criminal justice area. Most of them deal with parallel issues in welfare, however, which radicals also assume provide "control" strategies. See Peter Marris and Martin Rein, *Dilemmas of Social Reform* (New York: Basic Books, 1971); Peter Rose, *Betrayal of the Poor* (Cambridge, Mass.: Schenkman, 1976); Roland Warren, Stephen Rose, and Ann Bergunder, *The Structure of Urban Reform* (Lexington, Mass.: Lexington Books, 1974). For a recent analysis that challenges the "Marxian" connection between unemployment rates and welfare dependency see R. Richard Ritti, "The Administration of Poverty: Lessons from the Welfare Explosion 1967–1973," *Social Problems* 25 (Fall 1978): 157–175.

4. The terminology used here is admittedly ambiguous and will remain so for much of this first chapter. Suffice it for now that "criminal justice" and "criminal justice system" are to be understood here as they are traditionally used as loose designations for the activity of the criminal process. Some critics, notably the radicals, suggest that the criminal justice system is much wider than the system denoted by agencies of police, prosecution, judiciary, and corrections. They speak now of a social-industrial complex and a subunit or subsystem of that complex that deals with "social control." See Gregg Barak, "Community-Based Alternatives: A Change in Rehabilitation or the Developing Social Industrial Complex?" paper presented at the 1976 Annual Meeting of the American Society of Criminology, November 4–7, 1976, Tucson, Arizona. On the other side, some conservatives and liberals call the agencies of the criminal process a "nonsystem," denoting thereby that the agencies infrequently work together in a concerted manner in order to affect a unified policy. See James S. Campbell, Joseph R. Sahid, and David P. Stang, *Law and Order Reconsidered* (New York: Bantam Books, 1970).

The approach taken here, until we can reexamine the boundaries of the "criminal justice system" in chapters 7 through 10, is that agencies of police, courts, and corrections form a widely recognized "system" in the sense that the agencies do influence each other and that informal but observable feedback loops exist in the criminal process. This is the approach taken by Donald J. Newman in the introduction to Frank Remington, Donald J. Newman, Edward L. Kimball, Marygold Melli, and Herman Goldstein, *Criminal Justice Administration* (Indianapolis: Bobbs-Merrill, 1969), pp. 1–50.

5. I shall trace the development of the term "social control" in the next part of this chapter. Broadly conceived, social control is used here to denote activities that are *intended* or *designed* as "negative" or "redirective" feedback to groups or individuals whose behavior is defined by legislation and/or by official interpretation as deviating from prescribed rules, or from dominant norms. See Alexander Clark and Jack P. Gibbs, "Social Control: A Reformulation," *Social Problems* 12, 4 (1965): 398–415, and literature cited therein. The assumption, then, is that criminal justice is one of a set of activities that provide some stability to society. This assumption of stability is addressed in detail in Chapter 5.

6. E. A. Ross, *Social Control, A Survey of the Foundations of Order* (New York: Macmillan, 1914).

7. Recall that the juvenile justice system was not implemented until 1899 in Illinois and that there was much public debate at that time as to whether the government had a responsibility to control and protect juveniles through a process separate from the adult criminal system. See Anthony Platt, "The Rise of the Child-Saving Movement: A Study in Social Policy and Correctional Reform," *The Annals of the American Academy of Political and Social Science* 381, January 1969: 21–38. For discussion of police as a public function rather than a private problem, see Allan Silver, "The Demand for Order in a Civil Society: A Review of Some Themes in the History of Urban Crime, Police and Riot," in David Bordua, *The Police* (New York: Wiley, 1967), pp. 1–25; Cyril D. Robinson, "The Mayor and the Police—The Political Role of the Police in Society" in George L. Mosse (ed.), *Police Forces in History*, Vol. II. (London: Sage, 1975), pp. 277–315; Mark H. Haller, "Historical Roots of Police Behavior: Chicago, 1890–1925," *Law and Society Review* 10,2 (Winter 1976): 303–323; and Mark H. Haller, "Crime Reformers and Police Leadership: in Harlan Hahn (ed.), *Police in Urban Society* (Beverly Hills, Calif.: Sage, 1971), pp. 39–56.

8. Ray Madding McConnell, *Criminal Responsibility and Social Constraint* (New York: Charles Scribner's Sons, 1912), pp. 116–117.

9. George Homans, *The Human Group* (New York: Harcourt, Brace, and Co., 1950), p. 310.

10. Emile Durkheim, *The Rules of Sociological Method* (Glencoe, Ill.: The Free Press, 1950), pp. 60–70.

11. Morris Janowitz, "Sociological Theory and Social Control," *American Journal of Sociology* 91 (July 1975): 82–108.
12. See particularly L. L. Bernard, *Social Control in Its Sociological Aspects* (New York: Macmillan, 1939); Paul H. Landis, *Social Control: Social Organization and Disorganization in Process* (New York; Lippincott, 1939); and Richard T. LaPiere, *A Theory of Social Control* (New York: McGraw-Hill, 1954).
13. Platt, "The Rise of the Child-Saving Movement," and David Rothman, *The Discovery of the Asylum* (Boston: Little, Brown, 1971).
14. Gary L. Wamsley and Mayer N. Zald, "The Political Economy of Public Organizations," *Public Administration Review* 33, 1 (January/February, 1973): 70.
15. Homans, *The Human Group*, p. 284.
16. A. B. Hollingshead, "The Concept of Social Control," *American Sociological Review*, 2 (April 1941): 220.
17. Michael Banton, *The Policeman in the Community* (New York: Basic Books, 1964), also takes this point of view; see p. 2.
18. Richard Schwartz and James C. Miller, "Legal Evolution and Societal Complexity," *American Journal of Sociology* 70 (September 1965): 165–166.
19. *Ibid.*
20. *Ibid.*, p. 166
21. William J. Chambliss and Robert B. Seidman, *Law, Order and Power* (Reading, Mass.: Addison-Wesley, 1971), pp. 16–36.
22. Leslie Wilkins, *Social Deviance* (Englewood Cliffs, N.J.: Prentice-Hall, 1965), pp. 62–71.
23. Roland Warren, *Community in America* (Chicago: Rand McNally, 1963 [First Edition]), p. 180.
24. Brian Chapman, *The Police State* (London: Praeger, 1970), pp. 11–13.
25. *Ibid.*, pp. 12–13.
26. Silver, "The Demand for Order in Civil Society," p. 7.
27. H. L. Nieburg, "Violence, Law, and the Informal Polity," *The Journal of Conflict Resolution* 13, 2 (June 1969): 192.
28. Several accounts exist that contrast police organization and police behavior to the standards for police behavior prescribed in law. See James G. Wilson, *Varieties of Police Behavior* (Cambridge, Mass.: Harvard University Press, 1960), which relates police behavior to local socioeconomic conditions, and Jonathan Rubenstein, *City Police* (New York: Ballantine, 1973), which relates police behavior to the sociogeographic area it is to control.
29. Jerome Skolnick, *Justice Without Trial* (New York: Wiley, 1967) tends to emphasize the organizational influence on police behavior as determinant. See also Jerome H. Skolnick and J. Richard Wordworth, "Bureaucracy, Information, and Social Control: A Study of a Morals Detail" in D. Bordua, *The Police* (New York: Wiley, 1967), pp. 99–136, in which the authors demonstrate that enforcement of an unpopular law (statutory rape) from the police perspective is dependent upon interorganizational policy involving the police and the welfare department.
30. Tracing the community correctional movement to organizational motives rather than policy of the state is attempted in Peter B. Meyer and David Duffee, "Alternatives to Incarceration: Humane Correction or Low Cost Social Control?" paper presented at the National Conference on Criminal Justice Evaluation, Washington, D.C., March 10, 1977.
31. Van den Haag, *Punishing Criminals*, pp. 29–33.
32. Homans, *The Human Group*, p. 294.
33. John Rawls, *A Theory of Justice* (Cambridge, Mass.: Harvard University Press, 1973).
34. *Ibid.*, pp. 240–241.
35. *Ibid.*, p. 243.

36. There may be some "retributive" sanctions visible in civil law such as in the collection of damages at a multiple of the damages actually incurred. Nevertheless, most recent discussions of retribution limit it, by definition, to punishments of an offender in a way that symbolically uphold the law itself, rather than in ways that make a plaintiff better off. See Packer, *The Limits of the Criminal Sanction.*
37. Karl Menninger, *The Crime of Punishment* (New York: Viking, 1969); Ramsey Clark, *Crime in America* (New York: Pocket Books, 1971).
38. Packer, *The Limits of the Criminal Sanction,* p. 45; Van den Haag, *Punishing Criminals,* p. 64.
39. Ross, *Social Control: A Survey of the Foundations of Order,* pp. 106–107.
40. Charles Reith, *The Blind Eye of History: A Study of the Origins of the Present Police Era* (Montclair, N.J.: Patterson Smith, 1974), pp. 171–172.
41. Ross, *Social Control,* p. 114.
42. David Sudnow, "Normal Crimes: Sociological Features of the Penal Code in a Public Defender Office," *Social Problems* (Winter 1965), pp. 255–276.
43. Frank Remington, Donald J. Newman, Edward Kimball, Marygold Melli, and Herman Goldstein, *Criminal Justice Administration* (Indianapolis: Bobbs Merrill, 1969), pp. 884–896.
44. Dennis C. Sullivan, *Team Models for Probation* (Paramus, N.J.: National Council on Crime and Delinquency, 1969); Vincent O'Leary and David Duffee, "Correctional Policy—A Classification of Goals Designed for Change," *Crime and Delinquency* 17, 4 (October 1971): pp. 373–386.
45. Walter R. Nord, "The Failure of Current Applied Behavioral Science—A Marxian Perspective," *Journal of Applied Behavioral Science* 10, 4 (1974): pp. 575–576.
46. Jennie McIntyre, "Public Attitudes Toward Crime and Law Enforcement," *Annals of the American Academy of Political and Social Science* 374 (November 1967): p. 42. On the welfare side, see Morris and Rein, *The Dilemmas of Social Reform,* and Rose, *The Betrayal of the Poor,* both cited above. These analysts suggest that national programs aimed at redistributing power and resources became means of "rehabilitating" individuals on the local level of program implementation.

CHAPTER 2

1. See for example, David Duffee and Robert Fitch, *An Introduction to Corrections: A Policy and Systems Approach* (Pacific Palisades, Calif.: Goodyear, 1976), pp. 1–24; and John Kaplan, *Criminal Justice,* (Mineola, N.Y.: Foundation Press, 1973).
2. Ray Madding McConnell, *Criminal Responsibilities and Social Constraint* (New York: Charles Schribner's Sons, 1912), p. 326.
3. *Ibid.,* pp. 326–328.
4. Edward Alsworth Ross, *Social Control, A Survey of the Foundations of Order* (New York: Macmillan, 1914), pp. 107–108.
5. L. L. Bernard, *Social Control in its Sociological Aspects* (New York: Macmillan, 1939), p. 103.
6. *Ibid.,* p. 97.
7. Leon Radzinowicz, *Ideology and Crime* (New York: Columbia University Press, 1966), p. 105.
8. *Ibid.,* p. 109.
9. Herbert Packer, *The Limits of the Criminal Sanction* (Stanford, Calif.: Stanford University Press, 1968).

10. *Ibid.*, p. 3.
11. *Ibid.*, pp. 33–34.
12. *Ibid.*, pp. 69–70. John Rawls, in discussing the place of penal sanctions in a just society, also states that their inclusion may be necessary but lamentable. (*A Theory of Justice* (Cambridge, Mass.: Harvard University Press, 1973), pp. 240–241). Rawls's view is that the criminal sanction is required to seal the "contract" among men in a just society, meaning that even in a system of fairly distributed social advantages, men's temperaments might tempt them to seek more than their share of social advantages. Why Packer sees the criminal sanction as lamentable, however, might have different roots, since Packer admits that the actual distribution system is not fair. Could he mean that the criminal sanction is lamentable since it is the only means to maintain some level of stability in the unjust system? Compare with Van den Haag, *Punishing Criminals* (New York: Basic Books, 1975), who sees the criminal sanction as protective of a perhaps unjust but still "best" distributive system.
13. Packer, *The Limits of the Criminal Sanction*, p. 70.
14. *Ibid.*, p. 38.
15. *Ibid.*
16. For example, see Kaplan, *Criminal Justice*, pp. 18–25.
17. Nigel Walker takes a similar step in *Crimes, Courts, and Figures* (Baltimore: Penguin, 1971), pp. 117–118. Walker reserves deterrence to mean general deterrence and combines special deterrence—Packer's intimidation—and rehabilitation, calling both of these reformation. Walker argues that partitioning intimidation and rehabilitation involves the impossible task of selecting the motives that have led an offender not to commit new crimes.
18. Packer, *The Limits of the Criminal Sanction*, pp. 39–40.
19. *Ibid.*, p. 44.
20. This point is made forcefully by Leslie Wilkins, *Social Deviance* (Englewood Cliffs, N.J.: Prentice-Hall, 1965), pp. 46–48 and in the passage previously cited in Ross, *Social Control*, pp. 107–108.
21. Arnold M. Rose and Arthur E. Prell, "Does the Punishment Fit the Crime? A Study in Social Valuation," *American Journal of Sociology* 61 (November 1955): 247–259.
22. Packer, *The Limits of the Criminal Sanction*, p. 46.
23. *Ibid.*
24. Any elementary text cites numerous examples. One study known to the author that might support Packer demonstrates an apparent lower rate for persons in Pennsylvania released to parole from halfway houses rather than directly from institutions in Pennsylvania. David Duffee, Peter B. Meyer, Thomas R. Maher, and Kevin Wright, *Problems, Issues, and Outcome in a Community Placed Correctional System* (Harrisburg: Governor's Justice Commission, November 30, 1976). But generally less sanctions seem about equal in effect, compared to the more severe.
25. Douglas Grant and Marguerite Grant, "A Group Dynamics Approach to Non-Conformity in the Navy," *Annals of the American Academy of Political and Social Science* 322 (March 1959): 126–155.
26. Packer, *The Limits of the Criminal Sanction*, pp. 39–45.
27. A variety of studies compare the use of internal sanctions by middle-class parents and the use of external sanctions, notably punishment, by lower-class parents. See, for example, Lloyd Warner and Associates, *Democracy in Jonesville* (New York: Harper & Row, 1949) and A. B. Hollingshead, *Elmstown's Youth and Elmstown Revisited* (New York: Wiley, 1975).
28. Arthur L. Stinchcombe, "Institutions of Privacy in the Determination of Police Administrative Practice," *American Journal of Sociology*, 79 (September 1963): 152.

29. *Ibid.*, pp. 153–154.
30. Bernard Beck, "Welfare as a Moral Category," *Social Problems* 14, 3 (1967): 258–277.
31. See particularly Roland Warren, Stephen Rose, and Ann Bergunder, *The Structure of Urban Reform* (Lexington, Mass.: Lexington Books, 1974).
32. Herbert Packer, "Two Models of the Criminal Process," *University of Pennsylvania Law Review* 113 (1964): 1–23.
33. John Griffifths, "The Limits of Criminal Law Scholarship," *Yale Law Journal* 79 (1970), 1388.
34. Packer, *The Limits of the Criminal Sanction*, p. 150.
35. John Griffiths, "Ideology in Criminal Procedure or a 'Third' Model of the Criminal Process," *Yale Law Journal* 79, 3 (January 1970): 359–407.
36. Packer, *The Limits of the Criminal Sanction*, p. 296.
37. Donald J. Newman, *Criminal Justice* (Philadelphia: Lippincott, 1975), p. 2.
38. Packer, *The Limits of the Criminal Sanction*, p. 297.
39. See time and energy studies in James Q. Wilson, *Varieties of Police Behavior* (Cambridge, Mass.: Harvard University Press, 1968).
40. Packer, *The Limits of the Criminal Sanction*, p. 269.
41. Richard Korn, "Of Crime, Criminal Justice and Corrections," *University of San Francisco Law Review* 6 (October 1971): 27–75.
42. Van den Haag, *Punishing Criminals*, pp. 3–11.
43. *Ibid.*, p. 11.
44. *Ibid.*
45. *Ibid.*, pp. 16–17.
46. *Ibid.*
47. For a sociological discussion of the extent to which people are socialized with proper behavior rather than threatened into conforming, see Dennis Wrong, "The Oversocialized Conception of Man," *The American Sociological Review* 26: 184–193.
48. Van den Haag, *Punishing Criminals*, p. 20. The point that Van den Haag misses here is that the law can perform the stabilizing function only if deviance is marginal, or individual, rather than endemic to the system. H. L. Nieburg, "Vioence Law and the Informal Polity," *The Journal of Conflict Resolution* 13, 2 (January 1969): 192–209.
49. Van den Haag, *Punishing Criminals*, p.32. But here Van den Haag seems to ignore Rawls's limitations upon the separation of the distributive justice system and the penal system. The distinction makes sense, believes Rawls, only when the distributive system is just.
50. Van den Haag, *Punishing Criminals*, p. 32.
51. *Ibid.*, p. 34.
52. *Ibid.*, p. 53.
53. Emile Durkheim, *Suicide* (Glencoe, Ill.: The Free Press, 1949).
54. E.g., Karl Menninger, *The Crime of Punishment* (New York: Viking, 1969).
55. Van den Haag, *Punishing Criminals*, p. 64.
56. *Ibid.*, p. 117.
57. *Ibid.*, p. 69.

CHAPTER 3

1. Ray Madding McConnell, *Criminal Responsibility and Social Constraint* (New York: Charles Scribner's Sons, 1912), pp. 334–336.
2. E. A. Ross, *Social Control, A Survey of the Foundations of Order* (New York: Macmillan, 1914), p. 120.

3. L. L. Bernard, *Social Control in its Sociological Aspects* (New York: Macmillan, 1939), p. 580.
4. *Ibid.*, p. 581.
5. *Ibid.*, p. 582.
6. Paul Landis, *Social Control: Social Organization and Disorganization in Process* (New York: Lippincott, 1939), p. 430.
7. *Ibid.*, pp. 183–184.
8. George Dession, "Psychiatry and the Conditioning of Criminal Justice," *Yale Law Journal* 47, 3 (January 1938): 326–328.
9. *Ibid.*, p. 328.
10. Peter Nokes, "Purpose and Efficiency in Humane Social Institutions," *Human Relations* 13, 2 (May 1960): 153.
11. *Ibid.*, pp. 153–155.
12. Ramsey Clark, *Crime in America* (New York: Simon and Schuster, 1971), p. 3.
13. *Ibid.*, p. 6.
14. *Ibid.*, p. 6.
15. *Ibid.*, p. 21.
16. *Ibid.*, p. 22.
17. *Ibid.*, p. 39.
18. *Ibid.*, p. 141.
19. Peter Marris and Martin Rein, *The Dilemmas of Social Reform, Poverty and Community Action in the U.S.* (New York: Atherton, 1967).
20. Stephen M. Rose, *The Betrayal of the Poor, the Transformation of Community Action* (Cambridge, Mass.: Schenkman, 1972).
21. Karl Menninger, *The Crime of Punishment* (New York: Viking, 1969), p. 28.
22. *Ibid.*, pp. 3–15.
23. *Ibid.*, p. 113.
24. *Ibid.*, pp. 202–203.
25. *Ibid.*, pp. 209–210.
26. Marvin Frankel, *Criminal Sentences* (New York: Hill and Wang, 1972): Andrew von Hirsch, *Doing Justice* (New York: Hill and Wang, 1976); David Fogel, *We Are the Living Proof* (Cincinnati: Anderson, 1975).
27. Leon Radzinowicz, *Ideology and Crime* (New York: Columbia University Press, 1966); von Hirsch, *Doing Justice*, pp. 9–35.
28. *Ibid.*, pp. 254–258.
29. S. B. Sarason, *The Psychological Sense of Community: Prospects for a Community Psychology* (San Francisco: Jossey-Bass, 1974), p. 188.
30. Norval Morris, *The Future of Imprisonment* (Chicago, The University of Chicago Press, 1974); Anthony J. Mannochio and Jimmy Dunn, *The Time Game* (New York: Dell, 1970).
31. Menninger, p. 223.
32. *Ibid.*, p. 153.
33. *Ibid.*, pp. 228–235.
34. *Ibid.*, pp. 268–280.

CHAPTER 4

1. For a lengthy historical review of this scholarly tradition, and of some alleged shortcomings within it, see John Griffiths, "The Limits of Criminal Law Scholarship," *Yale Law Journal* 79 (1970): 1388–1474.

2. A large number of political science writings address the extent to which community and social structure is elitist or pluralist. See, for example, Willis D. Hawley and Frederick M. Wirt, *The Search for Community Power* (Englewood Cliffs, N.J.: Prentice-Hall, 1978, second edition).
3. See Ralph Dahrendorf, *Class and Class Conflict in Industrial Society* (Stanford, Calif.: Stanford University Press, 1959).
4. David Fogel, "... We Are the Living Proof...," (Cincinnati: Anderson, 1975); Norval Morris, *The Future of Imprisonment* (Chicago: The University of Chicago Press, 1974); Andrew von Hirsch, *Doing Justice* (New York: Hill and Wang, 1976); James Q. Wilson, *Thinking About Crime* (New York: Vintage, 1977).
5. It is interesting and informative to relate these basic assumptions on social change to the current debates about planning strategies in the United States. The best discussion of these is probably found in Amitai Etzioni, *The Active Society* (New York: The Free Press, 1968), pp. 249–282. This group seems to exhibit the same tendencies and preferences as the planners associated with Dahl, that is, the "incremental" planning approach.
6. This is true of the post-World War II manifestations of this tradition. Bernard, Landis, McConnell, Ross, to some extent Homans, and others cited in the introductory part of Chapter 4 were more elaborate in their attention to social structure, but as was pointed out in the first chapter, the early examinations of social control, which also downplayed the effectiveness and functionality of the law, became increasingly diffuse and refracted after Homans. The more modern work concentrates on problems and human service systems, not social structure.
7. Etzioni, *The Active Society*, p. 44.
8. Two other writers who are somewhat more explicit about this reshuffling of social resources are Matthew Dumont, *The Absurd Healer* (New York: Jacob Aronson, 1968); and Richard Korn, "Of Crime, Criminal Justice and Corrections," *University of San Francisco Law Review* 6 (October 1971): 27–75.

CHAPTER 5

1. See James N. Rosenau, "Intervention as a Scientific Concept," *Journal of Conflict Resolution* 13, 2 (June 1969): 155.
2. Note that these sources of error are either theoretical or empirical. The question of which social system is desirable for the future is an ethical question, or at least a question of values. Whether this ethical or value choice is, or can be thought of, as "correct" will not be covered here.
3. George Homans, *The Human Group* (New York: Harcourt, Brace, 1950), p. 295.
4. Norval Morris, *The Future of Imprisonment* (Chicago: The University of Chicago Press, 1974).
5. One presentation of equifinality is obtainable in Daniel Katz and Robert Kahn, *The Social Psychology of Organizations* (New York: Wiley, 1966), pp. 25–26.
6. Stafford Beer, *Decision and Control* (New York: Wiley, 1966), p. 254.
7. *Ibid.*
8. E. A. Ross, *Social Control, A Survey of the Foundations of Order* (New York: Macmillan, 1914).
9. Walter Buckley, *Sociology and Modern Systems Theory* (Englewood Cliffs, N.J.: Prentice-Hall, 1967).
10. Beer, *Decision and Control*, pp. 461–496.
11. Amitai Etzioni, *The Active Society* (New York: The Free Press, 1967).

12. Russell Ackoff and F. E. Emery, *On Purposeful Systems* (Chicago: Aldine-Atherton, 1972).
13. *Ibid.*, pp. 209–213.
14. Morris Janowitz, "Sociological Theory and Social Control," *American Journal of Sociology* 91 (July 1975): 82–108; Etzioni, *The Active Society*, pp. 60–83; Daniel Bell, *The Coming of Post-Industrial Society* (New York: Harper & Row, 1976).
15. Stephen M. Rose, *Betrayal of the Poor, The Transformation of Community Action* (Cambridge, Mass.: Schenkman, 1972) and Peter Marris and Martin Rein, *Dilemmas of Social Reform* (New York: Atherton, 1967).
16. Jerald Hage and Michael Aiken, *Social Change in Complex Organizations* (New York: Random House, 1970); Anant Negandhi, *Modern Organizational Theory in an Interorganizational Perspective* (Kent, Ohio: Kent State University Press, 1972); Matthew Trite, Roger Chisholm, and Michael Raduer, *Interorganizational Decision Making* (Chicago: Aldine-Atherton 1972).
17. Daniel Bell, *The Coming of Post-Industrial Society*, pp. 47–121, and Radovau Richta, *Civilization at the Crossroads: Social and Human Implications of the Scientific and Technological Revolution* (White Plains, N.Y.: International Arts and Sciences Press, 1969).
18. Buckley is perhaps the most vociferous critic of Parsons's systems analogues, *Sociology and Modern Systems Theory*; and Dahrendorf, *Class and Class Conflict in Industrial Society* (Stanford, Calif.: Stanford University Press, 1959) provides the conflict model of society as a substitute to the Parsonian model.
19. Morton Grozdins, *The American System: A New View of Governments in the United States* (Chicago: Rand McNally, 1963); Dahrendorf, *Class and Class Conflict in Industrial Society*; Roland Warren, *Community in America* (Chicago: Rand McNally, 1963).
20. Roland Warren, Stephen Rose, and Ann Bergunder, *The Structure of Urban Reform* (Lexington, Mass.: Lexington Books, 1974); Bell, *The Coming of Post-Industrial Society*, pp. 339–368.
21. Buckley, *Sociology and Modern Systems Theory*, pp. 205–207.
22. Talcott Parsons, *The Social System* (New York: The Free Press, 1964).
23. Geoffrey Vickers, *Making Institutions Work* (New York: Halsted, 1973), pp. 44–58.
24. Beer's explanation of this means of guidance of large systems is relatively clear (*Decision and Control*, pp. 461–495), but see also Vickers, *Making Institutions Work*, pp. 59–80, and Etzioni, *The Active Society*, pp. 387–428.
25. See W. Koehler, *The Place of Values in the World of Fact* (London: Liveright, 1938), pp. 314–328, and Daniel Katz and Robert Kahn, *The Social Psychology of Organizations* (New York: Wiley, 1966), pp. 14–29.
26. Beer, *Decision and Control*, pp. 289–298.
27. Several excellent examples of homostatic control in both physical and social systems is provided in Alfred Kuhn, *The Study of Society* (Homewood, Ill.: Irwin, 1963), pp. 10–49.
28. Homans, *The Human Group*, p. 303.
29. *Ibid.*, p. 298.
30. Theodore Mills, "Equilibrium and the Process of Deviance and Control," *American Sociological Review* 24, 5 (October 1959): 671–679.
31. *Ibid.*, pp. 673–674.
32. *Ibid.*, p. 674.
33. See Erving Goffman, *The Presentation of Self in Everyday Life* (Garden City, N.Y.: Doubleday Anchor, 1959), pp. 4–16; the coverage of the Scottish police in Michael Banton, *The Policeman in the Community* (New York: Basic Books, 1964); Homans, *The Human Group*.

34. Leslie Wilkins, *Social Deviance* (Englewood Cliffs, N.J.: Prentice-Hall, 1965), pp. 88–95; J. I. Kituse and D. C. Dietrick, "Delinquent Boys: A Critique," *American Sociological Review* 24, 2 (1959); Marvin Wolfgang and Franco Ferracuti, *The Subculture of Violence* (London: Tavistock, 1967), pp. 284–312.
35. One of the most straightforward accounts of this is provided by Clarence Schrag, "Contemporary Corrections—An Analytical Model," consultant's paper prepared for the President's Commission on Law Enforcement and the Administration of Justice (Washington, D.C., mimeo, 1966) and a revision of that paper in which Schrag emphasizes the limitations of a correctional system as a correctional or control device for society, *Annals of the American Academy of Political and Social Science*, January 1969.
36. Dahrendorf, *Class and Class Conflict in Industrial Society*, pp. 295–307; Bell, *The Coming of Post-Industrial Society*, pp. 366–367.
37. Parsons, *The Social System*, pp. 319–321.
38. Wilkins, *Social Deviance*, p. 66.
39. Mills, "Equilibrium and the Process of Deviance and Control," p. 678.
40. See Louis Wirth, "Urbanism as a Way of Life," *American Journal of Sociology* 44, 1 (July 1938): 1–24, generally considered one of the classic pieces on complex urban structure. For an empirical confirmation of this model of the city, see Albert J. Reiss, Jr., "Functional Specialization of Cities," in Paul K. Hatt and Albert J. Reiss, Jr. (eds.), *Cities and Society (The Revised Reader in Urban Sociology)*, Glencoe, Ill.: Free Press, 1957), pp. 555–575.

    Within the criminal justice literature, one of the finest articulations of the theory of urban social structure and police arrest practices is the previously cited paper by Arthur L. Stinchcombe, "Institutions of Privacy in the Determination of Police Administration Practice," *American Journal of Sociology* 49 (September 1963): 150–160.
41. Mills, "Equilibrium and the Process of Deviance and Control," p. 676.
42. *Ibid.*, p. 677.
43. Albert J. Reiss, Jr. and Donald J. Black, "Interrogation and the Criminal Process," *Annals of the American Academy of Political and Social Science* 374 (November 1967): 49.
44. *Ibid.*, p. 57.
45. Mills, "Equilibrium and the Process of Deviance and Control," p. 678.
46. Katz and Kahn, *The Social Psychology of Organizations*, pp. 71–110.
47. Bell, *The Coming of Post-Industrial Society*, pp. 212–232.
48. Leslie Wilkins, "Crime and Justice at the Turn of the Century," paper presented at the 77th Annual Meeting of the American Academy of Political and Social Science, Philadelphia, April 13, 1973.
49. Norton Long, "The Local Community as an Ecology of Games," *American Journal of Sociology* 64, 3 (November 1958): 251–261.
50. Robert McNamara's tenure in the Defense Department seems particularly important; see Bell, *The Coming of Post-Industrial Society*, pp. 357–358. See also Herbert Kelman, *A Time to Speak* (San Francisco: Jossey-Bass, 1968), pp. 43–45, 59–61, 92–98.
51. Not to change the intention of this emphasis on the system boundaries chosen and made legitimate by the President's Commission, one could also point to the work of the American Bar Foundation, in its criminal justice field studies directed by Frank Remington of Wisconsin Law School, as a forerunner of the President's Commission's approach. The Commission relied frequently on foundation reports and consultants who worked on the foundation survey. But in addition, the Commission added the general systems theory approach of Alfred Blumstein, who has then and since done system modeling of the criminal process under contracts from the U.S. Defense Department. See the *Science and Technology* report of the President's Commission (Washington, D.C.: Government Printing Office, 1967).

52. One of the best accounts of the growth of general systems theory and operations research in World War II is Beer, *Decision and Control*, pp. 33–37.
53. Bell traces this change in detail, with focus on the atomic bomb and the careers of the scientists involved in its creation. *The Coming of Post-Industrial Society*, pp. 386–408.
54. Wilkins traces the analogy from wartime operations research to strategies against crime with accuracy in *Social Deviance*, pp. 105–135.
55. *Ibid.*, p. 133.

CHAPTER 6

1. George H. Kuper, "Productivity: A National Concern," in Joan L. Wolfe and John F. Heaphey, eds., *Readings in Productivity in Policing* (Washington, D.C.: Police Foundation, 1975), p. 3. For a general discussion of the relationship between the tangibility of organizational goals and the predictability of organizational operations, see W. Keith Warner and A. Eugene Havens, "Goal Displacement and the Intangibility of Organizational Goals," *Administrative Science Quarterly* 12, 4 (March 1968): 539–555.
2. Michael Banton, *The Policeman in the Community* (New York: Basic Books, 1964), pp. 227–240. Banton tends to use the term "role" in this passage rather than "status." The latter term seems a more appropriate substitute, at least within American sociological usage.
3. *Ibid.*, and Leslie Wilkins, *Social Deviance* (Englewood Cliffs, N.J.: Prentice-Hall, 1965), pp. 65–71.
4. James Q. Wilson, *Varieties of Police Behavior* (Cambridge, Mass.: Harvard University Press, 1968).
5. Theodore Mills, "Equilibrium and the Processes of Deviance and Control," *American Sociological Review* 24, 5 (October 1959): 671–679; and for an application to corrections see Clarence Schrag, "The Correctional System: Problems and Prospects," *Annals of the American Academy of Political and Social Science* 381 (January 1969): 11–20.
6. Vincent O'Leary and Donald J. Newman, "Conflict Resolution in Criminal Justice," *Journal of Research in Crime and Delinquency* 7, 2 (July 1970): 99–119.
7. Roland Warren, Stephen M. Rose, and Ann F. Bergunder, *The Structure of Urban Reform* (Lexington, Mass.: Lexington Books, 1974).
8. Jerome Skolnick and J. Richard Woodworth, "Bureaucracy, Information and Social Control: A Study of a Morals Detail," in David Bordua (ed.), *The Police: Six Sociological Essays*, (New York: John Wiley, 1967), pp. 99–136.
9. Richard McCleary, "How Structural Variables Constrain the Parole Officer's Use of Discretionary Powers," *Social Problems* 23, 2 (December 1975): 209–225.
10. David Duffee and Barbara D. Warner, "Interorganizational Behavior and Correctional Programming," in D. Duffee, *Correctional Management* (Englewood Cliffs, N.J.: Prentice-Hall, 1980), pp. 289–315.
11. Patrick V. Murphy, "Police Accountability" in J. Wolfe and J. Heaphey (eds.), *Readings on Productivity in Policing* (Washington, D.C.: Police Foundation, 1975), p. 37.
12. Elmer K. Nelson and Catherine Lovell, *Developing Correctional Administrators* (Washington, D.C.: Government Printing Office, 1967).
13. Marvin E. Frankel, *Criminal Sentences* (New York: Hill and Wang, 1973), pp. 12–25.
14. See Wayne R. LaFave, *Arrest* (Boston: Little, Brown, 1965); Donald J. Newman, *Conviction* (Boston: Little, Brown, 1966); Donald M. McIntyre, Jr., Lawrence P. Tiffany,, and Daniel L. Rotenberg, *Detection of Crime* (Boston: Little, Brown, 1965); Frank W. Miller, *Prosecution* (Boston: Little, Brown, 1970); Robert O. Dawson, *Sentencing* (Boston: Little, Brown,. 1969).

15. Murphy, "Police Accountability," pp. 44–45.
16. President's Commission on Law Enforcement and the Administration of Justice, *Task Force on Courts* (Washington, D.C.: Government Printing Office, 1967), pp. 29–31.
17. *Ibid.*, pp. 34–35.
18. Albert J. Reiss and Donald J. Black, "Interrogation and the Criminal Process," *The Annals of the American Academy of Political and Social Science* 374 (November 1967): 48.
19. George C. Homans, *The Human Group* (New York: Harcourt, Brace and Co., 1950): 309–310.
20. William Reid, "Interagency Coordination in Delinquency Prevention and Control," *Social Service Review* 38 (March 1964): 418–428.
21. *Ibid.*, p. 427.
22. Malcolm Feeley, "Two Models of the Criminal Justice System: An Organizational Perspective," *Law and Society Review* 7, 3 (Spring 1973): 407–425.
23. *Ibid.*, p. 425.
24. Dennis Sullivan and Larry Tifft, "Court Intervention in Corrections: Roots of Resistance and Problems of Compliance," *Crime and Delinquency* 21, 3 (July 1975): 217–218. For a review of various external attempts to change police behavior and the means used by police to reduce the impact of such pressures, see Michael W. O'Neill, "The Role of the Police—Normative Role Expectations in a Metropolitan Police Department," unpublished doctoral dissertation, State University of New York at Albany, 1974, pp. 1–13.
25. Eugene Litwak and Lydia F. Hylton, "Interorganizational Analysis: A Hypotheses on Co-ordinating Agencies," in Y. Hasenfeld and R. English (eds.), *Human Service Organizations* (Ann Arbor: University of Michigan Press, 1974), p. 562.
26. See Morton Grozdins, *The American System* (Chicago: Rand McNally, 1963); Robert C. Wood, *Suburbia: Its People and Their Politics* (Boston: Houghton Mifflin, 1959); Peter Marris and Martin Rein, *Dilemmas of Social Reform, Poverty and Community Action in the United States* (New York: Atherton 1967).
27. Alvin W. Gouldner, "The Sociologist as Partisan: Sociology and the Welfare State," *American Sociologist* 3 (May 1968): 103–116.
28. On the "recycling" of conflicts, see L. R. Pondy, "Organizational Conflict: Concepts and Models," *Administrative Science Quarterly* 12, 2 (June 1967): 296–320. On this recycling problem within correctional agencies, Donald Cressey, "Limitations on Organization of Treatment in the Modern Prison," in R. Cloward and others, *Theoretical Studies in Social Organization of the Prison* (New York: Social Science Research Council, Pamphlet 15, March 1960), pp. 78–110.
29. One of the most insightful analyses of this situation relative to corrections is the Cressey article cited immediately above. See also Cressey, "Contradictory Directives in Complex Organizations: The Case of the Prison," *Administrative Science Quarterly* 4 (June 1959): 1–19, in which Cressey emphasizes the impact of negative sanctions applied to custodial officers on the ability of the prisons to control offenders. Similar problems among police departments are also frequently observed. See, for example, John McNamara, "Uncertainties in Police Work: The Relevance of Police Recruits' Background and Training," in D. Bordua, *The Police* (New York: John Wiley, 1965), pp. 163–252. The limitations of the criminal courts to negative sanctions in the control of either judicial or police behavior are fairly well known. Court sanctions are negatives, such as the exclusionary rule, which serve as guides rather than punishments only in a very indirect way.
30. Douglas McGregor, *The Professional Manager*, edited by Caroline McGregor and Warren Bennis (New York: McGraw-Hill, 1967), pp. 123–124. See also Alvin Gouldner, *Patterns of Industrial Bureaucracy* (New York: The Free Press, 1954), pp. 207–211.
31. McGregor, *The Professional Manager*, pp. 125–127.
32. *Ibid.*, pp. 142–143; Rensis Likert, *New Patterns of Management* (New York: McGraw-

Hill, 1961), pp. 16–25; Daniel Katz an Robert Kahn, *The Social Psychology of Organizations* (New York: John Wiley, 1966), pp. 347–368.
33. McGregor, *The Professional Manager*, pp.. 124–125.
34. Edward E. Lawler III and John Grant Rhode, *Information and Control in Organizations* (Pacific Palisades, Calif.: Goodyear, 1976), pp. 97–98.
35. McCleary, "How Structural Variables Constrain the Parole Officer's Use of Discretionary Powers," p. 224.
36. James P. Morgan, "Planning and Implementing a Productivity Program," in J. Wolfe and J. Heaphey, *Readings on Productivity in Policing* (Washington, D.C.: Police, Foundation, 1975), pp. 146–147.
37. David Sudnow, "Normal Crimes: Sociological Features of the Penal Code in a Public Defender's Office," *Social Problems* 12, 3 (Winter 1965): 255–276; John Kaplan, "The Prosecutorial Discretion—A Comment," *Northwestern Law Review* 60 (1965): 174–193.
38. Herman Goldstein, "Toward a Redefinition of the Police Function," in A. Cohn and E. Viano (eds.), *Police Community Relations, Images, Roles, Realities* (Philadelphia: Lippincott, 1976), pp. 125–130.
39. Johannes Andenaes, "General Prevention, Illusion or Reality," *Journal of Criminal Law, Criminology and Police Science* 43, 2 (July/August 1952): 179.
40. *Ibid.*, p. 180.
41. Frank Zimring and Gordon Hawkins, "Deterrence and Marginal Groups," *Journal of Research in Crime and Delinquency* 5, 2 (July 1968): 102.
42. *Ibid.*, pp. 104–105.
43. *Ibid.*, p. 108.
44. John Bennington and Paul Skelton, "Public Participation in Decision-Making by Governments," in *Application of Policy Analysis: Politics and Bureaucracy* (Chicago: Aldine, 1974), p. 442.
45. H. L. Nieburg, "Violence, Law and The Informal Polity," *The Journal of Conflict Resolution* 12, 2 (June 1969): 205.
46. Wilkins, *Social Deviance*, pp. 78–86.

CHAPTER 7

1. Edward Alsworth Ross, *Social Control, A Survey of the Foundations of Order* (New York: MacMillan, 1914), p. 109.
2. Johannes Andenaes, "General Prevention, Illusion or Reality," *Journal of Criminal Law, Criminology and Police Science* 43, 2 (July 1952): 176–198.
3. Jackson Toby, "Is Punishment Necessary?" *Journal of Criminal Law, Criminology and Police Science* 55, 3 (September 1964): 332–337.
4. Michael Banton, *The Policeman in the Community* (New York: Basic Books, 1964), pp. 368–369.
5. Richard Korn, "Of Crime, Criminal Justice and Corrections," *University of San Francisco Law Review* 6 (October 1971): 27–75.
6. Donald Cressey, "Contradictory Directives in Complex Organizations, The Case of the Prison," *Administrative Science Quarterly* 4 (June 1959): 1–19.
7. Herbert Packer, *Limits of the Criminal Sanction* (Stanford, Calif.: Stanford University Press, 1968).
8. Leslie Wilkins, *The Evaluation of Penal Measures* (New York: Random House, 1969), pp. 17–18.
9. Vincent O'Leary and David Duffee, "Correctional Policy—A Classification of Goals Designed for Change," *Crime and Delinquency* 17, 4 (October 1971): 373–386.

10. Elliot Studt, *Surveillance and Service in Parole* (Los Angeles: Institute of Public Affairs, U.C.L.A., 1971).
11. David Stanley, *The Prisoners Among Us* (Washington, D.C.: Brookings Institution, 1976).
12. Jennie McIntyre, "Public Attitudes Toward Crime and Law Enforcement," *Annals of the American Academy of Political and Social Science* 374 (November 1967): 34–46.
13. Louis Harris and Associates, *The Public Looks at Corrections*, survey undertaken for the Joint Commission on Correctional Manpower and Training, 1967.
14. David Duffee and R. Richard Ritti, "Correctional Policy and Public Values," *Criminology* 14, 4 (February 1977): 449–460.
15. National Advisory Commission on Criminal Justice Standards and Goals, *Corrections* (Washington, D.C.: Government Printing Office, 1973), pp. 141–143.
16. Herbert Simon, "On the Concept of Organizational Goal," *Administrative Science Quarterly* 9 (June 1964): 1–22, suggests a framework for the analysis of complex organizations under the assumption of inherent conflict.
17. Thurmond Arnold, "Law Enforcement—An Attempt at Social Dissection," *Yale Law Journal* 42 (1932): 8.
18. *Ibid.*, p. 12.
19. McIntyre, "Public Attitudes Toward Crime and Law Enforcement," pp. 36–37.
20. G. F. Kirchway, "Crime and Punishment," *Journal of Criminal Law and Criminology* 1 (January 1911): 718–734.
21. John W. Meyer and Brian Rowan, "Institutionalized Organizations: Formal Structure as Myth and Ceremony," *American Journal of Sociology* 83, 2 (September 1977): 340–341.
22. Simon, "On the Concept of Organizational Goal," p. 7.
23. *Ibid.*, p. 20.
24. Talcott Parsons, *The Social System* (New York: The Free Press, 1951), pp. 101–102.
25. David Sudnow, "Normal Crimes: Sociological Features of the Penal Code in a Public Defender's Office," *Social Problems* 12, 3 (Winter 1965): 255–276.
26. William A. Gamson, "Rancorous Conflict in Community Politics," *American Sociological Review* 41 (January 1966): 71.
27. H. L. Nieburg, "Violence, Law and The Informal Polity," *The Journal of Conflict Resolution* 13, 2 (June 1969): 192–209.
28. Gresham Sykes, *Society of Captives* (Princeton, N.J.: Princeton University Press, 1971).
29. Edward K. Hamilton, "Police Productivity: The View from City Hall," in J. Wolfe and J. Heaphey (eds.), *Readings in Productivity in Policing* (Washington, D.C.: Police Foundation, 1975), pp. 11–34.
30. James B. Jacobs and Norma Meachum Crotty, *Guard Unions and the Future of the Prisons* (Ithaca, N.Y.: Institute of Public Employment, Cornell University, Monograph 9), p. 1; Gilbert Geiss and Elvin Cavanagh, "Recruitment and Retention of Correctional Personnel," *Crime and Delinquency* 12, 3 (1966): 232–239.
31. John Bennington and Paul Skelton, "Public Participation in Decision Making by Governments," *Government and Program Budgeting: Seven Papers with Commentaries* (London: The Institute of Municipal Treasurers and Accountants, 1973).
32. Robert L. Crain and Donald B. Rosenthal, "Community Status as a Dimension of Local Decision Making," *American Sociological Review* 32, 6 (December 1967): 984.
33. Gamson, "Rancorous Conflict in Community Politics," p. 72.
34. *Ibid.*, p. 73.
35. Duffee and Ritti, "Correctional Policy and Public Value," pp. 455–456.
36. Andrew T. Scull, *Decarceration* (Englewood Cliffs, N.J.: Prentice-Hall, 1977).
37. Peter Marris and Martin Rein, *The Dilemmas of Social Reform* (New York: Atherton,

1967); Jeffrey L. Pressman and Aaron B. Wildavsky, *Implementation* (Berkeley, Calif.: University of California Press, 1973).
38. Robert C. Wood, *Suburbia: Its People and Their Politics* (Boston: Houghton Mifflin, 1959); Morton Grozdins, *The American System* (Chicago: Rand McNally, 1973); Roland Warren, Stephen Rose, and Ann F. Bergunder, *The Structure of Urban Reform* (Lexington, Mass.: Lexington Books, 1974).
39. Daniel Bell, *The Coming of Post-Industrial Society* (New York: Harper & Row, 1976), pp. 279–297.
40. For two examples of conflicting local/central interest in criminal justice administration, see David Duffee, Thomas Maher, and Steve Lagoy, "Administrative Due Process in Community Pre-Parole Programs," *Criminal Law Bulletin* 13, 5 (September 1977): 383–400; and Robert Sebring and David Duffee, "Who Are the Real Prisoners? A Case of Win-Lose Conflict in a State Correctional Institution," *Journal of Applied Behavioral Science* 13, 1 (February 1977): 23–40.
41. Roland Warren, *Community in America* (Chicago: Rand McNally, 1963), p. 155.
42. Kurt Lewin, *Field Theory in the Social Sciences*, Dorwin Cartwright, ed. (New York: Harper & Row, 1951).
43. F. E. Emery and E. L. Trist, "The Causal Texture of Organizational Environments," in R. E. Emery (ed.), *Systems Thinking* (Baltimore: Penguin, 1970), pp. 241–258.
44. Shirley Terreberry, "The Evolution of Organizational Environments," *Administrative Science Quarterly* 12, 4 (March 1968): 590–613.
45. Roland Warren, Stephen Rose, and Ann Bergunder, *The Structure of Urban Reform* (Lexington, Mass.: Lexington Books, 1976); and Roland Warren, "The Interorganizational Field as a Focus for Investigation," *Administrative Science Quarterly* 12, 3 (December 1967): 396–419.
46. Norton Long, "The Local Community as an Ecology of Games," *American Journal of Sociology* 64, 3 (November 1958): 251–261.
47. *Ibid.*
48. Nieburg, "Violence Law, and the Informal Polity," pp. 204–205.
49. William L. Blizek and Jerry Cederblom, "Community Development and Social Justice," *Journal of the Community Development Society* 4, 2 (1973): 49–50.
50. Bennington and Skelton, "Public Participation in Decision Making by Government," p. 432.
51. *Ibid.*, p. 444.
52. The literature that counters the traditional analytical mode of perceiving public programs as a delivery of effective services at least cost is sporadic. However, the reader might refer to Daniel Bell, *The Coming of Post-Industrial Society*, for his discussion of the economizing and the sociologizing modes of organization, pp. 274–284. See also Bernard Beck, "Welfare as a Moral Category," for a discussion of welfare client manipulation of requirements as a competence in controlling the environment, rather than an indication of moral weakness; and Charles Reich, "The New Property," *Yale Law Journal* 63 (1964) for a discussion of certain rights of citizenship and eligibility as the lower-class equivalent of property.
53. Marshall W. Meyer, "Organizational Domains," *American Sociological Review* 40 (October 1975): 600.
54. Nieburg, "Violence, Law, and the Informal Polity," p. 199.
55. Cyril D. Robinson, "The Mayor and the Police—The Political Role of the Police in Society," in G. Mosse (ed.), *Police Forces in History* (London: Sage, 1975), pp. 277–315.
56. George Dession, "Psychiatry and the Conditioning of Criminal Justice," *Yale Law Journal* 47, 3 (January 1938): 319–340.

57. D. Sullivan and L. Tifft, "Court Intervention in Correction: Roots of Resistance and Problems of Compliance," *Crime and Delinquency* 21, 3 (July 1975): 217.
58. Paul Lerman, *Community Treatment and Social Control* (Chicago: University of Chicago Press, 1974), pp. 189–191.
59. Ralph Dahrendorf, *Class and Class Conflict in Industrial Society* (Stanford: Stanford University Press, 1955), pp. 157–165.

CHAPTER 8

1. Roland Warren, *Community in America*, 1st ed. (Chicago: Rand McNally, 1963), p. 9.
2. *Ibid.*
3. E. T. Hiller, "The Community as a Social Group," *American Sociological Review* 6 (1941): 189–191.
4. George A. Hillery, Jr., "Definitions of Community: Areas of Agreement," *Rural Sociology* 20, 2 (June 1955): 118.
5. Warren, *Community in America*, p. 7.
6. *Ibid.*, p. 12.
7. Albert J. Reiss, Jr., "Functional Specialization of Cities," in Paul K. Hatt and Albert J. Reiss, Jr. (eds.), *Cities and Society: The Revised Reader in Urban Sociology* (Glencoe, Ill.: The Free Press, 1957), p. 562.
8. Reiss, "Functional Specialization," pp. 555–556.
9. Charles Perrow, "A Framework for the Comparative Analysis of Organizations," *American Sociological Review* 32, 2 (1967), p. 203.
10. Richard T. LaPiere, *A Theory of Social Control* (New York: McGraw-Hill, 1954), p. 311.
11. Albert Hunter, "The Loss of Community: An Empirical Test through Replication," *American Sociological Review* 40 (October 1975): 538.
12. See James Q. Wilson, *Varieties of Police Behavior* (Cambridge, Mass.: Harvard University Press, 1968).
13. Warren, *Community in America*, pp. 53–95.
14. Allan Silver, "The Demand for Order in Civil Society: A Review of Some Themes of Urban Crime, Police and Riot," in D. Bordua (ed.), *The Police* (New York: John Wiley, 1967), p. 22.
15. Peter B. Meyer, "Communities as Victims of Corporate Crimes," paper presented at the Second International Symposium of Victimology, Boston, September 8, 1976.
16. Mark H. Haller, "Historical Roots of Police Behavior: Chicago, 1890–1925," *Law and Society Review* 10, 2 (Winter 1976): 303–323.
17. National Advisory Commission on Civil Disorders, *Report of the National Advisory Commission* (New York: Bantam Books, 1968), p. 305.
18. William Vega, "The Liberal Policeman: A Contradiction in Terms," *Issues in Criminology* 4, 1 (Fall 1968): 27–28.
19. Bruce J. Terris, "The Role of the Police," *The Annals of the American Academy of Political and Social Science* 374 (November 1967): 62–64.
20. Louis Wirth, "Urbanism as a Way of Life," *American Journal of Sociology* 44, 1 (July 1938): 10.
21. *Ibid.*, pp. 14–15.
22. *Ibid.*, p. 12.
23. Arthur L. Stinchecombe, "Institutions of Privacy in the Determination of Police Administrative Practice," *American Journal of Sociology* 69 (September 1963): 152.
24. Wirth, "Urbanism as a Way of Life," p. 11.
25. William J. Chambliss and Robert B. Seidman, *Law, Order, and Power* (Reading, Mass.: Addison-Wesley, 1971), pp. 28–37.

26. Daniel Bell, *The Coming of Post-Industrial Society* (New York: Basic Books, 1973), p. xi.
27. Ralf Dahrendorf, *Class and Class Conflict in Industrial Society* (Stanford, Calif.: Stanford University Press, 1959), p. 138.
28. Warren's *Community in America*, is the major source for the following prescriptions, but the reader should not overlook a more recent work by Warren, Stephen Rose, and Anne Bergunder, *The Structure of Urban Reform* (Lexington, Mass.: Lexington Books, 1974).
29. Warren, *Community in America*, p. 9.
30. *Ibid.*, p. 10.
31. *Ibid.*, p. 10; Bell, *The Coming of Post-Industrial Society*, pp. 80-99.
32. Warren, *Community in America*, p. 11.
33. *Ibid.*, p. 11.
34. *Ibid.*, pp. 11, 186-191.
35. Martin R. Stein, *The Eclipse of Community: An Interpretation of American Studies* (Princeton, N.J.: Princeton University Press, 1960).
36. Robert C. Wood, *Suburbia: Its People and Their Politics* (Boston: Houghton Mifflin, 1959).
37. Warren, *Community in America*, p. 196.
38. Emile Durkheim, *The Division of Labor in Society*, trans. George Simpson (Glencoe, Ill.: The Free Press, 1947); Peter Kropotkin, *Mutual Aid: A Factor in Evolution* (Boston: Porter Sargent, no date).
39. Warren, *Community in America*, pp. 13-14.
40. D. E. Linder, J. Cooper, and E. E. Jones, "Decision Freedom as a Determinant of the Role of Incentive Magnitude in Attitude Change," in K. Thomas (ed.), *Attitudes and Behavior* (Baltimore: Penguin, 1971), pp. 221-239.
41. Warren, *Community in America*, pp. 12-13.
42. See Dahrendorf, *Class and Class Conflict in Industrial Society*, particularly the last chapter. Dahrendorf uses the terms pluralism and identity of authority to denote structures with high vertical and strong horizontal dimensions.
43. Warren, *Community in America*, pp. 237-266.
44. Leslie T. Wilkins, *Social Deviance* (Englewood Cliffs, N.J.: Prentice-Hall, 1965), pp. 190-226.
45. David Boorkman, Ernest J. Fazio, Jr., Noel Day, and David Weinstein, *Community Based Corrections in Des Moines* (Washington, D.C.: Government Printing Office, 1976).
46. Warren, Rose, and Bergunder, *The Structure of Urban Reform*.
47. Lawrence Sherman, Catherine H. Milton, and Thomas V. Kelly, *Team Policing, Seven Case Studies* (Washington, D.C.: Police Foundation, 1973).
48. David Duffee, Peter B. Meyer, and Barbara D. Warner, *Offender Needs, Parole Outcome and Program Structure in the Bureau of Corrections Community Services Division* (Harrisburg: Governor's Justice Commission, Fall 1977).

CHAPTER 9

1. Emile Durkheim, *Division of Labor in Society* (New York: The Free Press, 1964).
2. William Chambliss and Robert Seidman, *Law, Order, and Power* (Reading, Mass.: Addison-Wesley, 1971), p. 504.
3. Peter Kropotkin, *Mutual Aid, A Factor in Evolution* (Boston: Porter Sargent, no date).
4. *Ibid.*, pp. 252-259.
5. W. Lloyd Warner and J. O. Low, *The Social System of the Modern Factory, The Strike: A Social Analysis* (New Haven, Conn.: Yale University Press, 1947).

6. Amos H. Hawley, *Human Ecology: A Theory of Community Structure* (New York: Ronald Press, 1950), pp. 209–211.
7. Albert J. Reiss, Jr., "Functional Specialization of Cities," in Paul K. Hatt and A. J. Reiss, Jr. (eds.), *Cities and Society: The Revised Reader in Urban Sociology* (Glencoe, Ill.: The Free Press, 1957), p. 562.
8. *Ibid.*, pp. 555–556.
9. *Ibid.*, pp. 574–575.
10. Peter B. Meyer, "Communities as Victims of Corporate Crimes," paper prepared for the Second International Symposium on Victimology, Boston, September 8, 1976.
11. Chambliss and Seidman, *Law, Order, and Power*, pp. 484–485.
12. *Ibid.*, pp. 487–491.
13. *Ibid.*, p. 488.
14. Thomas C. Schelling, "What is the Business of Organized Crime?" *American Scholar* 40, 4 (Autumn 1971): 645–646.
15. *Ibid.*, p. 645.
16. *Ibid.*, pp. 650–652.
17. Chambliss and Seidman, *Law, Order, and Power*, p. 494.
18. *Ibid.*, p. 496.
19. James B. Jacobs, "The Politics of Corrections: Town-Prison Relations as a Determinant of Reform," *Social Service Review* (December 1976): 623–631.
20. Meyer, "Communities as Victims of Corporate Crimes."
21. Roland Warren, *Community in America* (Chicago: Rand McNally, 1963), p. 172.
22. *Ibid.*, p. 173.
23. Chambliss and Seidman, *Law, Order, and Power*, p. 495.
24. Warren, *Community in America*, p. 174.
25. David Street, Robert Vinter, and Charles Perrow, *Organization for Treatment* (New York: The Free Press, 1966), pp. 50–55.
26. Kropotkin, *Mutual Aid*.
27. See John Griffiths, "Ideology in Criminal Procedure or a 'Third' Model of the Criminal Process," *Yale Law Journal* 79, 3 (January 1970): 359–417 and Anthony Platt, "The Rise of the Child Saving Movement: A Study in Social Policy and Correctional Reform," *The Annals of the American Academy of Political and Social Science* 381 (January 1969): 25–28.
28. David Duffee and Vincent O'Leary, "Models of Correction: An Entry in the Packer-Griffiths Debate," *Criminal Law Bulletin* 7, 4 (May 1971): 329–352; Elliot Studt, *Surveillance and Service in Parole* (Los Angeles: Institute of Government and Public Affairs, U.C.L.A., 1972).
29. Griffiths, "Ideology in Criminal Procedure, or a 'Third' Model of the Criminal Process."
30. August B. Hollingshead, "Class Differences in Family Stability," *The Annals of the American Academy of Political and Social Science* 272 (1950): 39–46; Solomon Kobrin, "The Conflict of Values in Delinquency Areas," *American Sociological Review* 14 (1951): 653–661; W. I. Thomas and F. Znaniecki, *The Polish Peasant in Europe and America* (New York: Dover, 1927), pp. 1167–1170.
31. Kropotkin, *Mutual Aid*; Chambliss and Seidman, *Law, Order and Power*, pp. 28–35.
32. Mary Reistoffer, "A University Extension Course for Foster Parents," Children (Jan./Feb. 1968): 28–31; Child Welfare League of America on Fostering, *Fifteen Articles By and For Foster Parents* (New York: Child Welfare League of America, 1972).
33. Kropotkin, *Mutual Aid*.
34. *Ibid.*, and A. Maslow, *The Farther Reaches of Human Nature* (New York: Viking, 1971), pp. 299–308.

35. John Irwin and Donald Cressey, "Thieves, Convicts, and the Inmate Culture," *Social Problems* 10, 2 (Fall 1962): 142–155.
36. Andrew T. Scull, *Decarceration* (Englewood Cliffs, N.J.: Prentice-Hall, 1977), p. 31.
37. Marvin Wolfgang and Franco Ferracuti, *The Subculture of Violence* (London: Tavistock, 1967), pp. 299–305.
38. James Q. Wilson, *Varieties of Police Behavior* (Cambridge, Mass.: Harvard University Press, 1968).
39. Hans Toch, J. Douglas Grant, and Ray Galvin, *Agents of Change: A Study in Police Reform* (Cambridge: Schenkman, 1975), pp. 273–305.
40. T. Mills, "Equilibrium and The Processes of Deviance and Control," *American Sociological Review* 24, 5 (October 1959): 671–679.
41. See the discussion in Chapter 5.
42. Dennis C. Sullivan, *Team Models for Probation* (Hackensack, N.J.: National Council on Crime and Delinquency, 1971).
43. Street, Vinter, and Perrow, *Organization for Treatment*, 75–79.
44. Jules Henry, *Culture Against Man* (New York: Viking, 1965), pp. 182–322.
45. See Warren, *Community in America*, 177–185.
46. Dennis Wrong, "The Over Socialized Conception of Man in Modern Sociology," *The American Sociological Review* 26: 184–193. See also Daniel Katz and Robert Kahn, *The Social Psychology of Organizations* (New York: John Wiley, 1966), pp. 171–199.
47. David Reisman, *The Lonely Crowd* (New Haven, Conn.: The Yale University Press, 1961), pp. 3–31.
48. George Homans, *The Human Group* (New York: Harcourt, Brace, and Co., 1950); Chambliss and Seidman, *Law, Order and Power*; T. Mills, "Equilibrium and The Processes of Deviance and Control"; Michael Banton, *The Policeman in the Community* (New York: Basic Books, 1964).
49. August B. Hollingshead, "The Concept of Social Control," *American Sociological Review* 6, 2 (April 1941): 217–224.
50. Warren, *Community in America*, pp. 180–181. Warren relies heavily on William H. Form and Delbert C. Miller, *Industry, Labor, and Community* (New York: Harper and Bros., 1960).
51. Alfred Kuhn, *The Study of Society* (Homewood, Ill.: Irwin Dorsey, 1963); Katz and Kahn, *The Social Psychology of Organizations*, 94–96.
52. Amatai Etzioni, *The Active Society* (New York: The Free Press, 1968): Daniel Bell, *The Coming of Post-Industrial Society* (New York: Harper & Row, 1967).
53. Kropotkin, *Mutual Aid*, pp. 250–252.
54. See also Leslie Wilkins, "Directions for Corrections," in R. Carter and L. Wilkins (eds.), *Probation, Parole, and Community Corrections*, 2nd ed. (New York: John Wiley, 1976), pp. 60–70.
55. Talcott Parsons, *The Social System* (New York: The Free Press, 1964), p. 251; Katz and Kahn, *The Social Psychology of Organizations*, pp. 112–113.
56. T. Mills, "Equilibrium and The Processes of Deviance and Control"; Warren, *Community in America*, pp. 177–190; D. Wrong, "The Over-Socialized Conception of Man in Modern Sociology."
57. L. T. Wilkins, *Social Deviance* (Englewood Cliffs, N.J.: Prentice-Hall, 1965), pp. 132–135.
58. Albert J. Reiss, Jr. and David Bordua, "Environment and Organization: A Perspective on the Police," in D. Bordua (ed.), *The Police: Six Sociological Essays* (New York: John Wiley, 1967), pp. 25–26.
59. J. Q. Wilson, *Varieties of Police Behavior*; Egon Bittner, *The Functions of the Police*

in a Modern Society (Chevy Chase, Md.: National Institute of Mental Health, 1970).
60. Phillip Selznick, "Foundations for a Theory of Organization," *American Sociological Review* 13 (Fall 1948): 25–26.
61. Ray H. Elling and Sandor Halebsky, "Organizational Differentiation and Support: A Conceptual Framework," *Administrative Science Quarterly* 6, 2 (September 1961): 192.
62. *Ibid.*, pp. 209.
63. *Ibid.*, pp. 205–207.
64. Roland L. Warren, "The Integration of Community Decision Organizations: Some Basic Concepts and Needed Research," *Social Service Review* 41, 3 (September 1967): 266.
65. Chambliss and Seidman, *Law, Order, and Power*, p. 474.
66. *Ibid.*
67. Gilbert Geis and Elvin Cavanaugh, "Recruitment and Retention of Correctional Personnel," *Crime and Delinquency* 12, 3 (1966): 232–239; Milton Rokeach, Martin G. Miller, and John A. Snyder, "The Value Gap Between Police and Policed," *Journal of Social Issues* 27, 2 (1971): 155–171; Irving Piliavin, "Police-Community Alienation: Its Structural Roots and a Proposed Remedy," in A. Cohn and E. Viano (eds.), *Police Community Relations* (Philadelphia: Lippincott, 1976), pp. 589–603.
68. James Q. Wilson, "Police Morale, Reform, and Citizen Respect: The Chicago Case," in D. Bordua (ed.), *The Police: Six Sociological Essays*, p. 158.
69. *Ibid.*, pp. 156–158.
70. Michael Banton, "Authority in the Mass Society," *The Police Journal* 43, 7 (July 1970): 319–323.
71. Paul Lerman, *Community Treatment and Social Control* (Chicago: The University of Chicago Press, 1975), p. 214.
72. Jennie McIntyre, "Public Attitudes Toward Crime and Law Enforcement," *Annals of the American Academy of Political and Social Science* 374 (November 1967): 43.

CHAPTER 10

1. Roland Warren, *Community in America* (Chicago: Rand McNally, 1963), p. 188.
2. Steven Spitzer, "Punishment and Social Organization: A Study of Durkheim's Theory of Penal Evolution," *Law and Society Review* 9, 4 (Summer 1975): 613–637.
3. Warren, *Community in America*, p. 187.
4. Emile Durkheim, *Elementary Forms of Religious Life* (New York: The Free Press, 1955).
5. See the review in Daniel Bell, *The Coming of Post-Industrial Society* (New York: Harper & Row, 1973), pp. 181–188.
6. Morton Grozdins, *The American System* (Chicago: Rand McNally, 1963).
7. Robert C. Wood, *Suburbia: Its People and Their Politics* (Boston: Houghton Mifflin, 1959), p. 103.
8. *Ibid.*, p. 104.
9. *Ibid.*, p. 66.
10. Geoffrey Vickers, *Making Institutions Work* (New York: Halsted, 1973), pp. 81–92.
11. For Herbert Packer's analysis, see *Limits of the Criminal Sanction* (Stanford, Calif: Stanford University Press, 1968). For the argument that the due process approach to accuracy is deleterious to order, see Ernest Van den Haag, *Punishing Criminals* (New York: Basic Books, 1975), pp. 168–171.
12. E. L. Kimberly and D. J. Newman, "Judicial Intervention in Correctional Decisions: Threat and Response," *Crime and Delinquency* 14 (1968): 4.
13. Marvin Zalman, "Prisoners Rights to Medical Care," *The Journal of Criminal Law*

Criminology and Police Science 63, 2 (1972): 185–199; John W. Palmer, *Constitutional Rights of Prisoners* (Cincinnati: Anderson, 1973), pp. 126–133.
14. *Mempa* v. *Rhay*, 389 U.S. 128 (1967); *Morrissey* v. *Brewer*, 408 U.S. 471 (1972); *Gagnon* v. *Scarpelli*, 411 U.S. 778 (1973); *Wolff* v. *McDonnell*, 418 U.S. 539 (1974).
15. John Griffiths, "Ideology in Criminal Procedure or a 'Third' Model of the Criminal Process," *Yale Law Journal* 79, 3 (January 1970): 359–417.
16. H. I. Nieburg, "Violence, Law, and the Informal Polity," *Journal of Conflict Resolution* 12, 2 (June 1969): 205–206.
17. Packer, *The Limits of the Criminal Sanction*, pp. 43–44.
18. Nieburg, "Violence, Law and the Informal Polity," pp. 205–206.
19. Vincent O'Leary, "Some Directions for Citizen Involvement in Corrections," *Annals of the American Academy of Political and Social Science* 381 (January 1969): 99–108; Robert Trojanowicz and Samuel Dixon, *Criminal Justice and the Community* (Englewood Cliffs, N.J.: Prentice-Hall, 1974), pp. 279–326.
20. This is primarily the form of the argument as presented by the Welfare and Moralist groups.
21. Daniel Katz and Robert Kahn, *The Social Psychology of Organizations* (New York: John Wiley, 1966), pp. 211–212.
22. Warren, *Community in America*, pp. 195–207.
23. Peter Kropotkin, *Mutual Aid, A Factor of Evolution* (Boston: Porter Sargent, no date), pp. 290–291.
24. Arthur E. Morgan, *The Community of the Future* (Yellow Springs, Ohio: Community Service, Inc., 1957), p. 58.
25. J. Q. Wilson, *Varieties of Police Behavior* (Cambridge, Mass.: Harvard University Press, 1968), p. 18; Jim Munro, *Administrative Behavior and Police Organization* (Cincinnati: Anderson, 1974), pp. 9–19.
26. Hans Toch, J. Douglas Grant, and Ray Galvin, *Agents of Change: A Study in Police Reform* (Cambridge, Mass.: Schenkman, 1975), pp. 276–304.
27. National Institute of Law Enforcement and Criminal Justice, *Training Police as Specialists in Family-Crisis Intervention* (Washington, D.C.: National Institute, 1970); Trojanowicz and Dixon, *Criminal Justice and the Community*, pp. 310–324.
28. John A. Grimes, "The Police, The Union, and The Productivity Imperative," in J. L. Wolfe and J. F. Heaphy (eds.), *Readings in Productivity in Policing* (Washington, D.C.: Police Foundation, 1975), p. 77.
29. Toch, Grant, and Galvin, *Agents of Change: A Study in Police Reform*.
30. For an entire rationale and new organizational model of police as mutual support providers see Munro, *Administrative Behavior and Police Organization*. For an attempt to state how service need information can be run effectively incorporated in police management systems and policymaking, see William Brown, *Response and Responsibility*, manuscript in progress, School of Criminal Justice, State University of New York at Albany.
31. Bruce J. Terris, "The Role of the Police," *The Annals of the American Academy of Political and Social Science* 374 (November 1967): 67–68.
32. Frank J. Cannavale, Jr., *A Study of Witness Cooperation with District of Columbia Prosecutors* (Lexington, Mass.: D. C. Heath, in press), p. 92.
33. Alan T. Harland, "Restitution and Service by Offenders: A Summary of Previous Research," paper presented at the annual meetings of the American Society of Criminology, Dallas, November 1978.
34. Kropotkin, *Mutual Aid, A Factor of Evolution*, pp. 107–114, 130–137.
35. Robert Martinson, "What Works?: Questions and Answers About Prison Reform," *The Public Interest* 35 (Spring 1974): 25.

36. Michael Gottfredson, "Treatment Destruction Techniques," *Journal of Research in Crime and Delinquency* 16, 1 (January 1979): 39–54; Ted Palmer, "Martinson Revisited," *Journal of Research in Crime and Delinquency* 12, 2 (1975): 133–152.
37. David Duffee and R. Richard Ritti, "Correctional Policy and Public Values," *Criminology* 14, 4 (1977): 449–460.
38. Strategies by which to do this, offered up with apparently no realization that it is happening, are peppered throughout David Boorkman, Ernest J. Fazio, Jr., Noel Day, and David Weinstein, *An Exemplary Project, Community Based Corrections in Des Moines* (Washington, D.C.: Government Printing Office, November 1976).
39. David Duffee, Peter B. Meyer, and Barbara P. Warner, *Offender Needs, Parole Outcome and Program Structure in the Bureau of Corrections Community Services Division* (Harrisburg, Pa.: Governor's Justice Commission, 1977), p. 104.
40. *Ibid.*, p. 136.
41. *Ibid.*, pp. 145–146.
42. Elliot Studt, *Surveillance and Service in Parole* (Los Angeles: Institute of Government and Public Affairs, U.C.L.A., 1972).
43. Phillip Selznick, "An Approach to a Theory of Bureaurcracy," *American Sociological Review* 8, 1 (February 1943): 51.
44. Charles Perrow, "A Framework for the Comparative Analysis of Organizations," *American Sociological Review* 32, 2 (1967): 196–198.
45. The reader might also refer to Donald Cressey, "Contradictory Directives in Complex Organizations, The Case of the Prison," *Administrative Science Quarterly* 4 (June 1959): 1–19.
46. Paul Lerman, *Community Treatment and Social Control* (Chicago: The University of Chicago Press, 1975), pp. 129–199.
47. Richard McCleary, "How Structural Variables Constrain the Parole Officer's Use of Discretionary Powers," *Social Problems* 23, 2 (December 1975): 209–225.
48. David Fogel, ". . . We Are the Living Proof . . ." (Cincinnati: Anderson, 1975), pp. 112–126. See also Rudolph Moos, *Evaluating Correctional and Community Settings* (New York: John Wiley, 1974).

Bibliography

Ackoff, Russell, and F. E. Emery. *On Purposeful Systems*. Chicago: Aldine, 1972.
Andenaes, Johannes. "General Prevention, Illusion or Reality." *Journal of Criminal Law, Criminology and Police Science* 43, 2 (July/August 1952).
Arnold, Thurman. "Law Enforcement—An Attempt at Social Dissection." *Yale Law Journal* 42 (1932): 1–30.
Banton, Michael. "Authority in the Mass Society." *The Police Journal* 43, 7 (July 1920): 319–323.
———. *The Policeman in the Community*. New York: Basic Books, 1964.
Beck, Bernard. "Welfare as a Moral Category." *Social Problems*. (1967).
Beer, Stafford. *Decision and Control*. New York: John Wiley, 1966.
Bell, Daniel. *The Coming of Post-Industrial Society*. New York: Harper & Row, 1976.
Bennington, John, and Paul Skelton. "Public Participation in Decision-Making by Governments." *Application of Policy Analysis: Politics and Bureaucracy*. Chicago: Aldine, 1974.
Bensman, Joseph, and Israel Gerver. "Crime and Punishment in the Factory: A Functional Analysis." In Rosenberg, Gerver, and Houton (eds.), *Mass Society in Crisis*. New York: MacMillan, 1964, pp. 141–152.
Bernard, L. L. *Social Control in its Sociological Aspects*. New York: MacMillan, 1939.
Bittner, Egon. *The Functions of the Police in Modern Society*. Cambridge, Mass.: Oelgeschlager, Gunn & Hain, 1980.

Blizek, William L., and Jerry Cederblom. "Community Development and Social Justice." *Journal of the Community Development Society* 4, 2 (1973).
Boorkman, David, Ernest J. Fazio Jr., Noel Day, and David Weinstein. *Community Based Corrections in Des Moines*. Washington, D.C.: Government Printing Office, 1976.
Buckley, Walter. *Sociology and Modern Systems Theory*. Englewood Cliffs, N.J.: Prentice-Hall, 1967.
Campbell, James S., Joseph R. Sahid, and David P. Stang. *Law and Order Reconsidered*. New York: Bantam Books, 1970.
Cannavale, Frank, Jr. *A Study of Witness Cooperation with District of Columbia Prosecutors*. Lexington, Mass.: Lexington Books, in press.
Chambliss, William J., and Robert B. Seidman. *Law, Order and Power*. Reading, Mass.: Addison-Wesley, 1971.
Chapman, Brian. *The Police State*. London: Praeger, 1970.
Child Welfare League of America. *On Fostering: Fifteen Articles by and for Foster Parents*. New York: Child Welfare League of America, 1972.
Clark, Alexander, and Jack P. Gibbs. "Social Control: A Reformulation." *Social Problems* 12, 4 (1965): 398–415.
Clark, Ramsey. *Crime in America*. New York: Pocket B0oks, 1971.
Crain, Robert L., and Donald B. Rosenthal. "Community Status as a Dimension of Local Decision Making." *American Sociological Review* 32, 6 (December 1967): 970–984.
Cressey, Donald R. "Contradictory Directives in Complex Organizations." *Administrative Science Quarterly* 4, 1 (June 1959): 1–19.
———. "Limitations on Organization of Treatment in The Modern Prison." in R. Cloward et al., *Theoretical Studies in Social Organization of the Prison*. New York: Social Science Research Council, March 1960, pp. 78–110.
———. "The Nature and Effectiveness of Correctional Techniques." *Law and Contemporary Problems* 23 (Autumn 1958): 754–777.
Culombe v. Connecticut. 367 U.S. 568 (1971).
Dahrendorf, Ralf. *Class and Class Conflict in Industrial Society*. Stanford, Calif.: Stanford University Press, 1959.
Dawson, Robert O. *Sentencing*. Boston: Little, Brown, 1969.
Dession, George. "Psychiatry and The Conditioning of Criminal Justice." *Yale Law Journal* 47, 3 (January 1938).
Duffee, David, and Robert Fitch. *An Introduction to Corrections: A Policy and Systems Approach*. Pacific Palisades, Calif.: Goodyear, 1976.
Duffee, David, Frederick Hussey, and John Kramer. *Criminal Justice*. Englewood Cliffs, N.J.: Prentice-Hall, 1978.
Duffee, David, Thomas Maher, and Steve Lagoy. "Administrative Due Process in Community Preparole Programs." *Criminal Law Bulletin* 13, 5 (September 1977): 383–400.
Duffee, David, Peter B. Meyer, Thomas R. Maher, and Kevin Wright. *Problems, Issues, and Outcomes in a Community Placed Correctional System*. Harrisburg, Pa.: Governor's Justice Commission, November 1976.
Duffee, David, Peter B. Meyer, and Barbara D. Warner. *Offender Needs, Parole*

Outcome, and Program Structure in the Bureau of Correction Community Services Division. Harrisburg, Pa.: Governor's Justice Commission, 1977.

Duffee, David, and Vincent O'Leary. "Models of Correction: An Entry in the Packer-Griffiths Debate." *Criminal Law Bulletin* 7, 4 (May 1971): 329–352.

Duffee, David, and R. Richard Ritti. "Correctional Policy and Public Values." *Criminology* 14, 4 (February 1977): 449–460.

Duffee, David, and Barbara D. Warner. "Interorganizational Behavior and Correctional Programming." In D. Duffee, *Correctional Management*. Englewood Cliffs, N.J.: Prentice-Hall, 1980.

Dumont, Matthew. *The Absurd Healer*. New York: Jacob Aronson, 1968.

Durkheim, Emile. *Elementary Forms of Religious Life*. New York: The Free Press, 1955.

———. *Suicide*. Glencoe, Ill.: The Free Press, 1949.

———. *The Division of Labor in Society*. Trans. G. Simpson. Glencoe, Ill.: The Free Press, 1947.

———. *The Rules of Sociological Method*. Glencoe, Ill.: The Free Press, 1950.

Emery, F. E., and E. L. Trist. "Causal Texture of Organizational Environments." In F. E. Emery (ed.), *Systems Thinking*. Baltimore: Penguin, 1970, pp. 241–258.

Etzioni, Amatai. *The Active Society*. New York: The Free Press, 1968.

Feeley, Malcolm. "Two Models of the Criminal Justice System: An Organizational Perspective." *Law and Society Review* 7, 3 (Spring 1973): 407–425.

Fogel, David. ". . . We Are the Living Proof . . ." Cincinnati: Anderson, 1975.

Form, William H., and Delbert C. Miller. *Industry, Labor, and Community*. New York: Harper and Bros., 1960.

Frankel, Marvin. *Criminal Sentences*. New York: Hill and Wang, 1972.

Gagnon v. Scarpelli 411 U.S. 778 (1973).

Gamson, William A. "Rancorous Conflict in Community Politics." *American Sociological Review* 41 (January 1966).

Geis, Gilbert and Elvin Cavanaugh. "Recruitment and Retention of Correctional Personnel." *Crime and Delinquency* 12, 3 (1966): 232–239.

Goffman, Erving. *The Presentation of Self in Everyday Life*. Garden City, N.Y.: Doubleday, 1959.

Goldstein, Herman. "Toward a Redefinition of The Police Function." In A. Cohn and E. Viano (eds.), *Police Community Relations, Images, Roles, Realities*. Philadelphia: Lippincott, 1976, pp. 125–130.

Gottfredson, Michael. "Treatment Destruction Techniques." *Journal of Research in Crime and Delinquency* 16, 1 (January 1979): 39–54.

Gouldner, Alvin W., "The Sociologist as Partisan: Sociology and the Welfare State." *American Sociologist* 3 (May 1968): 103–116.

Grant, Douglas, and Marguerite Grant. "A Group Dynamics Approach to Non-Conformity in the Navy." *Annals of the American Academy of Political and Social Science* 322 (March 1959): 126–155.

Griffiths, John. "Ideology in Criminal Process, or a 'Third' Model of the Criminal Process." *Yale Law Journal* 79, 3 (January 1970): 359–417.

———. "The Limits of Criminal Law Scholarship." *Yale Law Journal* 79 (1970): 1388–1474.

246 / Bibliography

Grimes, John A. "The Police, The Union, and The Productivity Imperative." In J. L. Wolfe and J. F. Heaphey (eds.), *Readings on Productivity in Policing*. Washington, D.C.: Police Foundation, 1975.

Grozdins, Morton. *The American System: A New View of Governments in the United States*. Chicago: Rand McNally, 1963.

Hage, Jerald, and Michael Aiken. *Social Change in Complex Organizations*. New York: Random House, 1970.

Hamilton, Edward K. "Police Productivity: The View from City Hall." In J. L. Wolfe and J. F. Heaphey (eds.), *Readings on Productivity in Policing*. Washington, D.C.: Police Foundation, 1970.

Harland, Alan T. "Restitution and Service by Offenders: A Summary of Previous Research." Paper presented at the annual meetings of the American Society of Criminology. Dallas, November 1978.

Harris, Louis and associates. *The Public Looks at Correction*. Published for the Joint Commission on Correctional Manpower and Training. Washington, D.C.: Government Printing Office, 1967.

Hawley, Amos H. *Human Ecology: A Theory of Community Structure*. New York: Ronald Press, 1950.

Hawley, Willis D., and Frederick M. Wirt. *The Search for Community Power*, 2nd ed. Englewood Cliffs, N.J.: Prentice-Hall, 1978.

Henry, Jules. *Culture Against Man*. New York: Viking, 1965.

Hiller, E. T. "The Community as a Social Group." *American Sociological Review* 6 (1941): 189–202.

Hillery, George A. Jr. "Definitions of Community: Areas of Agreement." *Rural Sociology* 20, 2 (June 1955).

Hirschi, Travis, and Hannan C. Selvin. *Delinquency Research*. New York: The Free Press, 1967.

Hollingshead, A. B. *Elmstown's Youth and Elmstown Revisited*. New York: John Wiley, 1975.

———. "The Concept of Social Control." *American Sociological Review* 6, 2 (April 1941).

———. "Class Differences in Family Stability." *The Annals of the American Academy of Political and Social Science* 272 (1950): 39–46.

Homans, George. *The Human Group*. New York: Harcourt Brace, 1950.

Hunter, Albert. "The Loss of Community: An Empirical Test Through Replication." *American Sociological Review* 40 (October 1975): 537–552.

Irwin, John. *The Felon*. Englewood Cliffs, N.J.: Prentice-Hall, 1970.

Irwin, John, and Donald R. Cressey. "Thieves, Convicts and the Inmate Culture." *Social Problems* 10, 2 (Fall 1962): 142–155.

Jacobs, James B. "The Politics of Corrections: Town-Prison Relations as a Determinant of Reform." *Social Service Review* (December 1976): 623–631.

Jacobs, James B., and Norma Meachum Crotty. *Guards Unions and the Future of the Prisons*. Ithaca, N.Y.: Institute of Public Employment, Cornell University, Monograph 9.

Janowitz, Morris. *Social Control in the Welfare State*. New York: Elsevier, 1976.

———. "Sociological Theory and Social Control." *American Journal of Sociology* 91 (July 1975): 82–108.

Kamisar, Yale. "Equal Justice in the Gate Houses and Mansions of American Criminal Procedure." In Y. Kamisar, F. Inbau, and T. Arnold, *Criminal Justice in Our Time*. Charlottesville: University of Virginia Press, 1965.
Kaplan, John. *Criminal Justice*. Mineola, N.Y.: Foundation Press, 1973.
——. "The Prosecutorial Discretion—A Comment." *Northwestern Law Review* 60 (1965): 174–193.
Katz, Daniel, and Robert Kahn, *The Social Psychology of Organizations*. New York: John Wiley, 1966.
Kelman, Herbert. *A Time to Speak*. San Francisco: Jossey-Bass, 1968.
Kimberly, E. L., and D. J. Newman. "Judicial Intervention in Correctional Decisions: Threat and Response." *Crime and Delinquency* 14 (1968): 1–13.
Kirchway, G. F. "Crime and Punishment." *Journal of Criminal Law and Criminology* 1 (January 1911): 718–734.
Kittrie, Nicholas. *The Right to be Different*. Baltimore: Penguin, 1973.
Kituse, J. I., and D. C. Dietrick. "Delinquent Boys: A Critique." *American Sociological Review* 24, 2 (1959).
Kobrin, Solomon. "The Conflict of Values in Delinquency Areas." *American Sociological Review* 14 (1951): 653–661.
Koehler, W. *The Place of Values in the World of Fact*. London: Liveright, 1938.
Korn, Richard. "Of Crime, Criminal Justice and Corrections." *University of San Francisco Law Review* 6 (October 1971): 27–75.
Kropotkin, Peter. *Mutual Aid: A Factor in Evolution*. Boston: Porter Sargent, no date.
Kuhn, Alfred. *The Study of Society*. Homewood, Ill.: Irwin Dorsey, 1963.
Kuper, George H. "Productivity: A National Concern." In J. Wolfe and J. Heaphey (eds.), *Readings in Productivity in Policing*. Washington, D.C.: Police Foundation, 1975.
LaFave, Wayne R. *Arrest*. Boston: Little, Brown, 1966.
Landis, Paul H. *Social Control: Social Organization and Disorganization in Process*. New York: Lippincott, 1939.
LaPiere, Richard T. *A Theory of Social Control*. New York: McGraw-Hill, 1954.
Lawler, Edward E. III, and John Grant Rhode. *Information and Control in Organizations*. Pacific Palisades, Calif.: Goodyear, 1976.
Lerman, Paul. *Community Treatment and Social Control*. Chicago: The University of Chicago Press, 1975.
Lewin, Kurt. *Field Theory in the Social Sciences*. Ed. by D. Cartwright. New York: Harper & Row, 1951.
Lipton, Douglas, Robert Martinson, and Judith Wilks. *The Effectiveness of Correctional Treatment*. New York: Praeger, 1975.
Litwak, Eugene, and Lydia F. Hylton. "Interorganizational Analysis: A Hypothesis on Co-ordinating Agencies." In Y. Hasenfeld and R. English (eds.), *Human Service Organizations*. Ann Arbor, Mich.: University of Michigan Press, 1974.
Long, Norton. "The Local Community as an Ecology of Games." *American Journal of Sociology* 64, 3 (January 1958): 251–261.
Mannochio, Anthony J., and Jimmy Dunn. *The Time Game*. New York: Dell, 1970.
Marris, Peter, and Martin Rein. *Dilemmas of Social Reform*. New York: Basic Books, 1971.

Martinson, Robert. "What Works? Questions and Answers About Prison Reform." *The Public Interest* 35 (Spring 1974).

Maslow, Abraham. *The Farther Reaches of Human Nature.* New York: Viking, 1971.

McCleary, Richard. "How Structural Variables Constrain the Parole Officer's Use of Discretionary Powers." *Social Problems* 23, 2 (December 1975): 209–225.

McConnell, Ray Madding. *Criminal Responsibility and Social Constraint.* New York: Charles Scribner's Sons, 1912.

McGregor, Douglas. *The Professional Manager.* Ed. by Caroline McGregor and Warren Bennis. New York; McGraw-Hill, 1961.

McIntyre, Donald M. Jr., Lawrence P. Tiffany, and Daniel L. Rotenberg. *Detection of Crime.* Boston: Little, Brown, 1965.

McIntyre, Jennie. "Public Attitudes Toward Crime and Law Enforcement." *Annals of the American Academy of Political and Social Science* 374 (November 1967): 34–46.

McNamara, John. "Uncertainties in Police Work: The Relevance of Police Recruits' Background and Training." In D. Bordua (ed.), *The Police.* New York: John Wiley, 1965, pp. 163–252.

Mempa v. *Rhay.* 389 U.S. 128 (1967).

Menninger, Karl. *The Crime of Punishment.* New York: Viking, 1969.

Meyer, John W., and Brian Rowan. "Institutionalized Organizations: Formal Structure as Myth and Ceremony." *American Journal of Sociology* 83, 2 (September 1977): 340–363.

Meyer, Marshall W. "Organizational Domains." *American Sociological Review* 40 (October 1975): 599–615.

Meyer, Peter B. "Communities as Victims of Corporate Crimes." Paper presented at the Second International Symposium of Victimology, Boston, September 8, 1976.

Meyer, Peter B., and David Duffee. "Alternatives to Incarceration: Humane Correction or Low Cost Social Control?" Paper presented at the National Conference on Criminal Justice Evaluation, Washington, D.C., March 10, 1977.

Miller, Frank W. *Prosecution.* Boston: Little, Brown, 1970.

Mills, Theodore. "Equilibrium and the Processes of Deviance and Control," *American Sociological Review* 24, 5 (October 1959): 671–679.

Moos, Rudolph. *Evaluating Correctional and Community Settings.* New York: John Wiley, 1974.

Morgan, James P. "Planning and Implementing a Productivity Program." In J. Wolfe and J. Heaphey (eds.), *Readings on Productivity in Policing.* Washington, D.C.: Police Foundation, 1975.

Morris, Norval. *The Future of Imprisonment.* Chicago: The University of Chicago Press, 1974.

Morrissey v. *Brewer.* 408 U.S. 471 (1972).

Munro, Jim. *Administrative Behavior and Police Organization.* Cincinnati: Anderson, 1974.

Murphy, Patrick V. "Police Accountability." In J. Wolfe and J. Heaphey (eds.), *Readings on Productivity in Policing.* Washington, D.C.: Police Foundation, 1975.

National Advisory Commission on Civil Disorders. *Report of the National Advisory Commission.* New York: Bantam, 1968.
National Advisory Commission on Criminal Justice Standards and Goals. *Corrections.* Washington, D.C.: Government Printing Office, 1973.
National Institute of Law Enforcement and Criminal Justice. *Training Police as Specialists in Family Crisis Intervention.* Washington, D.C.: National Institute, 1970.
Negandhi, Anant (ed.). *Modern Organizational Theory in an Interorganizational Perspective.* Kent, Ohio: Kent State University Press, 1972.
Nelson, Elmer K., and Catherine Lovell. *Developing Correctional Administrators.* Washington, D.C.: Government Printing Office, 1967.
Newman, Donald J. *Conviction.* Boston: Little, Brown, 1966.
―――. *Criminal Justice.* Philadelphia: Lippincott, 1975.
New York Governor's Special Committee on Criminal Offenders. *Preliminary Report.* Albany, N.Y.: New York State, 1969.
Nieburg, H. L. "Violence, Law, and the Informal Polity." *The Journal of Conflict Resolution* 13, 2 (June 1969).
Nokes, Peter. "Purpose and Efficiency in Humane Social Institutions." *Human Relations* 13, 2 (May 1960).
Nord, Walter R. "The Failure of Current Applied Behavioral Science—A Marxian Perspective." *Journal of Applied Behavioral Science* 10, 4 (1974): 557–578.
O'Leary, Vincent. "Some Directions for Citizen Involvement in Corrections." *Annals of the American Academy of Political and Social Science* 381 (January 1969): 99–108.
O'Leary, Vincent, and David Duffee. "Correctional Policy—A Classification of Goals Designed for Change." *Crime and Delinquency* 17, 4 (October 1971): 373–386.
O'Leary, Vincent, and Donald J. Newman. "Conflict Resolution in Criminal Justice." *Journal of Research in Crime and Delinquency* 7, 2 (July 1970): 99–119.
O'Neil, Michael W. "The Role of The Police—Metropolitan Police Department." Unpublished doctoral dissertation, State University of New York at Albany, 1974.
Packer, Herbert. *The Limits of the Criminal Sanction.* Stanford, Calif.; Stanford University Press, 1968.
―――. "Two Models of the Criminal Process." *University of Pennsylvania Law Review* 113 (1964): 1–23.
Palmer, John W. *Constitutional Rights of Prisoners.* Cincinnati: Anderson, 1973.
Palmer, Ted. "Martinson Revisited." *Journal of Research in Crime and Delinquency* 12, 2 (1975): 133–152.
Parsons, Talcott. *The Social System.* New York: The Free Press, 1964.
Perrow, Charles. "A Framework for the Comparative Analysis of Organizations." *American Sociological Review* (1967): 194–208.
Pilliavin, Irving. "Police-Community Alienation: Its Structural Roots and a Proposed Remedy." In A. Cohn and E. Viano (eds.), *Police-Community Relations.* Philadelphia: Lippincott, 1976, pp. 589–603.
Platt, Anthony. "The Rise of The Child Saving Movement: Correctional Reform." *The Annals of the American Academy of Political and Social Science* 381 (January 1969): 21–38.

Pondy, L. R. "Organizational Conflict: Concepts and Models." *Administrative Science Quarterly* 12, 2 (June 1967): 296–320.
President's Commission on Law Enforcement and the Administration of Justice. *Task Force on Courts*. Washington, D.C.: Government Printing Office, 1967.
―――. *Task Force on Science and Technology*. Washington, D.C.: Government Printing Office, 1967.
Pressman, Jeffrey L., and Aaron B. Wildavsky. *Implementation*. Berkeley, Calif.: University of California Press, 1973.
Quinney, Richard. *Class, State and Crime*. New York: David McKay, 1977.
Radzinowicz, Leon. *Ideology and Crime*. New York: Columbia University Press, 1966.
Rawls, John. *A Theory of Justice*. Cambridge, Mass.: Harvard University Press, 1973.
Reich, Charles. "The New Property." *Yale Law Journal* 73 (1963): 733–787.
Reid, William. "Interagency Coordination in Delinquency Prevention and Control." *Social Service Review* 38 (March 1964): 418–428.
Reisman, David. *The Lonely Crowd*. New Haven, Conn.: Yale University Press, 1961.
Reiss, Albert J., Jr. "Functional Specialization of Cities." In P. K. Hatt and A. J. Reiss, Jr. (eds.), *Cities and Society (The Revised Reader in Urban Sociology)*. Glencoe, Ill.: The Free Press, 1957, pp. 555–575.
Reiss, Albert, J. Jr., and Donald J. Black. "Interrogation and the Criminal Process." *Annals of The American Academy of Political and Social Science* 374 (November 1967): 47–57.
Reiss, Albert J. Jr., and David Bordua. "Environment and Organization: A Perspective on the Police." In D. Bordua (ed.), *The Police*. New York: John Wiley, 1967, pp. 25–55.
Reistoffer, Mary. "A University Extension Course for Foster Parents." *Children* (Jan./Feb. 1968): 28–31.
Reith, Charles. *The Blind Eye of History: A Study of the Origins of the Present Police Era*. Montclair, N.J.: Patterson-Smith, 1974.
Remington, Frank, Donald J. Newman, Edward L. Kimball, Marygold Melli, and Herman Goldstein. *Criminal Justice Administration*. Indianapolis: Bobbs-Merrill, 1969.
Richta, Radovau. *Civilization at the Crossroads: Social and Human Implications of the Scientific and Technological Revolution*. White Plains, N.Y.: International Arts and Sciences Press, 1969.
Ritti, R. Richard. "The Administration of Poverty: Lessons from the Welfare Explosion 1967–1973." *Social Problems* 25, 3 (Fall 1978), pp. 157–175.
Robinson, Cyril D. "The Mayor and the Police—The Political Role of the Police in Society." In G. Mosse (ed.), *Police Forces in History*. London: Sage, 1975, pp. 277–315.
Rokeach, Milton, Martin G. Miller, and John A. Snyder. "The Value Gap Between Police and Policed." *Journal of Social Issues* 27, 2 (1971): pp. 155–171.
Rose, Arnold M., and Arthur E. Prell. "Does the Punishment Fit the Crime? A Study in Social Valuation." *American Journal of Sociology* 61 (November 1955): 247–259.

Rose, Stephen M. *Betrayal of the Poor*. Cambridge, Mass.: Schenkman, 1976.
Rosenau, James N. "Intervention as a Scientific Concept." *Journal of Conflict Resolution* 13, 2 (June 1969): 149–171.
Ross, E. A. *Social Control, A Survey of the Foundations of Order*. New York: Macmillan, 1914.
Rubenstein, Jonathan. *City Police*. New York: Ballantine, 1973.
Sarason, S. B. *The Psychological Sense of Community: Prospects for a Community Psychology*. San Francisco: Jossey-Bass, 1974.
Schrag, Clarence. "Contemporary Corrections—An Analytical Model." Consultant's paper prepared for the President's Commission on Law Enforcement and the Administration of Justice, Washington, D.C. Mimeo, 1966.
———. "The Correctional System: Problems and Prospects." *Annals of the American Academy of Political and Social Science* 381 (January 1969): 11–20.
Schwartz, Richard, and James C. Miller. "Legal Evolution and Societal Complexity." *American Journal of Sociology* 70 (September 1965): 159–169.
Scull, Andrew T. *Decarceration*. Englewood Cliffs, N.J.: Prentice-Hall, 1977.
Sebring, Robert, and David Duffee, "Who Are the Real Prisoners? A Case of Win-Lose Conflict in a State Correctional Institution." *Journal of Applied Behavioral Science* 13, 1 (February 1977): 23–40.
Selznick, Phillip. "Foundations for a Theory of Organization." *American Sociological Review* 13 (Fall 1948): 25–35.
Sherif, Muzafir, and Carolyn Sherif. *Social Psychology*. New York: Harper & Row, 1969.
Sherman, Lawrence, Catherine H. Milton, and Thomas V. Kelly. *Team Policing, Seven Case Studies*. Washington, D.C.: Police Foundation, 1973.
Silver, Allan. "The Demand for Order in a Civil Society: A Review of Some Themes in the History of Urban Crime, Police, and Riot." In D. Bordua (ed.), *The Police*. New York: John Wiley, 1967, pp. 1–25.
Simon, Herbert. "On the Concept of Organizational Goal." *Administrative Science Quarterly* 9 (June 1964): 1–22.
Skolnick, Jerome. *Justice Without Trial*. New York: John Wiley, 1967.
Skolnick, Jerome, and J. Richard Woodworth. "Bureaucracy, Information, and Social Control: A Study of a Morals Detail." In D. Bordua (ed.), *The Police*. New York: John Wiley, 1967.
Stanley, David T. *Prisoners Among Us*. Washington, D. C.: Brookings Institution, 1976.
Stein, Martin R. *The Eclipse of Community: An Interpretation of American Studies*. Princeton, N.J.: Princeton University Press, 1960.
Stinchcombe, Arthur L. "Institutions of Privacy in the Determination of Police Administrative Practice." *American Journal of Sociology* 49 (September 1963): 150–160.
Street, David, Robert Vinter, and Charles Perrow. *Organization for Treatment*. New York: The Free Press, 1966.
Studt, Elliot. *Surveillance and Service in Parole*. Los Angeles: University of California at Los Angeles, 1971.
Sudnow, David. "Normal Crimes: Sociological Features of the Penal Code in a Public Defender's Office." *Social Problems* 12, 3 (Winter 1965): 255–276.

Sullivan, Dennis C. *Team Models in Probation.* Paramus, N.J.: National Council on Crime and Delinquency, 1969.
Sullivan, Dennis C., and Larry Tift. "Court Intervention in Corrections: Roots of Resistance and Problems of Compliance." *Crime and Delinquency* 21, 3 (July 1975): 213–222.
Sykes, Gresham. *Society of Captures.* Princeton, N.J.: Princeton University Press, 1971.
Terreberry, Shirley. "The Evolution of Organizational Environments." *Administrative Science Quarterly* 12, 4 (March 1968): 590–613.
Terris, Bruce J. "The Role of the Police." *Annals of the American Academy of Political and Social Science* 374 (November 1967): 53–69.
Thomas, W. I., and F. Znaniecki, *The Polish Peasant in Europe and America.* New York: Dover, 1927.
Toby, Jackson. "Is Punishment Necessary?" *Journal of Criminal Law, Criminology and Police Science* 55, 3 (September 1964): 332–337.
Toch, Hans, J. Douglas Grant, and Ray Galvin, *Agents of Change: A Study in Police Reform.* Cambridge, Mass.: Schenkman, 1975.
Trite, Matthew, Roger Chisholm, and Michael Radner. *Interorganizational Decision Making.* Chicago: Aldine, 1972.
Trojanowicz, Robert, and Samuel Dixon. *Criminal Justice and the Community.* Englewood Cliffs, N.J.: Prentice-Hall, 1974.
U.S. News and World Report. "Big Change in Prisons, Punish—Not Reform." August 25, 1979: 21–25.
Van den Haag, Ernest. *Punishing Criminals.* New York: Basic Books, 1975.
Vega, William. "The Liberal Policeman: A Contradiction in Terms." *Issues in Criminology* 4, 1 (Fall 1968): 27–28.
Vickers, Geoffrey. *Making Institutions Work.* New York: Halsted, 1973.
Von Hirsch, Andrew. *Doing Justice.* New York: Hill and Wang, 1976.
Walker, Nigel. *Crimes, Courts, and Figures.* Baltimore: Penguin, 1971.
Wamsley, Gary L., and Mayer N. Zald. "The Political Economy of Public Organizations." *Public Administration Review* 33, 1 (January/February 1973): 000–000.
Warner, W. Keith, and A. Eugene Havens. "Goal Displacement and the Intangibility of Organizational Goals." *Administrative Science Quarterly* 12, 4 (March 1968): 539–599.
Warner, W. Lloyd, and J. O. Low. *The Social System of the Modern Factory. The Strike: A Social Analysis.* New Haven, Conn.: Yale University Press, 1950.
——— and associates. *Democracy in Jonesville.* New York: Harper & Row, 1949.
Warren, Roland. *Community in America.* Chicago: Rand McNally. First ed., 1963; 3rd ed., 1978.
———. "The Interaction of Community Decision Organizations: Some Basic Concepts and Needed Research." *Social Service Review* 41, 3 (September 1967): 261–270.
———. "The Inter-Organizational Field as a Focus for Investigation." *Administrative Science Quarterly* 12, 3 (December 1967): 396–419.
Warren, Roland, Stephen Rose, and Ann Bergunder. *The Structure of Urban Reform.* Lexington, Mass.: Lexington Books, 1974.
Whyte, William Foote. *Money and Motivation.* New York: Harper & Row, 1955.

Wilkins, Leslie T. "Crime and Punishment at the Turn of the Century." Paper presented at the 77th Annual Meetings of the American Academy of Political and Social Science, Philadelphia, April 13, 1973.

———. "Directions for Corrections." In R. Carter and L. T. Wilkins (eds.), *Probation, Parole and Community Corrections*, 2nd ed. New York: John Wiley, 1976, pp. 60–70.

———. *Social Deviance*. Englewood Cliffs, N.J.: Prentice-Hall, 1965.

Wilson, James Q. "Police Morale, Reform and Citizen Respect: The Chicago Case." In D. Bordua (ed.), *The Police*. New York: John Wiley, 1976, pp. 137–162.

———. *Varieties of Police Behavior*. Cambridge, Mass.: Harvard University Press, 1968.

Wirth, Louis. "Urbanism as a Way of Life." *American Journal of Sociology* 44, 1 (July 1938): 1–24.

Wolff v. *McDonnell*. 418 U.S. 539 (1974).

Wolfgang, Marvin, and Franco Ferracuti. *The Subculture of Violence*. London: Tavistock, 1967.

Wood, Robert C. *Suburbia: Its People and Their Politics*. Boston: Houghton Mifflin, 1959.

Wrong, Dennis. "The Oversocialized Conception of Man." *American Sociological Review* 26 (April 1961): 184–193.

Zalman, Marvin. "Prisoner's Rights to Medical Care." *The Journal of Criminal Law, Criminology, and Police Science* 63, 2 (1972): 185–199.

Zimring, Frank, and Gordon Hawkins. "Deterrence and Marginal Groups." *Journal of Research in Crime and Delinquency* 5, 2 (July 1968): 100–114.

Index

Achievement, contrasted with membership, 183
Ackoff, Russell, 80, 229n
Agnew, Spiro, 186
Aiken, Michael, 229n
Albany, New York, 105
American Bar Foundation, 108, 230n
American Correctional Association, 59
Amsterdam, New York, 105
Andenneas, Johannes, 113–114, 119, 233n, 243n
Arnold, Thurman, 122, 234n
Augustus, John, 143
Autonomy, of communities, 152

Banton, Michael, 103, 104, 120, 173, 178, 229n, 231n, 233n, 240n
Barak, George, 222n
Beck, Bernard, 30, 132, 226n, 235n
Beer, Stafford, 228n, 229n, 231n
Bell, Daniel, 87, 92, 132, 148, 229n, 231n, 235n, 237n, 239n, 240n
Bennington, John, 126, 132, 233n, 234n, 243n
Bergunder, Ann, 157, 209, 221n, 226n, 229n, 231n, 235n

Bernard, L. L., 25, 49, 223n, 224n, 227n
Bittner, Egon, 176
Black, Donald, 89, 230n, 232n
Blake, William, xi
Blizek, William, 132, 235n
Boorkman, David, 237n, 242n
Bordua, David, 176, 239n
Brandeis University, 130
Brown, William, 241
Buckley, Walter, 83, 228n, 229n
Bureaucracy, 197; and disappearance of community, 201
Bureaucratization, 144–148

California Department of Correction, 136
California Probation Subsidy, 135, 214, 221n
Campbell, James S., 222n
Cannavale, Frank, 241n
Cavanaugh, Elvin, 128, 178, 234n, 240n
Cederblom, Jerry, 132, 235n
Chambliss, William, 11, 160, 162–163, 165, 177, 178, 223n, 236n, 238n
Chapman, Brian, 13, 223n
Chicago Seven, 186
Chisholm, Roger, 229n

Civil rights, and corrections, 135
Civil law, retribution in, 224n
Clark, Alexander, 222n
Clark, Ramsey, 17–18, 23, 51–56, 63, 204, 227n
Class, and discipline, 225n
Coincidence, of service areas, 152
Community(ies): approaches to study of, 142–143, 204–211; autonomy of, 152; boundaries of, 129–130; as context of criminal justice, 136–137; and criminal justice, 109, 176; decision making in, 125–128; defined, 141–144; dimensions of, 152–154; disappearance of, and bureaucracy, 201; disorganized, 155; as ecological system, 130; elements of, 144; as forum for games, 128–136; fragmented, 155; goal polarity in, 119–125; as interaction field, 130–136; interdependent, 155, 157; locality-relevant functions of, 147; models of conflict in, 117–137; and mutual support, 149, 187–198; and organizations, 157; and police, 134; and production, 149, 159–166; psychological identification with, 152; rancorous conflict in, 125–128; role of in criminal justice analysis, 5; and social control, 154–158; and social participation, 149–150, 181–187; solidary, 155–156; stratification of, 176–177, 182; Warren's model of, 148–154
Community Decision Organizations, 209
Community Treatment Project, 135, 198, 219, 221n
Competition, as social control, 147
Control: concept of, 80–81; and equilibrium, 81–85; and feedback, 89; formal and informal, in simple and complex systems, 85; legitimate, 86; levels of, 82; and social deviance, 85–86; of a system, 111–113; and types of systems, 86
Convict culture, 169
Cooper, J., 237n
Corrections: and civil rights, 135; community programs, 158; constituencies, 194; judicial intervention in, 185; and schools, 171; separating functions of, 195
Courts, urban and rural differences, 108
Crain, Robert, 126, 234n
Cressey, Donald, 169, 232n, 233n, 239n, 242n
Crime, organized, 162–164
Crime control, war analogy, 96–97
Crime Control Model, 31–33

Crime(s): and health, 52–53; F.B.I. index, 35; mala in se, 35; and rationality, 43; street, 53
Criminal justice: and agency coordination, 110; alternatives to, 10; and community, 109; dramaturgical effects of, 186–187; federal–local relations in, 127; functions of, xiv; inertia and conflict, 126–128; as institution rather than organization, 101; as integrated system, 108–113; and management of community, 176; moralist approach to, xii; and mutual support, 189–191; needed research in, 211–214; normative analysis of, 100; perceived public ambivalence toward, 121–123; and political conservatives, 4; and political liberals, 4; and political radicals, 4; production functions, 162–166; related to the state, 13–15; restriction to negative sanctions, 11; as retributive justice, 16; and social complexity, 87–88; social control as function of, 6; and socialization, 169–172; and social participation, 183–187; and social welfare, 47–61; symbolic functions of, 122–123; and systems analysis, 77–97; as system control, 86–92; traditional meaning of, 1; as unitary system, 102–108; values toward, by class, 121–123; and vertical and horizontal dimensions, 152, 154–158, 202, 205, 210; welfare approach to, xii, 47–61
Criminal justice agencies: linkages outside criminal justice, 109; resistance to coordination, 111–113; service provision in, 196–198; and social control, 177–179; and socialization, 170–171;
Criminal justice analysis, 2–5; assumptions in, xiii; impact of commission studies, 94–95; and reductionism, 71; role of communities and public organizations in, 5
Criminal justice reform, 199–219; auspices of, 133; and domain enlargement, 131; healthy theme, 205; rational theme, 205; religious theme, 205; and social policy, 214–219; and social structure, 122
Criminal justice system, 2, 222n; boundary choices, 230n; control of, 111–113; misconceptions of, 99–102; as police-courts-corrections, 3; and retribution, 90
Criminal process, two models of, 31–33
Criminal sanction: and alternatives, 191; need for, 225n; overreach of, 34; Packer's

Limits criticized, 35–36; Packer's Limits on, 33–37; as social control, 42
Culture, shifts in, 183
Cybernetics, 80

Dahrendorf, Ralf, 87, 136, 148, 228n, 229n, 230n, 236n, 237n
Dallas, Texas, 3
Dawson, Robert, 231n
Day, Noel, 237n
Dershowitz, Allan, 204
Dession, George, 49–50, 134–135, 227n, 235n
Deterrence: appearance of, 115; conflict with humanization, 119–120; as cultural belief, 30; effectiveness of, 28–29; general, 27, 114; possibility of implementing, 90–91; and retribution, 40; special, 27
Deviance: marginal, 226n; reaction to, and stateless societies, 9–12; and social control, 85–86
Deviants, exclusion and inclusion, 88
Dietrick, D. C., 230n
Discipline, and class, 225n
Distributive justice, 16–21, 41; contrasted with retributive, 17
Dixon, Samuel, 241n
Due process, and social participation, 184–185
Due Process Model, 31–33
Duffee, David, 107, 115, 223n, 224n, 225n, 231n, 233n, 237n, 242n
Dumont, Matthew, 228n
Durkheim, Emile, 43, 151, 160, 182, 222n, 226n, 237n, 240n

Economic interdependence, 160
Economic specialization, of cities, 161–163
Economic structure, of American communities, 160–162
Elling, Ray, 176, 240n
Emery, Fred, 80, 130, 229n, 235n
Equilibrium, in social systems, 81–85
Etzioni, Amatai, 71, 80, 228n, 229n, 239n
Expiation, 27

Fazio, Ernest J., 237n, 242n
F.B.I. index, 35
Feedback: and control, 89; negative, 87
Feeley, Malcolm, 110, 232n
Ferracuti, Franco, 170, 230n, 239n
Fitch, Robert, 224n
Fogel, David, 69, 227n, 228n, 242n

Form, William H., 239n
Foster homes, 169
Frankel, Marvin, 227n, 231n

Gagnon v. *Scarpelli*, 241n
Galvin, Ray, 170, 190, 239n, 241n
Gamson, William, 125–128
Geis, Gilbert, 126, 177, 234n
General Electric Company, 161
General prevention, 113
General systems theory, 95, 231n
Gibbs, Jack P., 222n
Goffman, Erving, 229n
Goldstein, Herman, 113, 222n, 224n, 233n
Goldwater, Barry, 2
Good time, 186
Gottfredson, Michael, 242n
Gouldner, Alvin, 232n
Grant, Douglas, 170, 190, 225n, 239n, 241n
Great Depression, 8
Griffiths, John, 33, 186, 226n, 227n, 238n, 241n
Grimes, John A., 241n
Grozdins, Morton, 127, 182, 229n, 232n, 234n, 240n

Hage, Jerald, 229n
Halebsky, Sandor, 176, 240n
Halfway houses, 107, 195–196, 225n
Haller, Mark, 22n, 236n
Hamilton, Edward K., 234n
Hands-off doctrine, 185
Harens, A. Eugene, 231n
Harland, Alan, 241n
Harris, Louis, and Associates, 234n
Hartford, Connecticut, 161
Hawkins, Gordon, 114, 233n
Hawley, Amos, 161, 238n
Hawley, Willis, 228n
Health, and crimes, 52–53
Hearst, Patty, 186
Henry, Jules, 171, 239n
Hiller, E. T., 141, 236n
Hillery, George, 141, 236n
Hollingshead, August, 10, 225n, 238n
Homans, George, 7, 10, 16, 17, 109, 173, 222n, 223n, 228n, 229n, 232n, 239n
Hoover, Herbert, 94
Horizontal dimension: and production, 165–166; of community, 153, 202, 205, 210; and criminal justice, 154–158

Humane institutions, 50
Hunter, Albert, 236n
Hylton, Lydia, 232n

Illinois Juvenile Court, 55, 222n
Industrialization, 144–148
Interorganizational behavior, 212
Interorganizational conflict, 133
Interorganizational field, 106, 130–136
Interorganizational networks, 13
Interorganizational theory, 81
Intimidation, 28, 225n
Irwin, John, 169, 239n

Jacobs, James, 126, 164–165, 234n
Janowitz, Morris, 223n, 229n
Johnson, Lyndon, 2, 127
Jones, E. E., 237n
Judicial intervention, 185, 232n
Juries, and social participation, 187

Kahn, Robert, 174, 176, 188, 228n, 230n, 232n, 237n, 241n
Kaplan, John, 224n, 225n, 233n
Katz, Daniel, 174, 176, 188, 228n, 230n, 232n, 239n, 241n
Kelly, Thomas, 237n
Kelman, Herbert, 230n
Kennedy, John, 127
Kimball, Edward L., 222n, 224n
Kimberly, E. L., 240n
Kirchway, G. F., 123, 234n
Kituse, J. F., 230n
Koehler, W., 229n
Korn, Richard, 120, 226n, 228n, 233n
Kropotkin, Peter, 151, 167, 188, 237n, 238n, 239n, 241n
Kuhn, Alfred, 174, 229n
Kuper, George, 231n

Labor, specialization of, 160
LaFave, Wayne, 231n
Lagoy, Steve, 235n
Landis, Paul H., 49, 223n, 227n, 228n
LaPiere, Richard, 8, 223n, 236n
Law Enforcement Assistance Administration, 154, 183
Lawler, Edward, 233n
Legal specialization, 6–9
Lerman, Paul, 178, 198, 214, 221n, 236n, 240n, 242n
Lewin, Kurt, 235n

Likert, Rensis, 232n
Linder, D. E., 237n
Litwak, Eugene, 232n
Long, Norton, 131, 230n, 235n
Lovell, Catherine, 231n
Low, J. D., 237n

McCleary, Richard, 107, 113, 198, 231n, 233n, 242n
McConnell, Ray Madding, 7, 25, 49, 222n, 224n, 226n, 228n
McGregor, Douglas, 232n
McIntyre, Donald, 231n
McIntyre, Jennie, 121, 178, 224n, 234n, 240n
McNamara, John, 232n
McNamara, Robert, 230n
Macrosociology, 13
Maher, Thomas, 225n, 235n
Marris, Peter, 55, 221n, 224n, 227n, 232n, 234n
Martinson, Robert, 193, 241n
Marxists, assumptions of about criminal justice, 92–93
Marx, Karl, 81
Maslow, A., 238n
Melli, Marygold, 222n, 224n
Membership, contrasted with achievement, 183
Mempa v. *Rhay*, 241n
Menninger, Karl, 17–18, 56–61, 63, 204, 224n, 226n, 227n
Meyer, John W., 123, 234n
Meyer, Marshall, 235n
Meyer, Peter B., 162, 165, 195, 223n, 225n, 237n, 238n
Miller, Delbert C., 239n
Miller, Frank, 231n
Miller, James C., 11, 223n
Miller, Martin, 240n
Mills, Theodore, 85–93, 106, 171, 173, 229n, 230n, 231n, 239n
Milton, Catherine, 237n
Milton, John, xi
Monopsony, 214–215
Moos, Rudolph, 242n
Moralist approach: advantages of, 206–207; compared with community approach, 204–211; compared to welfare, 63–76; conception of current society, 65–69; conception of future society, 69; contrasted with welfare, 60–61; to control critiqued, 88–92; to criminal justice, xii; misconceptions

of socialization, 168–169; to punishment, 24–26; rational man construct, 70; and social control, 77–80; and social stability, 92–93
Morgan, Arthur, 241n
Morgan, James P., 233n
Morris, Norval, 69, 79, 227n, 228n
Morrissey v. *Brewer*, 241n
Multi-service centers, 200
Munro, Jim, 241n
Murphy, Patrick V., 107, 231n, 232n
Mutual aid, 151
Mutual support: as community function, 149, 187–198; and criminal justice, 189–191; and police, 190–191; and social control, 193–194

National Advisory Commission on Civil Disorders, 146
National Advisory Commission on Criminal Justice Standards and Goals, 183, 234n
National Institute of Correction, 1
National Institute of Law Enforcement and Criminal Justice, 1, 241n
Negandhi, Anant, 229n
Nelson, Elmer K., 231n
Newburg, New York, 105
Newman, Donald J., xi, 222n, 224n, 226n, 231n, 240n
New York City, 3
Nieburg, H. L., 132, 186, 223n, 233n, 234n, 235n, 241n
Nokes, Peter, 227n
Nord, Walter, 224n
Normative analysis, xiii
Norway, 114

Oakland, California, 105, 190–191
Offenders: access to serious, 195; needs of, 196; services to, 192–194
O'Leary, Vincent, 233n, 238n
Operations research, 231n
Organic solidarity, 151
Organizational strain, 177
Organization(s): constituencies of, 177; contrasted to state, 15–16; delegation of authority in, 177; domains of, 131, 133, 209; economizing and sociologizing, 235n; elaboration of, 197; goals of, 124, 231n; institutionalized, 123–124; and interdependent communities, 157; as instrumentalities, 212; public, 196–198;

and service delivery, 197–198; service management in, 194–198; and social control, 155; technology of, 197–198; Weberian, 202
Organized crime, 162–164
Orwell, George, 119, 174

Packer, Herbert, 4, 17–18, 23, 26–37, 51, 59, 63, 74, 185–186, 204, 221n, 224n, 225n, 226n, 233n, 240n; and criminal sanction, 33–37; definition of punishment, 26; definition of retribution, 27; rationale for deterrence, 26–31; and social control, 84, 90
Palmer, John W., 240n
Palmer, Ted, 242n
Parole, 186
Parole officers, and advocacy, 107
Parsons, Talcott, 87, 124, 176, 229n, 230n, 234n, 239n; model of society, 83, 229n
Pennsylvania, 121, 195
Perrow, Charles, 171, 197, 236n, 239n, 242n
Pilliavin, Irving, 178
Platt, Anthony, 8, 222n, 223n, 238n
Plea bargaining, 124
Police, 223n; as boundary spanning mechanism, 176; British, 19, 145; and community relations, 134; functions of, 105–107, 120; mobilization of, 146; and mutual support, 190–191; power of, 13, 20; professionalization of, 146; Roman, 13; as service providers, 189–191, 241n; training of, 232n; varieties of, 104–107
Police Act of 1829, 145
Police force, 13
Police Foundation, 190
Politics, and criminal justice, 4
Pondy, L. R., 232n
Power redistribution, 224n
Prell, Arthur, E., 225n
President's Commission on Law Enforcement and Administration of Justice, 2, 94–95, 108, 183, 230n, 232n
Pressman, Jeffrey L., 235n
Prisons: and societal integration, 188, organizational climate of, negative sanctions against staff, 232n
Probation, 185, 192; without conviction, 208
Production, as community function, 149, 159–166
Psychological identification with community, 152

260 / Index

Psychopaths, 43
Public organizations, role of in criminal justice analysis, 5
Public service delivery, 196–198
Punishment: conflict with treatment, 194–196; effectiveness of, 194; justifications for, 24–26; moralist approach to, 24–26; Packer's definition of, 26; and penalties, 57; as socially destructive, 60

Quality of life, 200, 212
Quinney, Richard, 4, 221n

Raduer, Michael, 229n
Radzinowicz, Leon, 25, 224n, 227n
Rationality, and crimes, 43
Rawls, John, 16, 223n, 225n
Reductionism, and criminal justice analysis, 71
Rehabilitation: Clark's argument for, 54–56; and intimidation, 225n; Menninger's justification for, 58–60; and technology, 70–71
Reich, Charles, 132
Reid, William, 110, 232n
Rein, Martin, 55, 221n, 224n, 227n, 232n, 234n
Reisman, David, 239n
Reiss, Albert J., 89, 161–163, 176, 230n, 232n, 236n, 238n, 239n
Reistoffer, Mary, 238n
Reith, Charles, 19, 224n
Release on recognizance, 208
Religion, and social participation, 182
Remington, Frank, 222n, 224n, 230n
Restitution, 192
Retribution: in civil law, 224n; and criminal justice system, 90; and deterrence, 40; need for, 39; Packer's definition of, 27; as revenge, 25; and social order, 40–41; and van den Haag, 37–46; van den Haag's definition of, 39
Retributive justice, 16–21; contrasted with distributive, 17
Rhode, John Grant, 233n
Richta, Radorau, 229n
Ritti, R. Richard, 221n, 234n, 242n
Robinson, April, 134, 222n, 235n
Rokeach, Milton, 178, 240n
Rose, Arnold, 225n
Rose, Stephen, 157, 209, 221n, 226n, 227n, 229n, 231n, 235n

Rosenau, James, 228n
Rosenthal, Donald, 126, 234n
Ross, E. A., 8, 18–19, 25, 80, 119, 222n, 224n, 226n, 228n, 233n
Rotenberg, Daniel, 231n
Rothman, David, 8, 223n
Rowan, Brian, 123
Russia, 175

Sahid, Joseph, 222n
Sanctions, reactions to negative, 112
San Diego Community Profile Project, 170
Sarason, S. B., 227n
Satisficing, 206
Schelling, Thomas, 163–165, 238n
Schenectady, New York, 161
Schools, and corrections, 171
Schrag, Clarence, 230n, 231n
Schwartz, Richard, 11, 223n
Scull, Andrew T., 221n, 234n, 239n
Sebring, Robert, 235n
Seidman, Robert, 11, 160, 162–163, 165, 177, 178, 223n, 236n, 238n
Selznick, Phillip, 197, 240n, 242n
Sentencing, 185
Service areas, coincidence of, 152
Service brokerage, 107
Service delivery: and organizations, 197–198; public, 196–198
Service management, in organizations, 194–198
Sherman, Lawrence, 237n
Shin, Huhn Joo, xi
Silver, Allan, 145, 222n, 223n, 236n
Simon, Herbert, 124, 206, 234n
Simple societies, 12
Skelton, Paul, 126, 132, 234n
Skolnick, Jerome, 106, 223n, 231n
Snyder, John, 240n
Social complexity, 6–9; and criminal justice, 87–88
Social control, 52, 222n; and community structure, 154–158; and community axes, 175–177; competition as, 147; and criminal justice agencies, 177–179; criminal sanction as, 42; and deviance, 85–86; early and later studies contrasted, 228n; early studies of, 6–7; emergence of, 174; as functional coordination, 174–175; as function of community, 149–150; as function of criminal justice, 6; and local access, 150; and moralist approach, 77–80;

and mutual support, 193–194; and organizations, 115; and socialization distinguished, 7, 173–175; and welfare approach, 77–80
Social deviance, and control, 85–86
Social goods, 218
Social harmony, 212
Social integration, 68
Socialization: and criminal justice, 169–172; as function of community, 149, 166–172; and horizontal dimension, 170–171; and social control, 7, 173–175; types of, 166–167
Social justice, 16; and partial compliance, 17
Social order, and retribution, 40–41
Social participation: as community function, 149–150, 181–187; and criminal justice, 183–187; and due process, 184–185; impact of state on, 182; and juries, 187; and religion, 182; and stratification, 182; and witnesses of crime, 187
Social policy, 214–219
Social structure, 122
Social system: American, 140; and administrative position, 114; and equilibrium, 81–85
Social welfare, and criminal justice, 47–61
Society, as integrated system, 113
Solidarity, organic, 151
Solitary confinement, 186
Specialization of labor, 160
Spitzer, Stephen, 182, 240n
Stang, David, 222n
Stanley, David, 234n
State(s): American, 140; compared to stateless societies, 11–12; contrasted to organization, 15–16; impact on social participation, 182; the rise of, 12–16
State-raised youth, 169
Stateless societies: compared to states, 11–12; and reaction to deviance, 9–12
State University of New York at Albany, Graduate School of Criminal Justice, xi
Stein, Martin, 237n
Stinchcombe, Arthur, 29, 225n, 230n, 236n
Stratification, and social participation, 182
Street, David, 171, 239f, 251b
Street crime, 53
Studt, Elliot, 234n, 238n, 242n
Suburbanism, 182–183
Sudnow, David, 224n, 233n, 234n
Sullivan, Dennis, 135, 224n, 232n, 236n, 239n

Supreme Court, of the United States, 89
Sykes, Gresham, 234n
Syracuse, New York, 1–5
Systems: and control, 85, 86, 111–113; equilibrium model, 86; goal-directed, 83; goal-oriented, 83; simple, 86–87; socio-technical, 83
Systems analysis, 77–97; development of, 93–95
System control, and criminal justice, 77–97

Team policing, 158
Terreberry, Shirley, 130, 235n
Terris, Bruce, 236n, 241n
Tiffany, Lawrence, 231n
Tifft, Larry, 135, 232n, 235n
Toby, Jackson, 120, 233n
Toch, Hans, 170, 190, 239n, 241n
Treatment, and conflict with punishment, 194–196
Trist, Eric, 130, 235n
Trite, Matthew, 229n
Trojanowicz, Robert, 241n

United States Department of Defense, 230n
Urbanization, 144–148, 149

van den Haag, Ernest, 4, 16, 17–18, 23–24, 37–46, 57, 59, 63, 69, 74–75, 204, 221n, 223n, 225n, 226n; and retribution, 37–46; and social control, 84, 90, 240n
Vega, William, 236n
Vertical dimension: of community, 152, 202, 205, 210; and criminal justice, 154–158; and organizational sponsorship, 177
Vickers, Geoffrey, 83, 183, 229n, 240n
Victims, services for, 191–192
Vienna, Illinois, 164–165
Vinter, Robert, 171, 239n
Volunteerism, in criminal justice, 187
Von Hirsch, Andrew, 69, 204, 227n, 228n

Walker, Nigel, 225n
Wamsley, Gary, 9, 223n
Warner, Barbara, 107, 195, 231n, 237n, 242n
Warner, Lloyd, 225n, 237n
Warner, W. Keith, 231n
War on crime, 95, 231n
Warren, Marguerite (Grant), 225n
Warren, Roland, 106, 141–142, 145, 148–154, 157, 160, 166, 172–173, 177, 181–182, 188, 209, 213, 221n, 223n, 226n, 227n, 231n, 235n, 236n, 237n, 238n, 240n

Washington, D.C., 192
Weiner, Norbert, 80
Weinstein, David, 237n
Welfare approach: advantages of, 206–207; compared and contrasted to moralist approach, 60–61, 63–76; compared with community approach, 204–211; conception of current society, 70–74; conception of future society, 74–76; to criminal justice, xii, 47–61; emphasis of on communication, 73–74; evolution of, 48–51; healthy man construct, 70; misconceptions of socialization, 168–169; and social control, 77–80; and social stability, 92–93
Welfare state, 37
Whyte, William F., 252–256
Wickersham Commission, 2, 94
Wildavsky, Aaron B., 235n
Wilkins, Leslie T., xii, 12, 88, 92, 104, 115, 203, 223n, 225n, 230n, 231n, 233n, 237n
Wilson, James Q., 69, 104–107, 120, 176, 178, 190, 204, 223n, 228n, 231n, 236n, 239n, 240n, 241n
Wirt, Frederick, 228n
Wirth, Louis, 146–147, 230n, 236n
Wisconsin Law School, 230n
Witnesses of crime, and social participation, 187
Wolff v. *McDonnell*, 241n
Wolfgang, Marvin, 170, 230n, 239n
Wood, Robert C., 127, 182–183, 232n, 234n, 237n, 240n
Woodworth, Richard, 106, 223n, 231n
World War II, 13, 95, 228n
Wright, Kevin, 225n
Wrong, Dennis, 239n

Youth, state-raised, 169
Youth Service Bureaus, 169

Zald, Mayer, 9, 223n
Zalman, Marvin, 240n
Zimring, Frank, 114, 233n

About the Author

David E. Duffee received his Ph.D. in criminal justice from the State University of New York at Albany, where he is currently Associate Professor of Criminal Justice. He previously taught in the Division of Community Development at the Pennsylvania State University. Professor Duffee has conducted a variety of research and action projects in prisons, halfway houses, courts, and schools.

אור הלב